JOHN ADAMS
UNDER FIRE

JOHN ADAMS UNDER FIRE

THE FOUNDING FATHER'S FIGHT FOR JUSTICE IN THE BOSTON MASSACRE MURDER TRIAL

DAN ABRAMS
AND DAVID FISHER

THORNDIKE PRESS
A part of Gale, a Cengage Company

LIBRARY OF CONGRESS CIP DATA ON FILE.
CATALOGUING IN PUBLICATION FOR THIS BOOK
IS AVAILABLE FROM THE LIBRARY OF CONGRESS

ISBN-13: 978-1-4328-8256-3 (hardcover alk. paper)

Published in 2020 by arrangement with Harlequin Books S.A.

Printed in Mexico
Print Number: 01   Print Year: 2020

I would like to dedicate this book to my brother and sister-in-law, Richard and Elise Langsam, extraordinary people who have spent their lives bringing credit to the law; and to my wonderful sister Bette Pricer, for her unfailing support and wise guidance.

— David Fisher

INTRODUCTION

I have long advocated for cameras in court-rooms, making the argument that like sunlight, they can be the best disinfectants. In particularly sensitive trials, where the outcome could inflame a community, it can be incredibly valuable for the public to see for themselves the arguments and witnesses in a trial, even if they can't make it to the courtroom. Closely observing the proceedings can help people better understand how jurors reached a verdict. Even one they find repulsive.

That principle in its 1770 form could not have been more apt in what became known as the Boston Massacre trials. Revolution was in the air and the events of March 5th, 1770, could have easily become the trigger to set off a war years before 1776. Instead, rather than turning to violence, a small courtroom served as a public theater for the battle. And because that battle was conducted conscientiously and was generally viewed as fair and proper, violence was averted, at least temporarily. A relatively new rule of law prevailed and set a standard for two hundred fifty years of jurisprudence to follow.

To truly understand how monumental an accomplishment that was, it is essential not just to understand the colonists' gripes with British oppression and arrogance as we do in Chapter One, but to also comprehend the Crown's mind-set coming into 1770. The previous century had seen four devastating world wars between England and France fought largely in North America. From 1689 to 1713 there were only five years of peace between what became known as King William's War and Queen Anne's War. In both, Massachusetts played a leading role among the colonies. Then what began as a war with Spain in 1739, in which Boston residents played a large role, morphed into a larger fight with the French again in King George's War, concluding in 1748. Then just six years later, skirmishes in the Ohio Valley broke out over control of the area west of the Appalachian mountains in what would become the greatest of the wars, eventually to be known as the Seven Years War.

The British finally prevailed again nine hard years later, and by the time the Treaty of Paris was signed in 1763, had expanded their footprint significantly through North America. But the victory led to a whole host of new challenges ranging from massive war debt to administration of the new territories to how they would fit into the now larger British Empire's mosaic of possessions. The war-weary British felt they had fought long and hard *for* the colonies, and while colonists had battled alongside them (including Lieutenant Colonel George Washington), they should now share in the financial and practical burdens. By 1770 the British were frustrated with what they felt were their freeloading, ungrateful subjects.

With tension reaching a boiling point, it became paramount to ensure this legal process was deemed to be just. So maintaining a written record was not just significant for historical purposes but also so those who could not attend the trial would be able to review the details of the proceedings.

In our first book, *Lincoln's Last Trial: The Murder Trial That Propelled Him to the Presidency,* we discussed how unusual it was in 1859 to have an entire trial transcribed. But at least there, scribe Robert Hitt had done so for a handful of other trials and even during the Lincoln-Douglas debates on behalf of Lincoln. In 1770, transcribing a trial wasn't just an anomaly, it was entirely new territory.

This book focuses on the two major Boston Massacre trials: that of Captain Thomas Preston, who led the British troops in Boston, and then that of eight soldiers. No transcription of Preston's trial has ever been found. John Adams wrote forty-six years later that Preston's trial "was taken down, and transmitted to England by a Scottish or English Stenographer, without any known authority but his own. The British government have never permitted it to see the light, and probably never will." Furthermore, a witness in the second trial seemed to refer to a transcript of the first proceedings.

In a letter to General Thomas Gage, who led all British forces in the colonies, the defendant Captain Preston ambiguously stated: "You desire to have the judges charges published in the newspapers . . . I am sorry to inform you that mine was not taken down, the court was so crouded, and but one man to be got that writes shorthand, that he had neither room, nor strength to execute it, being waried with taking the evidences, however he has taken that of the

10

mens which is more material." When he referred to "mine," was he talking about the charges or the trial testimony? We will never know for certain.

William Palfrey, a patriot and colleague of John Hancock who wrote about the events, reported that "Mr. Justice Murray . . . attended constantly at the trial and employ'd a Scotch underling of Mien the bookseller's to take down in shorthand all the witnesses said in favor of Capt. Preston, and the arguments of the counsel in his behalf, without noticing anything that was offer'd on the other side the question." That recollection, while hardly an endorsement of a full transcript, would certainly fit the description of Scottish-born John Hodgson, who transcribed the trial of the soldiers. Without that record in Captain Preston's trial, the quotes we use come from detailed notes taken by Adams and one of the prosecutors, Thomas Paine, as well as letters from Preston and a summary of the testimony, which survived.

But the transcript that serves as the heart of this book is the second and more historically significant trial, that of the eight soldiers. This 217-page transcription has since been maligned by many, including a controversial witness who claimed his comments were grossly misreported, and even by Adams himself, who wrote over four decades later, "I found so much inaccuracy, and so many errors, that I scratched out everything, but the legal authorities, and the testimonies of the witnesses." In other words, Adams was comfortable with the recounting of witness testimony but unhappy about the way arguments, including his own arguments, were recorded. In comparing the transcript to the thorough notes of the prosecutors and Adams, while there are differences in words, the central themes and points are consistent. And it should hardly come as a surprise that a lawyer would argue that his eloquence was not properly chronicled or that a colonist testifying for the defense would later claim that he did not intend to support the account of the British captain as indicated in the transcription. It is true, however, that Hodgson was unable to transcribe the entirety of the prosecution's closing argument (presumably because his hand became so tired) and asked them to recreate a portion of it for him.

But what really upset many colonists was the way the town was portrayed, and the transcript became a convenient scapegoat. After all, no matter what one believes actually transpired, there is no question that some inhabitants who gathered on King Street acted out and took an aggressive posture toward the soldiers. In 1771, according to historian Eric Hinderaker, at the first annual town meeting months after the verdicts, "residents considered the question of whether 'some steps may be taken to vindicate the character of the town inhabitants' who had been 'grossly injured by some partial and false publications relative to the tryals of Captain Preston & the soldiers.' A committee concluded that Hodgson had offered only a 'mutilated and partial account' of the soldiers' trial and recommended that the town should consider appointing another committee 'who shall be directed to prepare and draw up a true and full account of those tryals and what preceded them.' Tellingly, no action was taken."

In editing the transcript, we attempted to bring the flavor of the time to the page, especially in preserving sometimes more archaic language and spellings. At times, however, for clarity we made changes if a word could be misconstrued, and we edited punctuation and eliminated unnecessary capitalization, which was common at the time.

In the end, however, the quibbling over minutiae in the transcript is far less significant than the fact that this is the first time this fascinating historical document will have been accessible to a broader audience. Those who remember the acclaimed John Adams miniseries may recall the first episode that focused on this trial. They also may not recognize what is in this book, since that depiction was wildly inaccurate.

What we do hope that readers recognize is how significant these trials remain today. *Rex v. Wemms,* which was the official title for the soldiers' trial, was as important in the development of American jurisprudence as it was in the political history of this country. The nation's legal system was being born in this courtroom with John Adams leading the way, establishing the primacy of the rule of law.

In fact, he risked his career for it.

The Boston Massacre was not what many think it was, but be wary of those who claim they know exactly what happened and precisely who was to blame. This may be as close as we are going to get: a firsthand account of how a revered Founding Father defended the despised British soldiers for the killing of five patriots on a chaotic night two hundred fifty years ago.

CHAPTER ONE

John Adams, the thirty-four-year-old Boston lawyer, was passing a convivial evening with members of his longtime arts and social club at the home of Henderson Inches when the shots were fired. Gently lit by a quarter moon, March 5th, 1770, was a crisp night. A light snow had fallen earlier in the day, leaving a soft white blanket over a thick layer of ice. Adams and his compatriots sat by a warming fire in the South End of the city, a good distance from the Custom House where splashes of bright red blood stained the snow.

Just after nine o'clock, he would recall years later, he and his fellow guests were alarmed by the ringing of bells. Supposing it to be a signal of fire, they quickly put on their hats and cloaks "and went out to assist in quenching the fire or aiding our friends who might be in danger."

Within minutes, however, Adams would

learn the terrible truth. Or at least some version of it. There was no fire; British soldiers guarding the Custom House had fired into a crowd. Some number of inhabitants had apparently been killed while others were wounded.

Many residents of Boston had responded to the bells, quickly filling the wintery streets. Adams joined the stream of people flowing toward the top of King Street, the scene of the incident. His fears focused on Mrs. Adams, who was alone in their house with maids and their young son. It already was a difficult time for her; the Adamses had buried their young daughter, Susanna, only a month earlier and Abigail was hardly herself. This disconcerting news would, at the least, cause further upset.

His Majesty's troops were forming a protective barrier around their comrades. Adams quickly headed to his home on Cold Lane, walking down Boylston's Alley into Brattle Square, where he encountered "a company or two of regular soldiers drawn up in front of Dr. Cooper's old Church with their muskets all shouldered and their bayonets all fixed." He ignored them "as if they had been marble statues," and by the time he made it home, Abigail had been calmed.

Rumors were rampant about the incident but certain facts became indisputable. Three men had been killed in the street; Samuel Gray was shot in the head, his wound described as a hole as big as a hand, Crispus Attucks was struck twice in the chest, and James Caldwell was hit twice in his back as he fled the scene. Two others were grievously wounded and would eventually die. Six more had been hit by gunfire, several seriously, while earlier in the night an unknown number had been struck or cut with bayonets or cutlasses. Hearing the news, some of it accurate, other parts vastly exaggerated or just wrong, colonists raced with nailed sticks and muskets to the scene, determined to avenge their murdered brethren, while the entire British regiment turned out and hastily formed a defensive line, their muskets leveled, ready to fire. The two sides waited anxiously for a spark.

The discharge of weapons had taken only a few seconds, but it had been years in the making. These killings were the culmination of a decade of bitterness and anger.

In the early times of settlement, the bonds between Great Britain and her American colonies had been strong. Americans boasted of their allegiance to the Crown. More than simply faithful allies, the colonists considered themselves Englishmen, albeit at a great distance, but thus entitled to all the rights of every Englishman. The British military protected its settlements, and in return London benefitted greatly from the vibrant trade crossing the Atlantic. Wrote a visitor in 1725, "A gentleman from London would almost think himself at home in Boston when he observes the numbers of people, their houses, their furniture . . . their dress and conversation, which perhaps are as splendid and showy as those of the most considerable tradesmen in London." The colonies had been mostly self-governed, enjoying the same freedoms of speech, assembly and the press as allowed in England. Colonial assemblies were required to submit local legislation to Parliament for approval, but rarely was this other than a formality. In the years since America was settled, Parliament had passed fewer than one hundred statutes relating specifically to its thirteen distant possessions.

There were some trifling disagreements, but none that caused lasting harm. Trade statutes in force restricted colonial trade to England and its possessions and required all goods and raw materials be transported in British or colonial ships and allowed the imposition of duties on goods landed in

America. A small army of clerks on shore and powerful ships of the Royal Navy enforced these regulations.

The rancor between England and America might be traced to October 1760, when George III ascended to the throne. In 1761 the powerful political leader William Pitt decided that the colonies should financially assist the Empire in the cost of the European and American wars. He began by renewing writs of assistance, essentially search warrants that allowed customs officials to search any premises and open any "trunks, chests, boxes, fardells or packs" where contraband might theoretically be concealed.

It was a dire warning that British officials intended to crack down on smuggling and other trade that had been able to slip by under less-than-watchful officials. But it was not enough. As the English economy faltered, Pitt cracked down harder, claiming additional revenue was needed to pay for wars — ignoring completely that the vast lands captured in America and Canada were far more valuable than the cost of victory.

The Sugar Act in 1764 further alienated the colonists. That law sought to enforce parts of a previously ignored levy called the Molasses Act. While the tax wasn't direct, it further tightened trade restrictions and increased costs, while reducing legal options available to fight charges. In response, at a Boston town meeting, the seeds of a rebellion were sown: a committee of five men, among them the respected attorney Richard Dana and emerging patriot leader Samuel Adams, was appointed to draft instructions for the town's representatives to what was essentially the Massachusetts legislature. It was Samuel Adams who wrote, "If taxes are laid upon us in any shape without our having a legal representation where they are laid, are we not reduced from the character of free subjects to the miserable state of tributary slaves?" This was the first legislative body in the colonies to assert that Parliament had no legal right to impose these taxes.

The fraying relationship with England was made considerably worse when the Stamp Act of 1765 became the first true tax Parliament imposed on Americans. The Act required almost all written or printed documents, from books to playing cards, newspapers to deeds, diplomas to bail bonds, to carry a revenue stamp.

The passage of the Act led to boycotts and sent Massachusetts into a deep recession. Businesses closed, jobs were lost. It also led to the formation of a quasi-secret patriot organization known as the Sons of Liberty, which used intimidation and actual violence as tools to provoke confrontation with British authority. Eventually it consisted of as many as two thousand men in Boston and New York, among them Samuel Adams, John Hancock, James Otis, Paul Revere, Dr. Benjamin Rush, Patrick Henry, Dr. Joseph Warren and Benedict Arnold. While John Adams sympathized with their cause, he did not approve of their often violent methods and did not join with them, instead putting his faith in laws.

Riots broke out from New Hampshire to Georgia. British officials were forced to resign their posts. The Sons of Liberty in Boston hanged and burned an effigy of British official Andrew Oliver, whom the governor had commissioned to administer the Act, on an elm tree near the Common, a tree that became known throughout the colonies as the Liberty Tree and served as a gathering point for future protests. Oliver's home as well as a merchant building he had recently completed were ransacked, leading him to quickly and very publicly resign his position. Homes and businesses of Crown officials were plundered by mobs, including the magnificent residence of Oliver's brother-in-law, acting governor Thomas Hutchinson, which was stripped bare. Several thousand people rioted on November 5th, Guy Fawkes Day in England and Pope's Day in Boston, during which a boy was killed and many were hurt.

When the Stamp Act was finally repealed in March 1766, John Adams wrote that it "hushed into silence almost every popular clamour and composed every wave of popular disorder into a smooth and peaceful calm." But that calm was short-lived when the Act was quickly replaced in 1767 by the Townshend Act, which levied taxes on an array of imports and created a five-person Customs Board to ensure proper duties were paid and to take action against the small number of smugglers. John Hancock, one of the wealthiest merchants of Boston, led the opposition. When his vessel, *Liberty,* was taken into custody, mobs attacked several members of the Customs Board, causing them to flee the city with their families.

Minor distractions could be tolerated, but trade and taxes had become overly burdensome. New Englanders strained at the economic harness placed around their purses by the King. More and more, they wanted to be free of it all. Boston had become the hub of the nascent liberty movement in America. In 1768 the *Boston Gazette* published "The Liberty Song":

Come, join hand in hand, brave
    Americans all,
And rouse your bold hearts at fair
    Liberty's call;
No tyrannous acts shall suppress your
    just claim,
Or stain with dishonor America's name;
In freedom we're born and in freedom we
    shall live.
Our purses are ready; steady friends,
    steady;
Not as slaves but as Freemen our money
    we'll give.

Thomas Gage, commander of British forces in North America, decided the people of Boston "have now delivered their sentiments" and took action to put down the brewing rebellion. He ordered four regiments, two thousand troops, to occupy the city. In October 1768, fourteen warships, cannon loaded, sailed into Boston Harbor to discharge those soldiers. Each redcoat carried sixteen rounds of powder and ball, and they marched into town "with muskets charged, bayonets fixed, drums beating, fifes playing." The once-harmonious relationship was over.

Finding lodgings for those troops immediately became an issue. They pitched tents on the Common, but that would not suffice. There was not sufficient space anywhere in the city, so the soldiers were dispersed by unit. Stores and warehouses were rented to house enlisted men, while officers, many of whom had brought their families, rented rooms or space in private homes. The troops were spread like kindling through a dry forest.

The soldiers' presence changed the fabric of the town. Checkpoints were set up. Armed troops stood guard in front of military offices and barracks. Soldiers in and out of their redcoats filled the streets. Officers held "assemblies," social gatherings to which only the gentility and the most attractive single women were invited. Relationships developed, both good and bad. One captain eloped with a fifteen-year-old girl. Soldiers renting rooms in private homes established friendships. Other soldiers found work in the city to complement their meager salaries. While the occupation infused substantial monies into the city, with it came seemingly endless conflict. Rowdy soldiers assaulted people in the streets, attempted rapes were reported, arguments reached the point of confrontation, slaves were urged to turn on their masters, women were harassed, a musket was fired on a crowded street, and men complained of being cut by bayonets and cutlasses. British officers imposed strict discipline on their men, and meted out severe penalties when necessary — whippings became common. But with more than one soldier for every two Boston men, the sheer number of troops overwhelmed the city. Patriots like Samuel Adams continually poked and probed at the British, taking every opportunity to make their occupation even more unbearable. *The Journal of the Times,* a mostly weekly series of articles for newspapers throughout the colonies supposedly describing the occupation — often attributed to Sam Adams — tended to magnify and, on occasion, fabricate events. It warned, "Our enemies are waging war with the morals as well as the rights and privileges of the poor inhabitants."

Peter Oliver, a loyalist judge, saw the situation quite differently, writing later that these soldiers "restrained the rabble from committing their accustomed outrages . . . The inhabitants therefore used every art of irritation and soldiers . . . [were] met with

repeated abuses until, at last, provocations so thick upon one another that the soldiers . . . returned compliments for compliments and every blow was answered by a bruise."

Confrontation became inevitable. In the

fall of '69, bloodshed was barely avoided when a crowd threatened a British company, and its commander ordered his men not to strike anyone unless they were assaulted, but if they were, "put your bayonet through him." The crowd backed off.

But the spirit that had been planted in Boston had taken root and was blooming. In January of the new year, the Sons of Liberty in New York stopped British soldiers from posting handbills. Additional patriots rushed to the scene, greatly outnumbering and surrounding the soldiers. Hearing the commotion, redcoats came to the rescue. A minor altercation suddenly threatened to become a riot. Officers ordered their men back to the barracks. But when they reached an area known as Golden Hill, on which stood a wooden pole crowned with a golden vane bearing the word *Liberty,* the mob blocked their path. An officer ordered his men, "Soldiers, draw your bayonets and cut your way through them."

The jostling threatened to erupt into a riot. In the fighting, several men on both sides were cut and bruised; blood flowed from wounds. News of this Battle of Golden Hill spread rapidly, accounts of it sometimes exaggerated.

Several weeks later, the occupation of

Boston finally turned deadly. In late February, the Sons of Liberty had posted a large sign in front of a shop owned by Theophilius Lillie identifying him as a traitor for ignoring the boycott of British goods. Lillie was a loyalist, who had responded to previous demands that he cease importing those goods by pointing out the paradox: "It always seemed strange to me that people who contend so much for civil and religious liberty should be so ready to deprive others of their natural liberty — that men who are guarding against being subject to laws which they never gave their consent in person or by representative, should at the same time make laws, and in the most effectual manner execute them upon me and others, to which I never gave my consent . . ."

A short-tempered neighbor, Ebenezer Richardson, a known informer for the British (whom John Adams previously had vilified as "the most abandoned wretch in America," accusing him of adultery, incest and perjury), took hold of a cart and horse standing idly in the street and tried to run it into the sign. A group of young boys, somewhere between sixty and three hundred of them, went after Richardson, forcing him to flee to his own home. The crowd began hurling rocks at his house, smashing the door and windows. Richardson and a visiting sailor named George Wilmont took up muskets for protection. The situation escalated. Richardson fired birdshot at boys who had broken into his backyard; his shot hit eleven-year-old Christopher Seider, a German immigrant who died later that night.

The mob broke into the house and took hold of Richardson and Wilmont. Some in that crowd wanted to lynch the two men, but instead they were dragged through the town and delivered to justice. An impassioned town turned out for young Seider's funeral. The procession began at the Liberty Tree and snaked through the streets. "My eyes never beheld such a funeral," wrote John Adams. "The procession extended further than can be well imagined." The killing also served the needs of the liberty movement. Seider's death in February 1770 set the town on the tip of a blade, just waiting for a strong wind to blow it over. Following the boy's funeral, several brawls broke out between soldiers and townsmen.

On March 2nd, three days before the incident on King Street, a British soldier looking for part-time work asked men at John Grey's rope makers if there was work to be found there. Grey had previously hired soldiers for day work. This time, however, one of the rope makers responded that there was work to be done: "Go and clean my shithouse." The insulted soldier began brawling but quickly was overwhelmed and fled. Minutes later he returned with men from his unit, the 29th Regiment, this time carrying clubs. A melee broke out and the soldiers were sent scurrying back to their barracks.

The next night another fight took place, this time at MacNeil's Ropeworks, with a similar outcome: the soldiers retreating to the safety of their barracks. On March 4th redcoats were back at John Grey's rope makers, raiding it as they searched for a sergeant who was missing and rumored murdered. They found no evidence of any crime — the sergeant later reported for duty — but angry words and threats were exchanged. Grey asked the regiment's commander to restrain his men, and a rough agreement was reached. But the streets were rife with more rumor: a working man claimed he had heard four redcoats promising that many Boston men eating dinner that Monday night would not be eating dinner Tuesday night. Another soldier supposedly warned a woman whose brother he had befriended to keep him at home on Tuesday because there would be bloodshed that night.

At dusk on Tuesday, March 5th, 1770, a sizable crowd had gathered near the Liberty Tree in the South End. *The Boston Gazette and Country Journal* published earlier that day had reported, "The remains of young Seider, who was so barbarously murdered the 22nd of February last were decently interred . . . His tragical death and the peculiar circumstances attending it had touch'd the breaths of all with the tenderest sympathies [except those] void of the feelings of humanity . . ."

By nightfall, in groups of three to six, men carrying sticks began patrolling the snow-covered streets. Earlier in the evening there had been several nasty encounters between patriots and loyalists. A single sentry, Private Hugh White, was guarding the Custom House, a large brick building at the head of King Street, in which import duties were held. There was money there, but it was not the issue. White had gotten into an argument with a wigmaker's apprentice, Edward Garrick, who had publicly insulted Captain Lieutenant John Goldfinch by claiming the officer had refused to pay his master for dressing a wig. That night, Garrick was with a group of young men who began taunting

White, cursing him as a "Bloody lobster back" and "Lobster son of a bitch." This was a grave insult. Lobsters were scavengers of the oceans and considered the lowest form of animal life; the fact that they turned bright red when cooked made it easy to compare a lobster to the red coats worn by British soldiers. In response, the sentry swung his musket at Garrick, striking him hard on the side of his head.

A block away, two other young men, Edward Archbald and William Merchant, walked by a narrow alley leading to a sugar warehouse in which a contingent of the 29th was lodged. As they passed, reported the *Boston Gazette,* a soldier brandishing a broad sword "turned around and struck Archbald on the arm, then pushed at Merchant and pierced thro' his clothes inside the arm close to the arm-pit and grazed the skin." Hearing the commotion, young men rushed to the scene to reinforce both sides. A redcoat was knocked down, suffering a head wound, but soldiers armed with cutlasses, bayonets and clubs came to his aid and the crowd scattered.

Other assaults reportedly were taking place in dark streets. A small crowd gathered in front of Murray's Barracks and began haranguing the troops. A few officers tried to calm the situation, vowing to keep their men inside. But anger had taken hold and the shouting brought more people into the streets. In Boylston's Alley, snowballs hardened with ice were thrown at the troops. About two hundred people pushed into Dock Square from the north of the town. Those of them who did not bring sticks broke into the market stalls and grabbed hold of table legs. An unidentified man, standing in the middle of the darkened square wearing a white wig, jackboots and red cloak, stood shouting, further arousing the people. It was said by some that this figure was "Joyce Junior," dressed to be an incarnation of Cornet George Joyce, Oliver Cromwell's man famed for commanding the five hundred troops who held King Charles I in semi-captivity, and a popular political symbol. He was greeted with cheers and supportive whistles, and as the crowd began moving toward King Street, many of them ominously rattled their clubs on storefronts and walls. Then someone began ringing the bells of the Old Brick Meeting House.

Within minutes, other bells joined them, echoing that call for assistance, bringing even more men into the streets. Descriptions of the events that followed were loose and disputed. Stories got muddled and depended on which side of the lines a man stood. Many said the patriots were armed only with sticks and clubs, bottles and cracked ice against the British muskets, but Tory Peter Oliver described what the soldiers saw: "They provided themselves with massy clubs, a new manufacture of their own. Guns they imagined were weapons of death in the eye of the law, which the meanest of them was an adept in; but bludgeons were only implements to beat out brains with."

There were three large groups spread throughout the town, but by nine o'clock, at the ringing of the bells, they moved toward the Custom House on King Street, hooting, whistling, shouting as they came. Private White stood lonely in front of the building as even more men streamed into the square from the streets and alleys. The Custom House was both an office and the residence of a revenue official named Bartholomew Green and his family.

The size of the mob was later in dispute; the numbers varied from only a few dozen to three hundred, four hundred or more, all of them focused on White. They taunted him and shouted threats. They dared him to fire his musket. More snowballs were thrown. White was shaken. He retreated up the three steps to the door and made a show of loading his musket and fixing his bayonet. When a group of about twenty-five sailors carrying thick wooden clubs, led by a tall, broad man of mixed race calling himself Michael Johnson, joined the mob, White called for help.

Inside Custom House, Bartholomew Green and his family peered out the window with dismay. Green's daughter, Ann, and a friend had gone to the apothecary, accompanied by an apprentice named Bartholomew Broaders and his friend, the apprentice Edward Garrick. Green's son, Hammond, went into the street and brought the four of them inside for safety. After a time, the two apprentices slipped back into the street.

By regulation, troops were not permitted to become involved in civilian disturbances unless directly requested by civilian authority. But White's commanding officer, Captain Thomas Preston, believed his man to be in dire jeopardy, so he led a relief party, seven men, to assist White. Men of the 29th were renowned for their quick tempers: "such bad fellows," acting governor Hutchinson had once described them. Most of them were grenadiers, the biggest and toughest of the troops. They carried muskets nearly five feet long that fired fearsome lead balls; the guns were not loaded, but bayonets were fixed. As they pushed through the crowd to reach their beleaguered mate, those bayonets cut demonstrators who came too close.

Preston kept rein on his men. When one demonstrator refused to move, for example, the column split around him, going to either side. A young seller of science and military books, Henry Knox, a man of towering size, had been trying to keep the calm. "For God's sake," he warned Preston, "take care of your men. If they fire, you die."

"I am sensible of it," Preston acknowledged.

When the troops reached the sentry box at the Custom House, they loaded their weapons. Private White immediately fell into the column. Captain Preston attempted to march his men back to the Main Guardhouse, leaving Custom House unguarded. But the crowd had filled in and would not let them pass. Preston put his men in a defensive position, forming a single semicircular line in front of the building. According to Oliver, "the Rioters pelted the soldiers with brickbats, ice, oystershells and broken glass bottles."

Perhaps one body length separated the

troops and the demonstrators. There were moments of recognition; Private White saw a neighbor among the protestors. "Go home," he urged her, "or you'll be killed."

While men like Adams were enjoying a peaceful evening and families were gathered around the winter night fires in homes throughout the town, the streets of Boston were cold and alive with crowds. The number in front of the Custom House continued to grow, drawing courage from its size, feasting on rage. All the anger of the many months, brought to a head by the killing of young Seider, had finally been focused into one night, and one place.

Captain Preston took his commanding position in front of his men, facing the crowd, his men stirring anxiously behind him. All around them bells continued clanging, bringing out more men onto the streets, ready to fight a nonexistent fire. It was generally agreed that Preston stood firm, pleading with the crowd to disperse, even as snowballs were hurled at his men.

A man named Richard Palmes pushed his way to the front, carrying a club. He placed his free hand on Preston's shoulder and asked, "Are your soldiers' guns loaded?"

"With powder and ball," the captain responded. Powder made a show, smoke and thunder; balls killed. But His Majesty's officers knew the law: soldiers were not permitted to fire on civilians. Unspoken was the greater truth: a soldier, like a civilian, had the right to defend his life.

"Sir," Palmes responded, "I hope you don't intend the soldiers shall fire on the inhabitants."

"By no means," he said, then repeated it, "by no means." The fact that he was standing in front of his troops, between his men and the mob, was proof of that.

The crowd was feeling its power, daring the soldiers to shoot. The redcoats poked at those people close to them with bayonets, keeping them at a distance. Suddenly, a club sailed through the night and struck Private Montgomery directly, knocking him to the ground.

Enraged, Montgomery scrambled to his feet, picked up his musket and let loose the first shot. He fired into the air, hitting no one. But the inferno was sparked.

Palmes swung his club at Montgomery, slamming down on his left arm and knocking the gun from his hands. Then he turned and swung his club wildly at Captain Preston; Preston deflected the blow with his arm, "which for some time deprived me of the use of it," then lowered his musket and thrust his bayonet at Palmes.

Panic had taken hold. Clubs and ice were thrown. Some men stepped forward and were cut. Others fled. A few seconds or a few minutes passed, depending on who was telling the story, and then the soldiers began firing into the crowd; it was not an organized volley, but rather a series of individual shots. The sailor Michael Johnson, the son of a slave and an Indian mother, who was to be mourned by his true name, Crispus Attucks, was struck twice in his chest. One shot destroyed his liver and he died in the street. Private Matthew Killroy, who was said to have tussled with the laborer Samuel Gray at John Grey's rope making works, fired at him, blasting a hole in his head and killing him instantly. Another sailor recently arrived in port, James Caldwell, was hit twice in the back, perhaps fleeing, and died on that spot. Seventeen-year-old Sam Maverick, an apprentice ivory turner, was struck in his belly by a ricocheting shot and died the next day. Irish immigrant Patrick Carr, a leather smith just passing through the street, was struck in the hip; what appeared to be a nasty but survivable wound turned sour, and he died nine days later. In the barrage, others were hit and wounded, a few suffering permanent damage, but they lived.

The shooting stopped. As puffs of powder rose into the night, the redcoats reloaded as quickly as possible, preparing for whatever was to come. Preston moved up and down the line, imploring his men to stop firing.

In the horror of the events, time paused for an instant. Then men rushed back into the street to help the wounded. As bodies were being carried to homes and taverns to await physicians, or for some the coroner, Preston marched his men away from the Custom House to the Main Guard. He turned out all his men, placing them in a "street firing" formation suitable for a narrow lane. He ordered the drummer to beat "To Arms." If the Boston men wanted more of a fight, he was ready to give it to them.

All the bells of the town were ringing and a huge throng of townsmen answered, with four thousand or more men filling the streets. Soldiers caught isolated in distant parts of the town were endangered. Several officers had to fight their way back to the safety of the Main Guard. It was around this time that John Adams joined "the crowd of people . . . flowing down the street, to the scene of the action . . ." This was the explosion, he feared, "wrought up by designing men."

The acting governor of Massachusetts

Bay, Thomas Hutchinson, hurried to the scene from his home in North Square. "Unless I went out immediately," he remembered being told, "the whole town would be in arms and the most bloody scene would follow that had ever been known in America."

Of necessity he took a circuitous route, at times having to retrace his steps, passing through houses and dark backyards to avoid the mob. As he passed near the crowd in Dock Square, a bludgeon was aimed at his head. "Damn him!" his attacker shouted, "I'll do his business." But the blow was warded off, saving him. When he finally arrived safely at King Street, the mob was still in an uproar. He confronted Preston, demanding to know why his men fired on civilians without authority. "I was obliged to," the captain replied, "to save my sentry." Isaac Pierce, a bystander, then said pointedly, "Then you have murdered three or four men to save your sentry."

Hutchinson urged Preston to return the soldiers to their barracks, but he refused; they would not show weakness to the colonists. The situation was quickly becoming more chaotic and perilous; the crowd had continued to grow until it had become an overwhelming force.

Hutchinson was a Boston man. His family had been among the early migrants to the province and he had been born and raised there. After graduating from Harvard at age sixteen, he worked as a merchant, which enabled him to amass a great personal fortune. He went on to hold a variety of prominent public positions, including being elected the Speaker of the Massachusetts House of Representatives and receiving a royal appointment as chief justice of the superiour court. And while not especially well liked, he was well-known and his word was respected.

He rushed to the primary municipal building called the Town House just yards from the Custom House where the incident occurred. At the Main Guard, locked and loaded troops faced a furious mob armed with clubs and cutting weapons. News of the shootings had already spread beyond the city to neighboring towns, and more armed and determined men were coming to join the affray. Samuel Adams warned Lieutenant Colonel William Dalrymple to get his men off the streets. The King Street shootings threatened to be a prelude to a great bloody battle. Hutchinson eventually made his way to the balcony of the Town House and looked down upon the two sides.

He expressed concern about the tragedy, then gave the large crowd his word: "The law shall have its course. I will live and die by the law."

The law in the American colonies was still finding its place. It was a hazy thing, based loosely on the British model, with no clear borders, and too often had been bent to serve the needs of the powerful and wealthy rather than protect the interests of the common man. Hutchinson had no power to order the troops to return to their barracks, but at his request, Dalrymple and Lieutenant Colonel Maurice Carr did so. As the soldiers retreated down Pudding Lane, the crowd slowly faded into the darkness.

Hutchinson had persuaded both the townsmen and the soldiers to lower their weapons and retreat to their homes and barracks. No one else would die that night.

He immediately convened a hearing, inviting justices of the peace and military and civilian representatives. The killing was done, but the fight to turn those murders into political gain was just beginning. That very night many thousands of Bostonians gathered at Faneuil Hall to discuss an appropriate response. These deaths were the result of the military occupation, Sam Adams told them, and he warned that more would follow until both British regiments were driven out of Boston. The number of people in attendance swelled until Faneuil Hall could not hold them all and they reconvened in the larger Old South Meeting House.

At the Town House, Hutchinson was meeting with the selectmen, the town council. Several members urged him to order the troops out of Boston, warning of terrible consequences if he did not. Hutchinson delayed, claiming he lacked the power to give that order. He told the committee they had the power to calm the town, and issued his own warning to them in response: if "an attempt should be made to drive out the King's troops, everyone abetting and advising would be guilty of high treason."

Even in those first hours, John Adams understood the stakes. The people of Boston had entrusted their fate to the law, even while their faith in it wavered. This was to be a test of the power of the law to protect and defend the citizenry. He and Abigail spent the evening trying to understand the meaning of it all. "I suspected this was the explosion," he lamented. He also wondered about the consequences, knowing "If these poor fools should be prosecuted for any of their illegal conduct they must be punished.

If the soldiers [acted] in self-defense . . . they must be tried, and if the truth was respected and the law prevailed must be acquitted."

"Tuesday morning presented a most shocking scene," reported the *Boston Gazette.* "The blood of our fellow citizens running like water thro King Street and the Merchants Exchange." The battle to influence public opinion had begun.

Later that day, a delegation led by Sam Adams met with Hutchinson and the council. The town was near rebellion, the acting governor was told. Councilman Royall Tyler threatened that if the troops did not leave voluntarily, ten thousand men were ready to remove them forcefully. Hutchinson finally accepted the situation, that the possibility of a violent uprising was real, and in collaboration with the military commanders agreed that the soldiers would be removed to Castle William Island, three miles from the town in Boston Harbor.

Later in the day, Justice of the Peace John Tudor and Justice Richard Dana, after hearing sufficient evidence, issued a warrant for the arrest of British captain Thomas Preston of the 29th Regiment, alleging that he ordered his soldiers to fire on townsmen. Upon being informed of this, Captain Preston later said, "I instantly went to the Sheriff and surrendered myself, though for the space of four hours I had it in my power to have made my escape, which I most undoubtedly should have attempted and could have easily executed, had I been the least conscious of any guilt." By that afternoon all eight of his men also were taken into custody. It was as much to defuse the situation as to protect those men from mob justice.

While these combustible gatherings and rapid legal developments were occurring, a teary-eyed visitor was at the law office of John Adams, trying mightily to convince the young lawyer to represent the most unpopular of clients.

CHAPTER TWO

The city was still in an uproar the next day. Rumors spread quickly. Samuel Adams recognized the value of the incident for propaganda purposes and had already begun referring to it as a "horrid massacre." The provincial government, determined to maintain control, made certain it was known that all the accused were in custody and would be treated in accordance with the facts, whatever the outcome. Men had been killed and wounded, the violence was done, and now it was to be law and politics.

Adams was at work in his office on March 6th, which was near the steps of the Town House, when James Forrest called on him. Forrest was a successful merchant who was known, for some reason, as "the Irish Infant." He also was fervently loyal to the Crown. In fact, he had leased a building he owned at the West End of the city to the army to be used as barracks. He had been on King Street the night before and was acquainted with Captain Preston, which was the reason for this hurried visit. Preston, also an Irishman, had been generally well liked and even respected by the colonists up to this point. At forty years old, he had been serving in the military for fifteen years, and had been described as a "benevolent" and even "humane man."

"I am come with a very solemn message," Forrest began, tears streaming from his eyes. Captain Preston "wishes for counsel and can get none." Apparently others had already declined the engagement, but Josiah Quincy, Jr., and the well-respected Robert Auchmuty, Jr., had both agreed to accept the case on one condition: that John Adams join them.

It was not a simple decision. Adams knew there would be consequences and he had much to lose. Good men, working men, fellow New Englanders had been shot dead in the street by British troops. One of them shot in the back. The soldiers were an occupying force; many considered them the enemy. Any man who defended them would be risking his reputation in addition to his livelihood. Friends and potential clients certainly would take this case into consideration. To defend Captain Preston, a lawyer would have to make arguments against the victims. There was Abigail to consider too; she was in an emotional state having buried one baby and now being pregnant again. People might well take their passions out on her. In the extreme the Adamses might be forced to leave the city, to return to their former home in Braintree. And why? Money? Certainly not. His retainer would be one guinea, a coin weighing one quarter of an ounce of gold. Win or lose this case, there promised to be little pecuniary gain in it for him.

These were good arguments, which Adams casually dismissed. If the law was to gain a foothold in America it had to serve in the most troublesome instances. He would accept the case, he told Forrest. "Counsel ought to be the very last thing that an accused person should want in a free country . . . The bar ought . . . to be independent and impartial at all times and in every circumstance. That persons whose lives were at stake ought to have the counsel they preferred." But there was more than the fate of one man in this for him. As he later explained, "This would be as important a cause as ever was tried in any Court or Country of the world; and that every lawyer must hold himself responsible not only to

49

his country, but to the highest and most infallible of all tribunals for the part he should act. [Preston] must therefore expect from me no art or address, no sophistry or prevarication in such a cause, nor anything more than fact, evidence and law would justify."

Forrest was gratified. "As God almighty is my judge," he told Adams, "I believe him an innocent man."

"That must be ascertained by his trial," the lawyer quickly responded. "And if he thinks he cannot have a fair trial of that issue without my assistance, without hesitation he shall have it." Adams made sure to profess no sympathy for the accused officer, instead making it clear that he was not so much defending the man as he was defending the law.

He was committed. Not surprisingly, it was difficult for many to understand his decision. The outrage from the community was captured in a note from the esteemed Josiah Quincy to his son, who had agreed to serve with Adams as co-counsel. The Quincy family had been among the first settlers of Massachusetts. Adams had grown up with the Quincy family. He had played on the family estate and by a stretch had married into it: Abigail's mother was the elder Josiah

Quincy's cousin. And when the patriarch Quincy heard of his son's involvement, he expressed a combination of disbelief and disdain: "My Dear Son," he wrote, "I am under great affliction at hearing the bitterest reproaches uttered against you, for having become an advocate for those criminals who are charged with the murder of their fellow-citizens. Good God! Is it possible? I will not believe it . . . I have heard the severest reflections made upon the occasion, by men who had just before manifested the highest esteem for you, as one destined to be a savior of your country.

"I must own to you, it has filled the bosom of your aged and infirm parent with anxiety and distress, lest it should not only prove true, but destructive of your reputation and interest; and I repeat, I will not believe it unless it be confirmed by your own mouth or under your own hand."

Young Quincy's response echoed Adams's beliefs. Standing firmly on the law, he wrote back, "I have little leisure, and less inclination, either to know or to take notice of those ignorant slanderers who have dared to utter their 'bitter reproaches' in your hearing against me, for having become an advocate for criminals charged with murder . . . Before pouring their reproaches into the ear of the aged and infirm, if they had been friends, they would have surely spared a little reflection on the nature of an attorney's oath and duty . . . Let such be told, Sir, that these criminals, charged with murder, are not yet legally proved guilty, and therefore, however criminal, are entitled, by the laws of God and man, to all legal counsel and aid; that my duty as a man obliged me to undertake; that my duty as a lawyer strengthened the obligation; that from abundant caution, I at first declined being engaged; . . . until advised and urged to undertake it, by an Adams, a Hancock . . .

"This and much more might be told with great truth; and I dare affirm that you and this whole people will one day REJOICE that I became an advocate for the aforesaid 'criminals' charged with the murder of our fellow-citizens."

Joining Adams and Quincy, Jr., for the defense of Captain Preston, and the eight of his men, was the forty-five-year-old loyalist Robert Auchmuty, Jr. Auchmuty was another from a distinguished Massachusetts family, and was serving as a judge in the vice admiralty court.

The patriots of Boston railed against the three lawyers. It was said that rocks had been thrown through the windows of

Adams's home. The men were jeered in the streets. Clients were lost. Adams neither confirmed these stories nor complained about them. As Josiah Quincy, Jr.'s son would write years later, "The Boston Massacre had wrought the whole people of Massachusetts . . . to the highest pitch of rage and indignation. The populace breathed only vengeance. Even minds better instructed and of higher principles than the multitude . . . could not endure the doctrine that it was possible for an armed soldiery to fire upon and kill unarmed citizens, and commit a crime less than murder . . . The friends of freedom were loud in their indignation and clamorous for that justice which declares, 'Blood shall be the penalty for blood.' "

Adams confided privately to the Reverend William Gordon, Minister of the Third Parish Church of Roxbury, "It is impossible to realize the excitement of the populace, and the abuse heaped upon Mr. Quincy and myself for our defense of the British captain and his soldiers, we heard our names execrated in the most opprobrious terms whenever we appeared in the streets of Boston."

The indictment was drawn up by the King's attorney general Jonathan Sewall. If he had chosen to do so, he would prosecute the case. But it was not in his character; in the two years since the British had occupied the city he had refused to prosecute a single soldier-citizen case. Given that blood was still splashed in the packed snow, that position had become untenable. Rather than officially resigning, he simply left the city. Ironically, the court appointed a strong British sympathizer, the Tory Samuel Quincy, special prosecutor, pitting him against his younger brother as well as his longtime friend Adams. There was great irony in that choice, as Adams and Quincy, Jr., strong supporters of patriot causes, were to defend British soldiers, while Samuel Quincy, who held loyalist views, would prosecute them.

Samuel Adams and other patriot leaders lacked confidence that Quincy had sufficient zeal to prosecute the case as strongly as they desired, so these selectmen, as representatives of the town, agreed to "bear the expense" of adding the experienced lawyer Robert Treat Paine to the prosecution. Fearful that Quincy might resist, they insisted upon it, claiming Paine was representing the "Relatives of those person who were murdered."

While the trial would determine the fate of Preston and his eight soldiers, it had far greater importance for the Massachusetts colony and for the future of all Great Britain's thirteen American colonies. Boston had been founded 140 years earlier when Puritans from the small port city of Boston, England, settled at the mouth of the Charles River, on Massachusetts Bay. Given its ideal location for trade, it grew rapidly, and by 1770 its population was approaching twenty thousand, making it the third largest city on the eastern coast. The census five years earlier noted that more than half its population was under sixteen years old, the age at which white men qualified for militia duty, and included thirty-seven Indians.

John Adams had often made the thirteen-mile ride to Boston from his hometown in Braintree as a young man determined to study law. At first the chaos of the bustling port had dazzled him. The lively town impacted all his senses; "My eyes are so diverted with chimney sweeps, carriers of wood, merchants, ladies, priests, carts, horses, oxen, coaches, market men and women, soldiers, sailors, and my ears with the rattle gabble of them all that I can't think long enough in the street upon any one thing to start and pursue a thought."

It was a thriving place, a place where a man could find everything he needed, from finely carved furniture to silk stockings, much of it direct from England. There was an abundance of taverns, which served hearty fare, usually with tea, cider and liquor. It was, he wrote Abigail, a "noisy, dirty town . . . where parade, pomp, nonsense frippery, folly, foppery, luxury, politicks and the soul-confounding wrangles of the law will give me the higher relish for spirit, taste and sense . . ." And if a man was looking for trouble, he could find that too, which was one reason lawyering prospered there.

But Adams had mastered the pace of the town, gaining a sterling reputation as a man of learning and principles. Boston fit him well; it was a place of ideas as well as business. Harvard College, the first institute of higher education in America, had been established in nearby Cambridge in 1636, mostly to train men for the ministry. Adams had graduated from there in 1755, although after flirting with the ministry he had become a teacher.

The fact that Adams had chosen to swim against the rising tide by agreeing to defend Captain Preston and the soldiers should not have come as a great shock. The man was a lawyer, which already made him suspect. While lawyers were not considered a public nuisance, most of them were viewed with a mild distrust. They were men known to take advantage of people's misfortune, men who too often relied on fancy language and cunning to deceive the common folk. There were many among these lawyers who had learned just enough to be able to use the law for their own enrichment. At times lawyers seemed a lot more interested in raising their own status, and getting paid to do it, than getting to the truth of a matter.

In fact, some of the original colonies considered lawyers "base and vile" and enacted statutes prohibiting the practice of law. Legal questions were decided by judges appointed by the community leaders specifically because they had no legal training and therefore could be relied upon to apply common sense to settle a dispute. More than a century earlier, Thomas More had written in *Utopia,* "They have no lawyers among them, for they consider them as a sort of people whose profession it is to disguise matters."

Early in his life, Adams shared those sentiments. While studying at Harvard, he had written to a classmate, "Let us look upon a Lawyer. In the beginning of life we see him, fumbling and raking amidst the rubbish of writs, indictments, pleas, ejectments . . . and a thousand other lignum Vitae words that have neither harmony nor meaning. When he gets into business he often foments more quarrels than he composes, and enriches himself at the expense of impoverishing others more honest and deserving than himself. Besides the noise and bustle of the courts and the labor of inquiring into and pleading dry and difficult cases, have very few charms in my eye."

There was good reason for that opinion. The law was not yet a true profession. There were few universal standards, and it was governed as much by personal whim and accepted tradition as established guidelines and procedures. Lawyers were forced to compete for business with pettifoggers: local sheriffs and clerks who had no formal training or legal education yet were hired to handle small or "petty" legal matters such as drafting documents like deeds or wills and, on occasion, defending clients against small claims. To survive, many lawyers were forced to take additional employment, and the practice became a part-time vocation.

John Adams drifted into the law at first. The ministry did not suit him, he had decided, as the rigidity of church doctrine did not fit with his intense curiosity nor his ambition. And, at times, his own precepts of morality did not square with the demanding teachings of the church. There were other opportunities open to him: "I was like a boy in a county fair," he remembered decades later. "In a wilderness, in a strange country, with half a dozen roads before him, groping in a dark night to find which he ought to take. Had I been obliged to tell . . . the whole truth I should have mentioned several other pursuits. Farming, merchandise, law and above all, war. Nothing but want of interest (i.e. influence) and patronage prevented me from enlisting in the army."

The law, he decided, was the suitable place for him. At Harvard he had enjoyed the assigned readings and spirited debates. There were constant challenges in the law that would force him to further develop his mind. "The point is now determined," he wrote after making this decision, "and I shall have the liberty to think for myself."

Unlike England, where the law was taught in universities, in America it was considered a trade to be learned at the hand of a practitioner. No different than a cooper or a silversmith. To pay for his apprenticeship, he accepted a position as headmaster of a school in Worcester. Eventually he signed a contract with a young Worcester attorney, James Putnam, to study the law "under his inspection." The fee was $100.

Putnam provided no formal course of instruction. In fact, he did little more than suggest books that should be read. Adams pored over all the masters of the common law; Justinian's *Institutes,* Chief Justice Henry de Bracton's thirteenth century classic *On the Laws and Customs of England* in which he wrote, "The King [government] must not be under man but under God and under the law because law makes the King." He read Britton, a summary of English law supposedly written by order of Edward I. He read the works of Ranulf de Glanville, chief justice of England under Henry II, the late thirteenth century treatise on English common law known as the Fleta, and Sir Geoffrey Gilbert's *Treatise of Feudal Tenures,* and then the respected (and sometimes ponderous) Latin and Greek philosophers describing the importance and place of the law in government and society. And to learn about human nature he read the classics, from Ovid's *Art of Love* to Swift and Cervantes and all of Shakespeare. He took note of those things that appealed to him, among them Sir Edward Coke, the preeminent jurist of sixteenth century England. "Whose is the soil, his it is up to the sky," Coke wrote and Adams copied diligently. And, "The laws themselves require that they should be governed by right. Where the same reason exists, there the same right prevails."

Adams did not learn the mechanics of the law from Putnam, complaining, "Had he given me now and then a few hints concerning practice, I should be able to judge better at this hour than I can now." But during his apprenticeship Adams became familiar with the philosophical underpinnings of his profession and gained an understanding of the concept of justice that would shape his legal career. To learn the daily stuff of the law he would need to know, he sat in the courtrooms of Boston, watching "the greatest lawyers, orators . . . in short the greatest men in America, haranguing at the bar, and on the bench."

Having completed his apprenticeship Adams applied for admission to the bar; "the bar" was the physical barrier that separated spectators and participants (the judges, lawyers and clerks) in a courtroom, but it also was the term used to describe the loose association of lawyers who practiced law. It was an archaic word, believed by some to have derived from the great sandbar outside London Harbor. Once a vessel had passed over that bar it became subject to British law.

To gain admission to the bar Adams, like all applicants, was required to answer questions from Boston's leading lawyers. In November of 1758 Adams rode into the town, ironically, as events would prove, with his friend Samuel Quincy, to be admitted to the bar. The leading lawyer of the city, Jeremiah Gridley, advised him wisely to "pursue the study of law rather than the gain of it. Pursue the gain of it enough to keep out of the briars . . ." He also cautioned him about marrying early, as marriage would obstruct his career and "will involve you in expense."

As for the profession, Gridley advised, a young lawyer in America "must study common law and civil law and natural law and admiralty and must do the duty of a counselor, a lawyer, an attorney, a solicitor and even a scrivener . . ."

Adams and Sam Quincy then raised their right hands and took the lawyer's oath, swearing to honor "with all good fidelity as well to the court as to the client, and to delay no man for malice."

Adams threw himself into the practice of law with great enthusiasm, and met with immediate failure: his first case was a simple matter that might ordinarily have been resolved by town clerks familiar with Braintree's local procedures. Horses owned by Luke Lambert, a rough man whom Adams disliked, had broken into Joseph Field's yard, damaged crops and shooed out his horses. When Lambert refused to settle with his neighbor for the lost crops, Field sued. Once again ironically, the justice of the peace who would hear the case was Colonel Josiah Quincy, while Lambert was represented by the justice's son and Adams's friend, Samuel Quincy.

Adams warily prepared his first court document, "A Declaration in Trespass for a Rescue." Although he was now well-versed on the majesty and the history of the law, drawing up writs had not been part of his training. As a result, the case was lost because he had left out a few key words. It was an inauspicious beginning and, he feared, an embarrassing end. What use was a lawyer incapable of preparing simple papers?

But he had the decided advantage of being one of very few members of the bar in Braintree and gradually his practice grew. He worked hard at it, diving into a variety of cases, learning the law by the practice of it. He handled cases of fraud, embezzlement, trespass, assault, wounding, tarring and feathering, cruelty to an apprentice, and insurance claims. He represented accused tax cheats and debtors. He sorted out the case of a hat supposedly sold in a tavern and dealt with a challenge to a duel and an attempt to spread smallpox. He was involved in trials of murder and rape, buggery and bastardy. He defended thieves and smugglers. He represented Scottish seaman James Lowrie who was being sued by silversmith Paul Revere for "enticing and seducing an apprentice from his Master . . ." a case won by Revere (who may have regretted it after the unsavory apprentice married Revere's daughter.) He handled disputes over water rights and unreturned loans, settled family feuds and mediated disputes and finally mastered writs. To his own mind he was caught up in cases involving "two fools and two knaves [and] a lunatic." Years later he would write, "I believe no lawyer in America ever did so much business as I did afterwards . . . for so little profit."

He continued his study, making notes such as "Assumpsit: Sometimes signify's not only a promise but an actual undertaking of the business . . ." and "Warranty: If upon a sale of goods from a merchant A.B. to my friend C.D., I only make a collateral promise as a surety . . ."

John Adams was not a shy man; words always had come easily to him, sometimes in a torrent. He gained a reputation as a man who loved to talk. And then talk some more. He was also aspiring for recognition and maybe the fortune that came with it. To accomplish that he set out to make himself the most effective practitioner possible, at first trying to emulate Boston's leading lawyers, especially theatrical men like James Otis, whose courtroom eloquence he likened to "a flame of fire" or Jeremiah Gridley's "great learning and . . . his majestic manner," but over time discovered imitation did not suit him. And so he focused on developing his own skills and strengths, perhaps taking bits from the courtroom manner of the men he respected, and eventually creating a unique style. While he could bring the necessary fervor to the moment to persuade a judge or jury, his arguments were well reasoned, deliberate, and peppered with history, philosophy, precedent and prose.

In his diligence he had developed an almost unrestrained passion for the law, now feeling its power, and its potential. "To what higher object, to what greater character," he told the lawyer Jonathan Sewall, "can any mortal aspire than to be possessed of all this knowledge, well digested and ready to command, to assist the feeble and friendless, to discountenance the haughty and lawless, to procure redress to wrongs, the advancement of right, to assert and maintain liberty and virtue, to discourage and abolish tyranny and vice?"

His practice grew, expanding from Braintree to Boston and nearby towns. Within a decade he had become one of the busiest lawyers in Boston and accepted two young men to clerk in his office, although he wondered what he might do with two young men to train. As the law had not yet settled in many small towns, he joined other lawyers and judges to ride the circuit, traveling on horseback for weeks at a time to villages and outposts, bringing the law to the inhabitants. They carried justice with them, undertaking whatever legal tasks needed to be performed, filling the necessary variety of positions; living, eating, spending fireside evenings together and sometimes sharing a room. These journeys not only took him away from his increasingly busy practice but also separated him from his beloved wife, Abigail, whom he had married in 1764. While riding the circuit could be profitable, it was burdensome and too often dreary. As he complained in his diary, "This has been the most flat, insipid, spiritless, tasteless journey that I ever took . . . I have neither had business nor amusement nor conversation. It has been a moping, melancholy journey upon the whole."

Adams was experiencing the power of the law in all its variations. The law was the basis on which neighbors in a rural community might settle a dispute over a calf and, as he had learned in his studies, it also could bring kings to heel. In the hands of a clever man it was a sharp tool that could calm the present and shape the future. It could be employed just as readily to resolve the troubles of one man as it might to achieve the desires of a vast population. It was a set of rules to live by as well as the foundation on which to turn a political philosophy into practice. The great men of history had taught him this; they had showed him the path. So after firmly establishing his practice in Braintree he took a first small step into the public arena.

He began a campaign to limit the number of alehouses in Braintree. While seemingly a minor nuisance, to the people of the small town this mattered. Adams spoke for them, beginning by publishing an essay and continuing his campaign for a year, until the town meeting passed a resolution declaring it would issue only three liquor licenses.

At about the same time he became active in the campaign to turn the loose association of Massachusetts lawyers, with its barely regulated requirements, into a profession worthy of respect. Adams joined a campaign to rid the courts of pettifoggers. Although admittedly there would be financial gain in it for members of the bar if this "dirty, quacking practice," as he referred to it, could be eliminated, without question it also would raise the level of practice and procedures in the courts.

Those early forays into public service brought him attention, and the Braintree town leaders began to solicit his advice, and his services, on local matters like regulating highways and selling town land. He served on several committees and eventually was named surveyor of highways.

In 1761, Adams watched with awe as lawyer James Otis railed passionately in superiour court against the odious writs of assistance the Brits had implemented to enforce trade laws. These writs, Otis said, violated the natural rights of Englishmen, being "the worst instrument of arbitrary power, the most destructive of English liberty and the fundamental principles of law, that ever was found in an English law book." While these warrants were commonly used in England and were legal, Adams wrote later inside that courtroom, "Then and there the child independence was born."

As Adams's reputation grew, he and one other young lawyer were taken in hand by the aging Jeremiah Gridley, a revered legislator, editor and the Grand Master of the Masons in North Americas, who had committed to preparing them for the challenges he suspected were beyond his own horizon. In meetings of this weekly sodality, Gridley focused discussions on the medieval laws of the continent and urged his charges to prepare essays that might spark discussions among their colleagues.

By the time the oppressive Stamp Act was passed by Parliament in 1765, Adams was prepared to become a central figure in the greater public debate. He had already begun putting down his thoughts concerning canon and feudal law in a series of unpublished essays. In response to the act, Adams arranged for his revised and expanded essays to be published anonymously in four installments in the *Boston Gazette: A Dissertation on the Canon and Feudal Law* or, as they were titled when published in the

London Chronicle, True Sentiments of America.

Adams laid the foundation for a broad legal assault on tyranny in any form. "In the earliest ages of man," he wrote, "absolute monarchy seems to have been the universal form of government. Kings, and a few of their great counselors and captains, exercised a cruel tyranny over the people, who held a rank . . . little higher than the camels and elephants that carried them and their engines to war."

Canon law and feudal law were created to allow the church and the palace to retain control over the people, he argued. The church "persuaded mankind to believe . . . that God had entrusted them with the keys to heaven . . . with a power of dispensation over all the rules and obligations of morality, with authority to license all sorts of sins and crimes . . . with a power of procuring or withholding the rain of heaven and the beams of the sun . . .

"Thus was human nature chained fast for ages in a cruel, shameful, and deplorable servitude to him, and his subordinate tyrants . . ."

The feudal laws did no better, he wrote. While the original purpose, "the necessary defense against barbarous people," might have been necessary, the result was "the common people were held together . . . in a state of servile dependence on their lords . . . bound . . . to follow them wherever they commanded, to their wars, and in a state of total ignorance . . ."

As a result of the confederacy between these "two systems of tyranny . . . one age of darkness succeeded another."

In his essays, Adams summed up all that he had learned in his readings and discussions and finally, like gathering up pebbles in a pouch and pulling closed the drawstring, brought together all the disparate pieces of philosophy, religion and history into his own powerful statement about the law.

From the time of the Reformation to the settlement of America, he continued, the people threw off those shackles. In fact, "it was a love of universal liberty, and a hatred, a dread, a horror of the infernal confederacy . . . that projected, conducted and accomplished the settlement of America."

Through centuries those malignant systems of common and feudal law had been overcome by the spreading of knowledge, Adams argued, knowledge that had been spread by printers, "who have done important service to your country" by resisting those who would "destroy the freedom of thinking, speaking and writing." This Stamp Act, he continued, was an attempt to "strip us in a great measure of the means of knowledge, by loading the press, the colleges, and even an almanac and a newspaper, with restraints and duties . . ."

In closing he called upon his fellows to act. "Let the bar proclaim 'the laws, the rights, the generous plan of power' delivered down from remote antiquity . . . British liberties, are not the grants of princes or parliaments, but original rights, conditions of original contracts . . ."

Allowing this to be published was a brave act, even if done so anonymously at first. John Adams had laid out a legal and moral defense against Parliament's attempt to impose taxes upon the colonies. It would not pass muster in England, so he presented his legal argument against the tax to a committee of Braintree residents. These Braintree Instructions, as they were known, directed the town's representative to the general court, the legislature, to vote against the Stamp Act. It accused Parliament of violating principles of English law that had been respected since the passage of the Magna Carta in 1215. "The maxims of the law," it read, ". . . no freeman can be separated from his property but by his own act or fault. We take it clearly, therefore, to be inconsistent with the spirit of the common law, and of the essential fundamental principles of the British constitution, that we should be subject to any tax imposed by the British Parliament because we are not represented in that assembly . . ."

The Instructions was passed unanimously and published, and soon forty other Massachusetts towns adopted it and ordered their own representatives to vote for it. With this extraordinary show of colonial unity, John Adams had become a public man, a leader of the growing independence movement.

His standing was solidified several months later, after the Act had taken effect. The town was essentially shut down when residents refused to pay the tax. Courts and businesses were shut. Adams's practice came to a halt and he lamented he "had but just become known and gained a small degree of reputation when this execrable project was set on foot for my ruin as well as that of America . . ." His newly achieved status became evident when the Boston town meeting asked him to join the venerable Gridley and Otis to represent the city in demanding the governor and council remove the tax so the courts of law might be opened. While this petition was denied by the governor, the continued boycott finally achieved its purpose and the Stamp Act was repealed.

Early in his career Adams had wondered to his diary what his purpose in life was meant to be. Now he had found it. In addition to his growing practice he was elected town selectman, bringing his legal expertise to bear on the myriad problems of local government, from schools to roads. It was the application of the law in the most relevant way: how to make the lot of his fellow man better.

He was leading the good lawyer's life: his practice was expanding, so broadly it was necessary to add a third clerk; he was utilizing his abilities for the community and remained active in improving the standards of the profession. But it was a time of unease: there was a resolution coming to this hostility between England and her colonies, which was becoming inevitable, but what form it might take was as hazy as the summer's morning mist rising in Boston Harbor. Adams was determined that whatever was to come, for the colonists to achieve their aims it must be done lawfully.

Colonists were being forced to choose

their side, patriot or loyalist. Adams's patriotism was only slightly tested in 1768 when his close friend, Jonathan Sewall, a loyalist who had risen to become attorney general of the province, presented him with an offer from Governor Francis Bernard to become advocate general in the admiralty court. It was a prestigious and lucrative post. It would bring him into the King's government, with all the rewards that promised. And while Sewall stated that the governor made this offer with full awareness of Adams's sympathies and it should not be construed as a passive bribe, Adams refused. Several weeks later Sewall again made the offer, and again was rebuffed.

Only months later Adams found himself standing up as a defense attorney for the merchant John Hancock against Sewall in that same court. In May, Hancock was accused of smuggling one hundred pipes of Madeira wine aboard his sloop *Liberty* to avoid duties payable under the Revenue Act. After that ship had been seized by the crew of *H.M.S. Romney,* and secured under its fifty guns, Hancock hired Adams to contest it.

Adams initially was appointed by the town of Boston to help draft instructions to its representatives on the general court, the first effort to find a conciliatory path. When that attempt failed, the admiralty court declared Hancock's *Liberty* forfeit and the Royal Navy put it into a service as a revenue cutter.

Hancock then was personally charged as an accessory to the violation and threatened with a massive fine of £9,000, three times the value of the smuggled wine. The trial took place in admiralty court, where verdicts were reached by the presiding judge, instead of a jury. In this case it was Robert Auchmuty, Jr., who would later become Adams's co-counsel in the Massacre case.

Rather than disputing the facts of the case, Adams used it to attack the entire relationship between England and America, giving voice to the frustrations of the colonists. He challenged the entire legal structure under which the action had been brought. His client was being denied his fundamental right of trial by jury, he argued, under a statute that was unjustly passed without the consent of the people. "My client, Mr. Hancock," Adams pointed out, "never consented to it; he never voted for it himself and he never voted for any man to make such a law for him."

The case rambled on for so long, Adams wrote, "I was thoroughly weary and disgusted with the Court, the Officers of the Crown, the cause and even with the tyrannical bell that dongled me out of my house every morning." Whether it was the strength of his arguments, a lack of evidence connecting Hancock to the event or sheer exhaustion, Sewall eventually caused the case against Hancock to be dropped.

Fate, ambition, skill, intelligence and opportunity had come together to make John Adams the legal advocate for what was to come. His reputation was soaring. In September 1768 he had defended a man named Samuel Quinn, who had been accused of rape, a charge carrying the death penalty. After being acquitted of that capital crime, Quinn had said, "God bless, Mr. Adams. God Bless his soul I'm not to be hanged."

As the political situation worsened, he found himself enmeshed in most local matters in dispute, and became the acknowledged leader of the legal aspect of the growing liberty movement. When four American sailors were accused of killing British Naval Lieutenant Henry Panton in April 1769, for example, it was natural that Adams would defend them. The men were aboard a brig at sea, the *Pitt Packet,* when it was boarded by sailors and marines from *H.M. Frigate Rose.* They had come aboard that ship to impress those men, forcing them into Royal Navy service. Four crew members hid in the *Pitt Packet*'s forepeak and when discovered refused an order to come out, vowing to defend themselves. After threats were made and a shot was fired by a British seaman, crewman Michael Corbett ran through Panton with a harpoon. The four men were taken into custody.

There was little precedent to cover this event, and it took place at sea, so there was a question of which jurisdiction applied. What laws were broken? In what court should the case be heard? Should a jury sit in judgment or was this a military action? It was a knotty situation, and Adams dived into it.

It was decided the trial would be held in special admiralty court, which would convene in the newly constructed courthouse on Queen Street. Governor Bernard and acting governor Hutchinson would sit with other officials in judgment. Boston was fixated on this trial. As Adams later recalled, "No trial had ever interested the community so much before, excited such curiosity and compassion or so many apprehensions of the fatal consequences of the supremacy of parliamentary jurisdiction . . ."

This was clearly self-defense, Adams

decided. In his preparatory notes he wrote, "Self preservation is the first law of nature," and "Self love is the strongest principle in our breasts, and self-preservation not only our unalienable right but our clearest duty, by the law of nature."

Adams contested all of the jurisdictional issues and the court heard witnesses for three days. Then Adams rose to begin his summation. He had prepared copious notes to guide his argument: "The first question to be made . . ." he wrote, "is whether impresses in any cases . . . are legal. For if impresses are always illegal . . . Corbett and his associates had a right to resist him and if they could not otherwise preserve their liberty to take away his life. His blood must lye at his own door, and they be held guiltless . . ." He then cited the statute under which impresses were illegal. Later in his notes, Adams referred to William Hawkins's seminal *A Treatise of the Pleas of the Crown:* " 'Not only he who on assault retreats to a wall, or some such straight beyond which he can go no further, before he kills the other, is judged by the law to act upon unavoidable necessity . . .' "

Adams intended to raise questions the Crown did not want debated. The right to impress crewmen was sticky and based more in history and tradition than statute. A legal decision against it might cause long and unexpected ramifications. So unexpectedly, moments after Adams rose to present his argument, Hutchinson sought an adjournment. Since it was not granted, Hutchinson found another route, arguing that Panton specifically did not have the authority to impress anyone, rather than fighting Adams's more general attack on the right itself. After four hours of deliberation, the court reached the verdict of justifiable homicide. The men were acquitted, although the verdict was never published.

It was a victory for the Americans, but Adams was not satisfied. He represented the seaman whose arm had been broken by the pistol shot, John Ryan, in an action against the shooter — and won a £30 judgment.

It was less than a year later that British soldiers fired upon Boston men, killing five of them. Undoubtedly it came as a great surprise to the town, perhaps even disbelief, when John Adams, patriot, agreed to defend the killers. While others demanded blood, he would defend the British soldiers with all his ability and tools, but he would do so for the good of Americans.

With the immediate action done, the

propaganda war began. The Boston Massacre, as it quickly became known to the patriots, became the Incident on King Street to the British. The two sides made great efforts to gather support for their position. Thousands of Bostonians turned out for the funeral; it was reportedly the largest number of mourners for any funeral on the American continent. Four of the victims were interred together, and when Carr died several days later, "the fifth life that has been sacrificed by the rage of the soldiery," wrote the *Boston Gazette,* he was buried in the same mass grave in the Granary Burying Ground.

The *Gazette* pitched dry wood on the fire, reporting in its front page coverage several different acts of violence leading to the shootings, among them a confrontation between Samuel Atwood and ten or twelve soldiers, during which he "asked them if they intended to murder people? They answered yes, by G-d, root and branch! With that one of them struck Mr. Atwood with a club . . ."

As for the killings, "the soldiers continued the fire, successively, till 7 or 8, or as some say 11 guns were discharged. By this fatal maneuver, three men laid dead on the spot, and two more struggling for life; but what shewed a degree of cruelty unknown to British troops . . . was an attempt to fire upon or push with their bayonets the persons who undertook to remove the slain and wounded . . .

"Tuesday morning presented a most shocking scene, the blood of our fellow citizens running like water thro' King Street . . ."

That same edition of the patriot-leaning journal carried an advertisement placed there by Captain Preston. It appeared to be his effort to soften the feelings against him. "My thanks in the most public manner," it read, "to the inhabitants in general of this town — who throwing aside all party and prejudice, have with the utmost humanity and freedom stept forth advocates for truth in defense of my injured innocence."

To document the patriot's version of the massacre, on the morning of March 7th the town meeting appointed a fifteen-man committee, supervised by two justices, to take down the depositions of eyewitnesses to the entire event. Almost a hundred people gave their versions of what transpired that night, including Samuel Condon, who described witnessing the killings. He was standing "nigh the west end of the Custom House . . ." he recalled. "In a few minutes after having placed myself aforesaid, a musket was fired by the soldier who stood next to the corner, in a few seconds after another was fired and so in succession until the whole was discharged . . .

". . . when the firing ceased I turned and went up to the head of the lane where I saw people carrying off one dead person and two more laying lifeless on the ground, about two muskets length from the soldiers, inhumanly murdered by them, the blood then running from them in abundance. A person asked the soldier who fired first the reason for his doing so, the soldier answered, 'Damn your bloods, you boogers, I would kill a thousand of you . . .' "

They told their stories, which were recorded without question. Admittedly, some of the accounts contradicted others, perhaps properly reflecting the confusion in the town. But what emerged was another shocking claim, hints of a darker conspiracy: several people testified they had seen guns fired from the second story of the Custom House, supposedly from the windows of Green's home. The inference was clear; customs officials, government men, had taken part in the massacre. Charles Bourgatte, a fourteen-year-old French-speaking boy indentured to a customs official, said that he had been taken inside by Hammond Green and forced to fire out the window, although he added that he had fired harmlessly into the air. As he left the room, he continued, his master, Edward Manwaring, had fired one more shot.

A carpenter named Benjamin Andrews declared he found a musket ball buried two-and-a-half inches deep in a doorpost almost directly opposite the Custom House, the inference being it had been shot at a downward angle. That was consistent with other eyewitness claims, and led to Edward Manwaring, the French boy's master; his friend John Munro; Hammond Green, who lived in an apartment there with his family; and Thomas Greenwood, a customs employee, being indicted for participation in the event.

Seemingly in confirmation of this startling claim, artist Henry Pelham produced a fanciful illustration of the shooting; it was so woefully inaccurate that it even depicted the wrong number of soldiers. Paul Revere apparently copied the distorted engraving and three weeks later released for sale his own print, titled "Bloody Massacre Perpetrated in King Street in Boston." Both versions included a gun extending from a second-story window surrounded by a cloud of smoke. Below the illustration,

Revere printed a poem he had written, reinforcing the prevailing emotions: "While faithless P — n and his savage bands, with murd'rous rancor stretch their bloody hands," adding, "The patriots copious tears for each are shed, a glorious tribute which embalms the dead."

"These depositions," concluded the committee, "show clearly that a number of guns were fired from the Custom House." It was Revere's popular print that gave Bostonians the most widely accepted description of what happened under the dim light of the quarter moon. Sam Adams and his Sons of Liberty had helped lay the foundation for the prosecution in the court of public opinion.

Forty-eight-year-old Samuel Adams was seemingly a shadow moving behind every significant event on the path to liberty. There were some who suspected he might have been directing events on the night of March 5th, then helped collect the depositions and determine how to use the event to further the patriot cause. Sam and John Adams were second cousins; and while not especially close, they shared many of the same beliefs and desires, but they followed very different paths to achieve them. Sam Adams was a fiery political agitator, never taking a step back or shying away from confrontation, while his less flamboyant cousin fought within the confines of the law. John Adams respected Samuel, observing that he "was zealous and keen in the cause" of liberty, a man of "steadfast integrity" and "universal good character," who had "the most thorough understanding of liberty."

Acting governor Hutchinson was not about to let the patriots' version of events stand without a challenge. When he became aware that the town was taking depositions, he empowered a more friendly justice to receive additional testimony, taken mostly from the troops. Those statements, presenting a picture of soldiers doing their duty attacked by zealots, were secretly sent by man o' war to London and delivered to the ministry.

The patriots' version of that night was edited and bound into a pamphlet entitled *A Short Narrative of the Horrid Massacre in Boston* and printed at the town's expense. But supposedly to prevent potential jurors in the coming trials from forming an early opinion, this was not circulated in America. Instead about forty copies were sent to London, where it was hoped it might influence government policy, specifically con-

The town was stunned when British troops fired into a crowd of rowdy protestors, killing five men. Within days, artist Henry Pelham had published an inaccurate and inflammatory engraving of "The Fruits of Arbitrary Power, or The Bloody Massacre." Three weeks later, silversmith Paul Revere offered for sale a similar print. "The Bloody Massacre Perpetrated in King Street Boston on March 5th 1770" became a popular propaganda piece, fueling anti-British sentiment. COLLECTION OF THE MASSACHUSETTS HISTORICAL SOCIETY

cerning the presence of troops in the province.

Only after the ninety-six-page *Short Narrative* arrived in England were the loyalist statements collected and bound into a volume entitled *A Fair Account of the Late Unhappy Disturbance at Boston.* To provide the false impression that these statements were a valid extension of the first pamphlet, simply adding more statements, its pages were numbered beginning at ninety-seven. Among those loyalists who gave a deposition was Captain Preston, who swore, "About 9 some of the guard came to and informed me the town inhabitants were assembling to attack the troops, and that the bells were ringing as the signal for that purpose and not for fire, and the beacon intended to be fired to bring in the distant people of the country." While he proceeded to the Main Guard, which was stationed in a building near the Town House, a mob in front of the Custom House "surrounded the sentry posted there, and with clubs and other weapons threatened to execute their vengeance on him. I was soon informed by a townsman their intention was to carry off the soldier from his post and probably murder him . . . I immediately sent a non-commissioned officer and 12 [sic] men to protect both the sentry and the king's money, and very soon followed myself to prevent, if possible, all disorder, fearing lest the officer and soldiers, by the insults and provocations of the rioters, should be thrown off their guard and commit some rash act."

Coincidentally, on the day the killings took place, the 5th of March, Lord North, the new prime minister, had requested Parliament partially repeal the hated Townshend Acts, which had led to so much distress. That request had nothing at all to do with the violence that came later that night; it was instead a logical response to reality. The colonial nonimportation strategy had proved successful; collections had been reduced by more than £700,000 while the cost of maintaining a military presence in Massachusetts to enforce the act had risen. The act had brought colonists to the tip of rebellion while proving devastating to British manufacturers and merchants. In April, Parliament voted for this partial repeal. Duties on all products other than tea were eliminated.

Tea was excepted because it was not grown in England, and thus a boycott did not affect British merchants. Far more important, Parliament wanted to reinforce its legal argument that England had an absolute right to tax its colonies. But the repeal of the most onerous portions of the act, and the immediate increase in trade, significantly reduced confrontations between customs officials and colonists.

With the regiments out of reach on Castle William, a fortified island in Boston Harbor, and Preston and his men in prison awaiting trial, the immediate crisis had been abated. Now it was time for the lawyers to try to set things right. Murders had been committed. And many in the city felt strongly, blood required blood.

CHAPTER THREE

More than a decade earlier John Adams had written in his journal: "No man is entirely free from weakness and imperfection in this life. Men of the most exalted genius and active minds are generally most perfect slaves to the love of fame. They sometimes descend to as mean tricks and artifices in pursuit of honor or reputation as the miser descends to in pursuit of gold . . . I will stand collected within myself and think upon what I read and what I see. I will strive with all my soul to be something more than persons who have had less advantages than myself."

While Adams was highly ambitious, he was also keenly aware of the perils associated with actively seeking notoriety. And his representation of the British soldiers was already bringing him far more infamy than reputational gain among the people whom he encountered on a regular basis. The fact that he chose to involve himself in this case was hardly surprising. He ranked high among the most respected lawyers in the area, as the ever-increasing pace of his practice reflected, but still involved himself in those issues he believed important.

Only two months earlier, on the evening of January 3rd, 1770, for example, in an effort to bring professionalism to the practice of law, he joined a dozen other attorneys and barristers at the Bunch of Grapes Tavern on the corner of State and Kelly streets to form the Suffolk County Bar Society. It was the first such organization in Massachusetts and he was elected secretary. The initial concern of the men was to set reasonable standards for admission to the bar, and to accomplish that, they began meeting somewhat regularly.

A month later, Adams's one-year-old daughter, Suky, as he called her, died. It was a harsh blow. But Adams contained his emotions, barely referring to this tragedy. Only once, many years later, did he speak his child's name in public. He remained busy. In the first few months of 1770 his office produced more than one hundred writs; whatever his defects had been as a young lawyer through the years, they had been addressed. In addition to representing Captain Preston and his eight men facing an array of very serious charges, in March he was involved in forty-three other cases, ranging from illegal searches to property disputes.

While the political bickering continued publicly, both the prosecution and the defense were maneuvering quietly to gain an advantage. Trials were popular entertainment and this one, a murder trial that touched so many people of the town, was going to be a great show. Most times the spectators were passive observers, but in this case there was an emotional involvement. Everyone in Boston had suffered through the occupation: they had heard the taunts and the insults, they had watched the soldiers parading through their streets with arrogance, they had seen the redcoats dismiss the local laws, they had watched as their liberties were challenged.

The trials of Captain Preston, of the soldiers, and of the men who had been on the second floor of the Custom House, would be an excitable spectacle. And there was reason to believe the town would be quite satisfied with the outcome: the soldiers had fired their weapons at innocent men standing only a few feet away. They had killed people. Whether or not Captain Preston had actually given the order to fire made little difference to most; as their officer he bore the responsibility for their actions. There was almost no sympathy for any of the accused. A fair trial would be held and then, as the renowned author and Anglican cleric Jonathan Swift had written years earlier, "There will be the devil and all to pay."

The situation for the men upstairs in the Custom House was less clear. The French boy, Charles Bourgatte, continued to insist that he had been forced to fire a musket from the second floor and that he had seen other men firing. But the other people present there, including the Green family and their servants, refuted that. All of them were brought before the grand jury several times. There were even reports that threats were made to compel them to confirm the boy's story, but they remained steadfast in their denials. Nevertheless, seven witnesses swore that guns were fired from the window and the grand jury finally indicted them on March 27th.

Trials generally were held as quickly as possible, while the witnesses were in place and their memories untainted. It was expected that the trials of Preston and the soldiers would take place within weeks and last no longer than a day. The jury would be selected in the morning, testimony would be given, evidence would be heard through the afternoon, there would be a summing up, and the jury would render its verdict. Two days, at most.

But in this case, the timing mattered more than usual. As Sam Adams pointed out, many of the prosecution witnesses were seamen and did not have the luxury of remaining ashore. To assist the court, two justices had already taken written eyewitness depositions. The court was currently in adjournment but was scheduled to resume its work on March 17th; it was expected these trials would soon be on the docket.

The defense wanted to delay the trials as long as possible, allowing sufficient time to pass for passions to cool. But there was another, equally important reason: by tradition, British army officers convicted of crimes committed in the line of duty could expect to be pardoned by the Crown. But pardons could not be issued before a verdict had been rendered. The distance between London and New York could be measured in months, so if the redcoats were convicted of murder and sentenced to death, it would be difficult to delay the carrying out of that sentence long enough for a pardon to arrive. In a similar circumstance in Edinburgh, rather than waiting, the town had carried out the sentence, taking the prisoner by force and hanging him. There was speculation that should the men be convicted, several hundred soldiers would be brought back into the city to protect them until the King could make his wishes known, an outcome that would add new complications to an already dire situation. As an obedient servant of the King, Governor Hutchinson secretly wrote to London and asked for instructions.

Most of the colonists wanted revenge more than justice. The clergy declared the defendants guilty from their pulpits. Loyalist Peter Oliver quoted the senior minister of Boston, the Reverend Dr. Charles Chauncy, declaring of Preston, " 'If I was to be one of the jury upon his trial, I would bring him in guilty, evidence or no evidence.' " Hutchinson wrote, "The minds of the people are so inflamed that it is much to be desired that the trials of the officers and soldiers should be deferred," adding in another missive his desire to "keep [the people] in expectation of it until they were somewhat cooled and could be diverted by some other subject for their attention."

The law was silent on how long those diversions could last. The right of a defendant to a speedy trial had been sewed into the fabric of law in 1166, when Henry II had issued a series of ordinances known as the Assize of Clarendon, in which it was stated that when a man was accused of a crime, "if the justices are not about to come speedily enough," the sheriffs must make arrangements for a judge to be present. The Magna Carta enshrined that right, declaring, "wee shall not . . . deny or delay Justice and right, neither the end, which is Justice, nor the meane, whereby we may attaine to the end, and that is the law."

Sir Edward Coke in his *Institutes* wrote that the law was clear on the subject: it was the obligation of justices to provide for prisoners (which included the accused even though they had not been convicted) "full and speedy justice . . . without detaining him long in prison."

But nowhere was that further explained, nor was there any specific guidance for the defense seeking to delay the proceedings. There was little in recent legal history for either side to base an argument as to how quickly the trial must be held. It was left to the parties to make the fight any way possible. Both sides made efforts to intimidate the judges. Adams's Suffolk County Bar Society supported an adjournment, claiming they, as well as the judges, "had been fatigued with the business of the term in this county," and that a new term was fast approaching. When the judges agreed to a postponement to the first week in June, the patriots were outraged. A delegation led by John Hancock, Sam Adams and Dr. Joseph Warren, the patriot leader who weeks earlier had conducted the autopsy on young Christopher Seider, trailed by "a vast concourse of people," marched into the courtroom and, recalled Hutchinson, "press[ed] the judges physically as well as morally." They "harangued" the judges, they put them "under duress"; according to Governor Francis Bernard, they faced the possibility of "being torn to pieces" should they counteract the will of this sovereign committee. The risk became so great that Attorney General Jonathan Sewall left town and acting chief justice Benjamin Lynde, Jr., tried twice to resign his position, but that resignation was not accepted. Hutchinson offered his own resignation but it too was rejected.

The judges finally acquiesced; had they not, explained Judge Oliver, "It was rather more than an equal chance that the prisoners would have been murdered by the rabble, and the judges exposed to assassination." The trials were set for April. All of the prisoners, including Captain Preston, were held in the Boston Gaol, which had opened only three years earlier. It was a brick building, with walls three feet thick, situated just off Court Street in the center of the town.

Perhaps to "divert the attention" of the town, as Hutchinson desired, on April 20th the trial of Ebenezer Richardson for the slaying of young Seider began. It provided at least a temporary release for the fury Sam Adams had built up and allowed the soldiers' trial to be delayed again until the end of May. Richardson and co-defendant Wilmot had struggled to find a man to defend them; every lawyer in the town had refused their request, the first court-appointed lawyer had taken sick twice, and the burden finally fell upon Josiah Quincy, Jr., who was assisted by Sampson Salter Blowers, a loyalist who had studied the law in Hutchinson's office. The prosecution was handled by Quincy's older brother, Solicitor General Samuel Quincy, and Sons of Liberty member Robert Treat Paine, the same team who would be prosecuting Captain Preston and the soldiers. The trial began some weeks after the shooting but anger was still at a high pitch. The defendants claimed they had been attacked on Richardson's property, there was reason for them to fear for their lives and thus they were justified in protecting themselves in any way possible. The right of self-defense was a natural right given to every man, particularly in his home. The people who truly were guilty, they argued, were those who had encouraged these boys to act. And even if the jury did not believe they acted in self-defense, because the mob was acting illegally the worst charge against Richardson should be manslaughter. The prosecution ridiculed that argument, contending that the so-called attackers were nothing more than rowdy schoolboys, and that neither defendant's life had ever been in jeopardy.

Several times during the trial, spectators shouted warnings to the jurors, reminding them that "Blood requires blood." After hearing the evidence, at least one judge told the jury, as was common practice at the time, that he believed this was a case of justifiable homicide, a legal term that included self-defense. The prisoner was attacked in his own house by a number of people and he had a natural right to defend his life. The onlookers disagreed: when the prisoners were returned to jail — while the jury deliberated — another attempt was made to take them and hang them. The crowd even hissed and abused the judges as they left the courtroom.

The jury found George Wilmot not guilty and Richardson guilty of murder. At the reading of the guilty verdict, spectators burst into hurrahs. Then the gears of the law took hold. The judges did not agree with the verdict, believing the jury had been unduly influenced by the spectators. There was little that could be done to change it, though; the defense requested a new trial, but under the law, that did not fit the circumstances. The judges found a suitable compromise, court was adjourned and sentencing was delayed several months.

Further investigation proved the jury had been confused. The final holdout had agreed to find Richardson guilty only after being assured by his fellow jurors, after arguing through the night, that "if the verdict was not agreeable to law, the court would not receive it." The court found reasons to put off sentencing, while the authorities wrote to England, requesting the King issue a pardon. Richardson remained in jail for two years. Knowing the defendant's life remained in jeopardy, the court waited until a town meeting was in progress, then brought Richardson into court and essentially freed him. He fled Boston before anyone knew about the hearing. Furious men pursued him, intending to impose their own law, but he escaped.

Among those taking note of this trial was John Adams; while he had no professional involvement in it, he certainly recognized that at least some of the legal arguments presented in Richardson's defense might prove beneficial in his own cases. The defense had reminded the jury, quoting Sir Edward Coke, that the law was clear: "A man's home was his castle and he may defend it by himself or with such as he calls to assist him."

For precedent, the colonists mostly looked to English common law for guidance and direction. In Richardson's defense, his counsel cited the 1707 case *Reg. v. Mawgridge,* in which violence was considered justifiable in response to an assault. In that affray, Mawgridge, a guest of Lieutenant Cope, an officer at the Tower of London, quarreled with his host over a woman. After heated words, Mawgridge threw a bottle of wine at Cope's head, then drew his sword. Cope apparently retrieved the bottle and hurled it back at Mawgridge, striking him and wounding him. Mawgridge then stabbed and killed Cope, and was arrested for murder. "If upon angry words," read the notes, "one man assault another either by pulling him by the nose or even filliping him on the forehead, and he who is so assaulted immediately runs the other through, it is but manslaughter, for the peace is broken by him that is killed; and he that receives such indignity may reasonably apprehend a further design upon him."

The defense in the Richardson case referred to several other cases that touched upon elements of this precedent, but given the climate in the town, none of that truly mattered. There was little doubt about the verdict.

The massacre trial was scheduled to be held in late May, when the Massachusetts Superiour Court of Judicature returned to Boston from its regular sittings in Plymouth and Barnstable in the south of the province. But on his ride from Middleborough, Judge Peter Oliver conveniently had fallen from his horse and was unable to attend, while Justice Trowbridge had taken ill. On May 31st, Chief Justice Benjamin Lynde adjourned the court *sine die,* meaning without designating a new date. But it would not be soon; the court would not be in session again in Boston until the very end of August. The loyalists had won their delay but Captain Preston and the soldiers were hardly able to relax. Rumors were floated that a mob might storm the jail to lynch Captain

Preston and the soldiers. The concern so great that acting governor Hutchinson wrote to Sheriff Stephen Greenleaf, recommending that he take the keys to their jail cells home each night so the jail guard "himself, if they should be demanded, may not have it in his power to deliver them." Hutchinson even went as far as to consider transforming parts of Castle William island into a prison, just to keep the British soldiers safe.

Meanwhile, Adams was moving deftly through this difficult time. After dealing with the brickbats of the town, he had still been asked to run for an open seat representing Boston in the general court, Massachusetts's representative body. Simply being invited to run for the seat was itself a strong statement from Sam Adams and the Sons of Liberty that they accepted his principled stand. The months that had passed already had the intended impact of calming the initial fury. But Adams was ambivalent about the offer; until this moment he had avoided direct political involvement, happily expressing his patriotic sentiments through his legal work and public statements. He worried about the price of a public career, writing that in his mind, "I was throwing away as bright prospects as any man ever had before him . . . and that for nothing, except what indeed was and ought to be in all a sense of duty." He discussed the offer with Mrs. Adams, whom, he admitted, burst into tears but told him she was willing to place her trust in him and in Providence.

On May 29th, a week before the election, Abigail gave birth to their second son, named Charles. As was the practice, candidate Adams had not campaigned. But his reputation and the support of second cousin Sam Adams was sufficient. In June, he was elected to the court with 418 of the 536 votes cast. Upon being informed of his victory, he thanked supporters at Faneuil Hall and launched immediately into his first political battle. Parliament had determined that the influence of Sam Adams and his followers might be reduced by moving the general court out of Boston to Cambridge. Six years earlier that body had met outside the town during a smallpox outbreak, but never before had it done so for political reasons. In his newly elected position Adams led the successful legal fight to block that attempt.

Even with the new addition to his family, his election and continuing preparations for the trials, Adams worked hard at his basic law practice. Bills could not be paid with prestige. His other cases might have lacked the life-and-death urgency of Captain Preston's, but they were necessary to support his family. Although he had gained significant renown in the town, and was leading the defense in the most important trial in American history, days after the legislature adjourned he climbed into his one-man buggy, his Desobligeant, and joined his fellow attorneys on the circuit, bringing the law to the people.

Even while arguing matters of property and insults and injuries, while filing writs and the array of legal papers, while getting embroiled in other criminal cases, decisions had to be made about trial strategy. Adams would be defending both Captain Preston and his men, which created a legal dilemma. The best defense for each of them was to place the responsibility on the other. Preston had not shot anyone; he had been indicted for ordering his men to fire. His men had done the killing. Preston certainly would deny he had given any such order, thus placing the blame squarely on his men. While serving his defense, it would weigh heavily against those troops.

The best defense those soldiers could offer was that they were following Captain Preston's orders, which they were bound to do under penalty of death. Either Preston ordered his men to shoot, in which case he would be guilty and they were obeying legal orders or he did not order his men to shoot, in which case he might be acquitted or receive a lesser verdict but his men could be guilty of murder.

If Captain Preston and his troops were tried together, the inevitable accusations and counters might so disturb the jury that its only option was to find all of them guilty. To prevent that situation from happening, one of the first legal decisions made was to sever them and hold two separate trials. Preston would be tried first, then his soldiers. His conviction would likely result in the acquittal of the troops, while should he be found not guilty, additional pressure would come to bear on the soldiers.

The only path that would serve the interests of all the accused was to prove that either together or individually they were in fear for their lives and acted in self-defense, and that there was sufficient justification for them to believe that.

As a student of the law, Adams had a complex history on which to create his strategy. He was an avid collector of books, often referring to it as his passion; his library included most of the important legal books, and he was a regular subscriber to London booksellers. In his preparation, Adams reviewed his newly arrived copies of Sir William Blackstone's *Commentaries of the Laws of England.* The four volumes had been published in England between 1765 and 1769. Adams could not wait for the American publication, instead paying a then whopping $26 for the Oxford edition. The *Commentaries* had created quite a hullaballoo among lawyers and judges; Blackstone was considered the foremost authority on the law, having been a lawyer, a law professor, a judge and then serving in Parliament. These volumes set forth the established common law from its natural derivation to its courtroom application. And while the man himself was a strong supporter of the King and his right to impose the Stamp Tax on England's possessions, his scholarship delighted colonists by stressing the immutable rights of individuals to security, liberty and property.

Adams took special note of Blackstone's conclusions about self-defense: "The defence of one's self, or the mutual and reciprocal defence of such as stand in the relations of husband and wife, parent and child, master and servant. In these cases if the party himself, or any of these his relations, be forcibly attacked in his person or property, it is lawful for him to repel force by force; and the breach of the peace, which happens, is chargeable upon him only who began the affray. For the law, in this case, respects the passions of the human mind, and (when external violence is offered to a man himself, or those to whom he bears a near connection) makes it lawful in him to do immediate justice, to which he is prompted by nature, and which no prudential motives are strong enough to restrain . . .

"Self-defense . . . is justly called the primary law of nature, so . . . [it cannot be] taken away by the law of society." He also cautioned that the level of response must be limited to defense and prevention, as anything beyond that would be an act of aggression. It was a solid foundation on which Adams, Quincy and Auchmuty might build the defense.

The prosecution faced its own challenges: no one contested the facts that the soldiers fired their weapons and men were killed, but simply proving that was hardly the critical issue. While the soldiers stood trial together, there could not be a single verdict covering all of them. Legally, each man was on trial. To convict any one of them, it had to be shown that he had killed one or more of the victims. There was no hard evidence beyond the provable fact that the guns had been fired to link a soldier and a victim. In fact, the numerous eyewitness claims that civilians had fired on the crowd from the Customs House made proving soldiers had actually fired the lethal shots even more complicated.

As spring eased into summer, there still was no firm date set for the trials to begin but both the prosecution and defense continued to make their case with the people. Preston himself, who remained in prison this whole time, hurt his position when it was revealed that at the same time he was complimenting the town, he was sending an entirely different message to supporters in England. In a letter published in British newspapers he wrote, "So bitter and inveterate are many of the malcontents here they are industriously using every method to fish out evidence to prove it was a concerted scheme to murder the inhabitants. Others are infusing the utmost malice and revenge into the minds of the people who are to be my jurors . . ." Publication of this letter in the *Boston Gazette* served Sam Adams's desire to influence the jury pool far better than anything he might have written. Preston finished by admitting he expected to be convicted and sentenced to hang "in a very ignominious manner, without the interposition of his Majesty's Royal Goodness."

Preston's situation was made even worse when he claimed his letter had been edited and now included words he hadn't written, a claim that eventually was shown to be untrue. These were his own words and they stuck to him. The patriot narrative was given even greater reinforcement when the copies of the *Short Narrative* were circulated in the colony.

John Adams was also at work for the defense, quietly collecting evidence and currying favor among officials. While the particulars were not explained, in his account submitted to the Crown for reimbursement he listed £25 as payment "to certain people employed to enquire about town and collect affidavits and evidences," £21 "to turnkey fees and civility money," and an additional £21 for "small presents to particular people in Boston."

That "evidences" of necessity would be limited to eyewitness accounts of the events and the ability of jurors to understand how it applied to the circumstances. Courts tended to be somewhat loose about the rules of evidence; in 1630, Pilgrim John Billington had been the first Englishman in America convicted of murder and hanged, a conviction supposedly based solely on circumstantial evidence as there were no witnesses to the shooting. Six decades later, a court in Salem had permitted "spectral evidence," witness testimony that he or she had seen the accused person's spirit or specter, which had been sent by the devil, to be considered by a jury as evidence of witchcraft. Ironically, the chief justice in the witchcraft trials was Samuel Sewall, a distant relation to Adams's close friend Jonathan Sewell, the attorney general who fled town rather than prosecute Preston and his men.

These cases would turn on the testimony of witnesses. The only physical evidence was the few musket balls recovered from the scene. A standard for evaluating that testimony had been described by Chief Justice Sir Matthew Hale, who wrote in 1677, "that which is reported by many eyewitnesses hath greater motive of credibility than that by light and inconsiderable witnesses; that which is reported by a person disinterested than that which is reported by persons whose interest is to have the thing true or believed to be true . . ." It was a reasonable

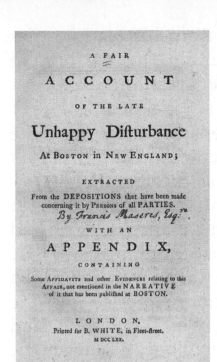

A FAIR

ACCOUNT

OF THE LATE

Unhappy Difturbance

At Boston in New England;

EXTRACTED

From the DEPOSITIONS that have been made concerning it by Persons of all PARTIES.
By Francis Maseres, Esq.re.

WITH AN

APPENDIX,

CONTAINING

Some Affidavits and other Evidences relating to this Affair, not mentioned in the NARRATIVE of it that has been publifhed at BOSTON.

LONDON,
Printed for B. WHITE, in Fleet-ftreet.
M DCC LXX.

A Short

NARRATIVE

OF

The horrid Maffacre in Boston,

PERPETRATED

In the Evening of the Fifth Day of March, 1770;

BY

Soldiers of the XXIXth Regiment ;

WHICH WITH

The XIVth Regiment

Were then Quartered there :

WITH SOME

OBSERVATIONS

ON THE

STATE OF THINGS

PRIOR TO THAT

CATASTROPHE

Printed by Order of the Town of BOSTON,
And Sold by EDES and GILL, in Queen-Street,
And T. & J. FLEET, in Cornhill, 1770.

While previously there had been countless insults and assaults exchanged between soldiers and townsmen, this raised the stakes. Patriot leaders immediately took depositions from ninety-six witnesses and published a pamphlet entitled "A Short Narrative of the Horrid Massacre," which was sent to England to influence opinion. Loyalists responded with their own version of events, "A Fair Account of the Late Unhappy Disturbance at Boston in New England," which included the testimony of thirty-one people.
COLLECTION OF THE MASSACHUSETTS HISTORICAL SOCIETY

standard for weighing testimony; the more people whose descriptions coincide the more likely it is to be true, and a person with nothing to gain from his testimony is more likely to be telling the truth than someone who has a personal interest.

While Adams was preparing his case, there also was continuous communication about the precarious situation between British officials in Boston and their advisors in London. Although the Hancock trial had attracted attention in England and the colonies, this trial was being watched much more intently throughout America and the vast British Empire, which by then had spread across the entire globe. Whatever the verdict, it would have widespread ramifications. Parliament already was struggling to maintain power over the colonies. Various suggestions were being offered about controlling the political impact of the coming trial, with the aim being to make certain that the impression of justice being done was clear while the actual consequences were minimal. London could not be seen to have abandoned its men. British soldiers around the world had interest in the proceedings, as they expected the Crown to protect troops doing their duty in the most distant parts of the Empire. They undoubtedly sympathized with the men of the 29th and, in the many countries around the world in which they served, could imagine themselves caught in a similarly precarious situation.

Of course, the 2,210,000 people living under British rule in America also were carefully watching the proceedings. To varying degrees they all had suffered the British deprivations and had risen against them. Virginia and Pennsylvania, among others, had joined the fight against taxation without representation. In Virginia, George Washington and Patrick Henry had led the struggle, with Henry inspiring patriots with his brave retort in the House of Burgesses when warned after criticizing the King, "If this be treason, make the most of it." Sam Adams's 1768 response to the Townshend Acts, the "Circular Letter" called upon colonists to unite to fight for their rights and had been quickly endorsed by the assemblies in New Hampshire, Connecticut and New Jersey — even after warnings from London. Massachusetts and Virginia's boycott of British imports, from luxury items to slaves, had spread to New Jersey, Rhode Island and North Carolina. Maryland, South Carolina and Georgia had joined the other colonies in a nonimportation agreement. While the level of participation in these various actions grew or waned at times, the undeniable result was that the thirteen colonies, some of them with little in common with others, had been forced into an undefined alliance against Parliament.

In 1754, Benjamin Franklin had published a cartoon depicting a snake severed into pieces, each segment labeled with the name of a colony, above the slogan, "Join or die." It was his desire that the colonies unify under an elected government in America with the power to levy taxes and raise a military, presided over by a president general appointed by the King. That attempt had failed, but a decade later the cartoon had been resurrected with quite a different meaning: meeting the threats from Parliament required a united front. All of the colonies had watched with growing trepidation as British troops marched ashore in Boston and gradually stripped away the existing civil liberties, wondering if the same fate was in their future.

Their worst fears had come to fruition that night on King Street. British soldiers had shot and killed protesting Americans. Newspapers and pamphlets had spread the news throughout the colonies, usually repeating the patriot viewpoint. Philadelphia's *Pennsylvania Gazette* reported that after his soldiers were pelted with snowballs, "the Captain commanded them to fire, and more snowballs coming he again said Damn you fire, be the consequence what it will . . ."

"Plenty of evidence will prove the soldiery to have been wholly the aggressor," wrote the Annapolis *Maryland Gazette,* "and that the inhabitants have been treated by them with unexampled barbarity." (In direct response to this report, England's *Leeds Intelligencer and Yorkshire General Advertiser* informed its readers, "Military discipline has been supported in Boston with unusual severity, and while the townsmen took the most cruel and barbarous advantage of abusing the troops, not only with impunity, but with applause. The soldiers . . . have been flogged all round hand the blood of the 29th has flown so plentifully that [it] goes under the denomination of bloody-backs . . .")

But when the court session resumed in Boston in late August, rather than the massacre case, it almost immediately took up arguments against the Richardson verdict. On September 6th, after enjoying a meal at John Adams's home, the judges returned to the courtroom and heard evidence that the holdout juror had been coerced into joining the majority in finding Richardson guilty. The judges were in an untenable position;

the law did not allow them to revisit the verdict, even though it did not reflect the unanimous belief of the jurors, and the mandated sentence for that verdict was death by hanging. Rather than being forced into that ruling, the judges once again delayed sentencing.

The next day, though, the prisoners were brought to the bar in the Queen Street courtroom. "Captain Thomas Preston, Esq; William Wemms, James Hartegan, William McCauley, Hugh White, Matthew Killroy, William Warren, John Carrol and Hugh Montgomery, laborers all," as defined by the court, were "charged by the grand jurors for the body of this county with having feloniously and of malice aforethought, shot and thereby murdered Samuel Maverick, Samuel Gray, James Caldwell, Patrick Carr and Crispus Attucks, against the peace, crown and dignity of our Sovereign Lord the King."

The men were accused of "not having the fear of God before their eyes, but being moved and seduced by the instigation of the devil and their own wicked hearts."

Each man was asked in turn how he pled. Not guilty, they replied one by one. "How will you be tried?" asked the clerk. "By God and my country," was the response, "country" in this instance meaning by a jury.

"God send thee a good deliverance," the clerk intoned, meaning grant them a fair trial.

Also indicted that day were the four men accused of shooting from the Custom House windows, Hammond Green, boat builder, Thomas Greenwood, laborer, Edward Manwaring, Esq., and John Munroe, gentleman. It was expected that the trials would begin within the next days, but to great surprise and without explanation the court adjourned again until the end of October.

As part of the effort to keep colonists' passions alive during this long period of waiting, beginning with the funerals there had been efforts to ensure that the victims were remembered as real men to be mourned rather a list of names. Samuel Adams would have them remembered as martyrs to the cause of liberty. Patrick Carr was a thirty-year-old Irish immigrant, the only Catholic among the victims. As he lay dying he had told the doctor he had seen mobs confronted by soldiers in Ireland, but admitted he had never seen soldiers "bear half so much before they fired." Carr worked as a leather smith, making breeches, in John Field's shop.

Seventeen-year-old seaman James Cald-well had been learning the art of navigation as a mate on Captain Morton's brig, *Young Hawk,* sailing between the town and the West Indies. Although he was not a Boston man, on the night of March 5th he had been courting the young daughter of "a reputable person" with an honorable intent, when his life was ended.

Samuel Maverick also was seventeen years old, an apprentice to the carpenter Isaac Greenwood. He was learning to be an "ivory turner," a craft in which a great variety of objects, from delicate fans to durable teeth, were carved on a lathe. In partial payment for his work, he lived at the Greenwood home, sharing a bedroom with his master's fifteen-year-old son, John. The two young men had become fast friends, and after Maverick's death John Greenwood admit-ted, "I used to go to bed in the dark on purpose to see his spirit, for I was so fond of him and he of me."

At fifty-two years old, Samuel Gray was the oldest victim; he was a laborer at John Grey's ropeworks and previously had fought with the soldiers. His hobby, it was said, was scrimshaw, the carving of whale bone, ivory or even shells. He was the first man shot and there were many who believed he had been targeted by the soldiers. The ball wounds to his head were described in gruesome detail, "a hole as big as my hand," perhaps to further inflame anger.

Crispus Attucks, the imposing "mulatto man" commonly known as Michael Johnson, was second to be killed. It was not unusual that there was confusion about Attucks's identity. Boston was a thriving port in which it was easy for a man to lose his past; its streets were filled with traders and seafaring men of all the varying shades and colors of the Americas, the Caribbean and Africa, who lived together mostly without problem. The first black men had arrived in the area more than a century earlier as indentured servants, and after working off their debt settled there and owned land. Attucks was believed to be about forty-seven years old, and reportedly was the son of a black father and Native American mother, a member of the Wampanog tribe from Natick. The *Gazette* claimed Attucks had been "born in Framingham, but lately belonged to New-Providence" and was working in Boston as a rope maker while waiting to ship out. He was known to have worked on whalers, but there was reason to believe he was an escaped slave. Two decades earlier William Brown of Framingham had posted a £10 reward in the *Gazette* for his runaway named Crispus, whose description, six-foot-two and "knees nearer together than common" fit the slain man. Attucks was a common Native American name, meaning *deer.* The color of his skin made little difference to the patriots. What mattered was that he had been a victim of British guns.

The wounded too served the cause. Seventeen-year-old apprentices Christopher Monk and John Clark survived what were believed at first to be fatal wounds, while merchant Edward Payne, John Greene the tailor, wheelwright apprentice David Parker, and seaman Robert Patterson were also shot.

The British too had made an effort to personalize the incident; but rather than naming specific patriots, it placed blame for the incident on the entire town. It was the unrelieved antagonism, the relentless name-calling and threats, the daily cuts and open displays of hatred that had led to the soldiers' rational fears for their lives when under attack that night on King Street. The defense was going to show that it was elements of Boston itself that instigated and supported this violence.

The story had been played out for almost seven months, dragged through the hot summer in the town. Both sides had gotten something from the delay, as Hutchinson and Parliament had hoped the burning hot passion had been reduced to smoldering embers, and Sam Adams and his Sons of Liberty had used the killings to help build anti-British sentiment and embrace the possibility of liberty.

But there was one more bit of legal business to be done before the trials would begin. Against the wishes of Adams and Quincy, three of the soldiers, believing their fate was tied inexorably to Captain Preston, petitioned the court to be tried alongside him. "May it please your honor," wrote these men, "we poor distressed prisoners beg that ye would be so good as to let us have our trial at the same time as our Captain, for we did our Captain's orders and if we did not obey his command we should have been confine'd and shot for not doing it . . . We only desire to open the truth before our Captain's face for it is very hard he being a gentleman should have more chance for to save his life than we poor men that is obliged to obey his command."

The petition was rejected. Now, finally, the trials would take place in late October. And Captain Preston suddenly seemed prepared, even eager, to begin the proceedings.

CHAPTER FOUR

The trial of Captain Thomas Preston, 29th Regiment of Foot, for murder, began on the 24th of October. The town was still reeling from the massive nor'easter that had rolled through only four days earlier, cutting off Boston from the mainland, flooding streets and storage rooms with massive tides, destroying boats and wharves, spoiling stocks of imported goods and resulting in as many as twenty deaths in the harbor.

After seven months of preparation, the outcome of these proceedings might have been determined on the first day. There are many advantages an attorney seeks at trial, but none of them outweigh a sympathetic jury. The concept of a defendant being judged by his peers stretches back to the 13th century, before even the end of trial by ordeal. Prior to that, God was assumed to be the judge, a man was subjected to a grueling trial by ordeal, which included tests by water, fire and duels, and his guilt or innocence determined by whether or not he survived.

Juries came to England with the Normans, who brought with them a procedure known as an "inquest." When a crime was charged, men with knowledge of the events were summoned to appear before a jury of as many as twenty-three men; they took an oath to reply truthfully to inquiries. A vote of one more than half a jury, twelve men, was sufficient to indict. Over centuries that would evolve into grand juries as well as a regular system of trial juries, which consisted of men who did not have direct knowledge of a crime coming together to hear testimony from others who did, and from that reach a conclusion as to the facts.

The Pilgrims brought the jury system to the new world with them. In 1623, only three years after landing in Plymouth, they issued a decree stating, "All criminal facts, and also all matters of trespasse and debts between man and man should be tried by the verdict of twelve honest men to be impaneled by authority in forme of a jury upon their oath."

Jurors were to be selected by "the freemen of the town where they dwell." And under colonial law, any person chosen who "shall refuse to serve in, or take upon him any such office, being legally chosen thereunto, he shall pay for such refusal, such fine and the town shall impose not exceeding twenty shillings for one offense."

It was not until 1696 that defendants were permitted to be represented by counsel, men who might help sway the opinion of a jury, although initially that right was limited to charges of treason. But by 1770 a fully functioning jury system was in place. "The method of chusing them is the most fair and impartial that the wit of man could possibly devise," merchant William Palfrey, a colleague of John Hancock, wrote to radical British politician John Wilkes. According to the law, selectmen from several towns submitted lists that named a total of twenty-four men qualified to sit in judgment. Adams and Quincy peremptorily challenged seventeen of them, meaning they did not have to explain their reasoning for excusing these men from serving. Of the seven that remained, only two were Bostonians known to be friends of the Sons of Liberty.

To complete the jury, the sheriff and his deputies were empowered by law to find spectators or passersby, "talesmen," and compel them to serve. At that time, William Palfrey continued, "a number of his [Preston's] friends and most intimate acquaintances stood ready and were accordingly return'd by the sheriff." Among these talesmen was Philip Dumaresq, who previously had been quite outspoken about his beliefs. Initially he had been picked by lot at the Boston town meeting, but asked to be excused from the panel because he was "an intimate acquaintance of Captain Preston" and "had repeatedly declared in presence of diverse witnesses that he believed Captain Preston to be as innocent as the child unborn, and that if he happened to be upon the jury he would never convict him if he sat to all eternity."

Among the other jurors was Gilbert Deblois, a merchant known to be friendly with British officers (and who had previously advised Preston which members of the original panel to challenge); the baker William Hill, who sold bread to the 14th Regiment and after an earlier altercation had stood surety for several indicted soldiers; Deblois's brother-in-law William Wait Wallis; and another quite open loyalist, Joseph Barrick. It was a jury the defense might have conjured up in a dream.

Adams was known to be steady in a courtroom, relying on his knowledge of the law rather than a grand display of emotion. At the outset he demanded clarification of the indictments against his client. The charges were specific, he pointed out, alleging that a certain soldier shot or killed a named victim. But what if it were proved that a different soldier had fired that fatal shot? Would Captain Preston still be responsible for aiding and abetting a false charge? It was a legal point well-taken; the court certainly was aware that its rulings in this trial would apply equally to the soldiers' trial. Eventually the court simply applied a far more general standard: if it could be proved that any soldier was guilty of murdering any victim, all who were present could be equally guilty of aiding and abetting the murder.

The men at the bar knew each other well, having appeared together and in opposition in many courtrooms. More than that, prosecutor Samuel Quincy would be arguing against his younger brother, Josiah, and his longtime friend Adams. The great affection that once had existed between Sam Quincy and Adams had started to wane, a casualty of the political situation. Alone in his distinguished family Sam Quincy had remained a loyalist, while his old friend Adams was a patriot.

Adams did not have great respect for some

of the other lawyers: even on his own side, he had once described the loyalist Robert Auchmuty, Jr., the oldest member of his defense team and a justice of the Massachusetts Vice Admiralty Court, as a man who argued with "voluble repetition and repeated volubility," and noted that the fact he was held in such high regard by the bar was "a libel upon it — a reproach and disgrace to it." Auchmuty, for his part, had little faith in the defense case and shared that openly with Governor Hutchinson. "I am afraid poor Preston has but little chance," the governor wrote back in March. "Mr. Auch[muty] who is his counsel tells me the evidence is very strong to prove that the firing upon the inhabitants was by his order and he doubts whether the assault could be an excuse for it."

But the bigger challenge would be dealing with the other prosecutor, Robert Treat Paine. Adams's relationship with Paine had been long, complicated and difficult. After working as a seaman, a merchant, and even a chaplain during the Seven Years War, Paine had wobbled along in his legal career. He and Adams had known each other since Adams's days as a schoolmaster. They were friends, at various times colleagues and sometimes bitter rivals. Their personalities clashed; Adams was reticent, Paine was boisterous; Adams savored his privacy, Paine was too often loud and outgoing. Adams clearly was ambivalent about him, having written, "Bob Paine is conceited and pretends to more knowledge and genius than he has. I have heard him say that he took more pleasure in solving a problem in Algebra than in a frolick . . . He makes himself a great many enemies . . . He is an impudent, ill-bred, conceited fellow. Yet he has witt, sense, and learning, and a great deal of humour, and has virtue and piety except his fretful, peevish, childish complaints against the disposition of things . . ."

Paine at times held an equally poor opinion of Adams, once telling a table of superiour court justices that Adams was "a numbskull and a blunder buss." Now they would be facing each other in a courtroom with a life at stake, with the outcome certain to affect the relationship between England and Massachusetts, and perhaps the future of all the colonies.

The trial was held in Boston's new Suffolk County Courthouse on Queen Street, which had been dedicated only a year earlier and apparently had escaped serious damage from the storm. The concept of a building dedicated solely to the law, a courthouse,

Robert Treat Paine, who would prosecute Captain Preston and the soldiers, had met John Adams in 1756. The men had long been friendly rivals who respected each other. Adams described Paine as an "an impudent, ill-bred, conceited fellow," although admittedly with "witt, sense and learning . . . a great deal of humour, virtue and piety." Paine became a patriot leader and eventually signed the Declaration of Independence for Massachusetts. COLLECTION OF THE MASSACHUSETTS HISTORICAL SOCIETY

was growing in America; in most towns and villages, trials and hearings still were held in town houses and taverns. On the traveling circuit, trials might be held in any space with sufficient room for spectators to pile in. Boston had opened a new courthouse with great pride. It was considered an important step in further recognizing the law as a respectable profession. Built at a cost of more than £2,400, it was an imposing structure; "It is a large, handsome building of brick," wrote author Thomas Pemberton, "three stories high and has on the roof an octagon cupola. The lower floor is used partly for walking . . . In the second story the floor of which is supported by pillars of the Tuscan order are held the courts of law."

The second floor courtroom was based loosely on a traditional British design. In addition to the well, where the business of the law was done, it contained a raised spectator gallery. The chief justice sat on a great chair made of walnut in the front of the room, giving him prominence over the other justices and participants. There was a chimney and fireplace behind his seat. The small courtroom also contained a lawyer's table, the first such special seating for lawyers in the colony, which was placed directly in front of the justice's bench.

Four judges would be presiding in this case. They would be wearing the somber red robes that signified this was a death penalty case. The Massachusetts Superiour

Court of Judicature, which had been established in 1692, consisted of four associate justices and a chief justice, all of them appointed by the governor. The fifth member of the court here, the chief justice, who was also the acting governor Thomas Hutchinson, had declined to participate in the trials. Adams was on good terms with the judge who would be acting as the chief justice, Benjamin Lynde. Lynde was known to be a "nervous man," a "high-strung" man, and twice in the previous few months had tried to resign his office, it seemed so he would not have to adjudicate this case; but Hutchinson had talked him out of it. Adams on occasion had dined at Justice Lynde's home in Salem, and he remembered being there when Lynde received his commission as chief justice. "Judge Lynde entertained me for some time," he recalled, "with conversation about making Salem the Seat of Government, and with the probable effects of such a measure one of which he said would be the translation of a great part of the trade from Boston to Salem. But he said he did not want to have Troops in Salem."

Associate Justice Peter Oliver was a former member of the legislature and secretary of the colony until he was named to the superiour court in 1756. Judge Oliver was a wealthy man, and only a month before the shootings his son, his namesake, had married Governor Hutchinson's daughter Sara. He knew John Adams well, but on a professional level had mixed feelings; "His genius is in the practice of law," he wrote. "He is a man of sense and made a figure at the bar; but whether nature had neglected him, or he had acquired, his self, an acrimony of temper . . . he was determined to raise hisself to a superiority which he had no claim to, and he unguardedly confessed, in one of his sallies of pride, that 'he could not bear to see anyone above him.' "

As for Adams's politics, he was, "being a sensible lawyer . . . friendly to government." That had changed, Oliver believed, when he was refused a commission by then governor Barnard, which "touched his pride and from that time resentment drove him into every measure subversive of law and of government . . ."

Ironically, Adams felt quite the opposite about Oliver, describing him as "The best bred gentleman of all the judges by far."

At the beginning of Adams's career he had been in awe of another associate justice, Judge Edmund Trowbridge, writing that he "had the power to crush, by his frown or his nod, any young lawyer in his country." Most others shared that sentiment, as his peers believed Trowbridge to be the most accomplished lawyer in New England. Adams knew him well, dined with him on occasion and the two men had enjoyed long conversations. Adams also had appeared in several courtrooms with him; in a 1762 case in which the province had brought an action against several persons "for building and covering their buildings not with slate or tile, but with shingles," it was, Adams noted, "a long wrangle, as usual when Trowbridge is in a case . . ."

Associate Justice John Cushing had no formal legal training, but after serving as a representative in the general court followed his eminent father onto the superiour court bench. As with the other justices, Adams had known him for some time and had appeared in courtrooms before him. In 1768, for example, Adams successfully represented the heirs of one Samuel Clap against claims by others that the deceased had not been of sound mind when he wrote his will. One witness testified that for several weeks before his death, "I could not get any other words from him but these, 'God blast the corn . . .' " Adams also had observed Judge Cushing preside over a complex 1766 slavery case, in which a black female slave won her freedom by proving her mother had been a free white woman. Adams also enjoyed a close friendship with Judge Cushing's son, William, and within a two-year period preceding the trial the two young lawyers had worked together on at least thirteen cases and opposed each other once.

So this was a courtroom in which all of the legal participants knew each other well; regardless of any personal differences through the years, they had been brought together by an appreciation of, and respect for, the law.

When the trial began at 8 a.m., the courtroom was filled with townsmen as well as British officers, sailors and customs officials. As many as sixty spectators crowded into the gallery. All of them, though, respected the decorum of the proceedings, and no problems arose among them.

The American legal system had deep British roots, and even as it grew naturally away from that source it continued to follow many of the basic procedures. Among the most significant differences in the two systems was that in England, defendants were not afforded the presumption of innocence; rather it was believed that an innocent man should be able to prove it. But in 1657, the earliest days of the Massachusetts colony, its legislative body, the general court had decreed, "In all civil cases . . . it behoveth both court and jury to see the affirmation be proved by sufficient evidence, else the case must be found for the defendant; and so it is also in a criminal case, for in the eyes of the law every man is honest and innocent unless it be proved legally to the contrary."

It was a fundamental and powerful right; a man is considered innocent of any charge until a jury of his fellowmen had been convinced of his guilt. And New Englanders were ready to fight for it: the nascent liberty movement had first gained strength in 1764 with the passage of the Sugar Act, under which accused smugglers would be tried in admiralty court rather than the regular town courts. This was an attack on the basic rights of New Englanders; in these special courts an accused man had to prove his innocence and a single judge, rather than twelve men, would render the verdict.

Just as Captain Preston's trial would have begun in London's Old Bailey, the Central Criminal Court for England and Wales, the clerk read the original March 7th indictment for the murder of Crispus Attucks; Captain Preston (and his men) were accused of "feloniously, willfully, and of their malice aforethought [being] present, aiding, helping, abetting, comforting, assisting and maintaining the said William Warren, to do and commit the felony and murder aforesaid."

While the presence of lawyers was still a somewhat new addition to criminal trials, they already had developed methods of making their presence known; a means of introducing themselves and perhaps impressing the jury with their skill. Adams and Paine made their preliminary arguments, debating somewhat technical points of the law. Why wasn't Preston's counsel given the names of the entire jury panel two days before selection began? Should all of the homicides be included in a single indictment? What questions might be asked about previous encounters and threats? To make his arguments, Adams cited several century-old cases that helped establish the prevailing rules.

Samuel Quincy made the opening statement for the prosecution. The position of public prosecutor was fairly new to New England courtrooms. Previously it had been the job of victims and their families to arrange for a private attorney to present the case. To make certain the passions of the public were gratified, a private lawyer, Paine, had been hired by the town to assist Quincy. His case would be presented through the words of the men who had been on King Street on March 5th. There had been a disturbance in the town that night, snowballs had been thrown at soldiers, who had swiped their bayonets at townsmen, and the fire bells brought more people into the streets. Then, under order from Captain Preston, the soldiers had fired on the people, killing five of them.

Perjury was considered a serious crime, so serious that a man bearing false witness put in jeopardy his immortal soul, and the courts did not hesitate to prosecute, so it was presumed that witnesses would be testifying truthfully as to what they believed occurred. Although there were certain classes of people who, because of their religious background, could not take the oath, including Quakers and Indians, the presumption of truthfulness was widely accepted. As chief justice, Sir Francis North had told a witness during an 1681 treason trial, "You are not to be sworn, but when you speak in a court of justice you must speak as if in the presence of God, and only speak what is true."

The Crown's first witness was young

Edward Garrick, the wigmaker's apprentice who admitted he may have sparked the night by trading insults with a soldier, Captain Lieutenant Goldfinch, over a supposedly unpaid bill to his master, the barber John Piemont. In response to his insolence, Private Hugh White, the sentry on guard in front of the Custom House had struck Garrick, he said, bringing him to tears. A main body of troops was alerted and turned out carrying naked swords, ready for confrontation. There were redcoats in the streets, and so the confrontation began.

The next witness for the prosecution was a well-known patriot and leading citizen of the town, Thomas Marshal. In addition to his quite successful tailor shop, Marshal was a colonel in the Ancient and Honorable Artillery Company of Massachusetts, having served as a member of that militia since 1761. Colonel Marshal was no stranger to violence, admittedly having swung a shovel at a loyalist while enforcing the nonimportation boycott a year earlier. He picked up the thread from Garrick, recounting how on that night he had heard a noise at some distance; he opened his door and saw two groups of soldiers in the streets, shouting warnings. He seemed certain those threats preceded the ringing of the bells, but when pressed admitted he wasn't certain. He did conclude that there was sufficient time between the first shot and subsequent shots for an officer to have stepped forward and stopped the killing rounds from being fired.

The prosecution's next several witnesses told the story of the whole ruckus; great noise, redcoats running through the streets with bayonets, patriots fleeing, finally a shot, then several shots. Fifty-eight-year-old Ebenezer Hinkley, a man who could trace his lineage to the Mayflower, testified he saw the whole confrontation; one soldier "kept pushing his bayonet at the people to stab 'em . . . I saw a stick, a few pieces of snow or snowballs thrown. The stick hit the soldier and he thereupon fired . . ." Especially important, he put Captain Preston between the people and his soldiers and said he had never seen him behind his men.

Peter Cunningham testified that he heard Captain Preston order his men to prime and load, although when questioned a bit further he admitted his lack of certainty made him only "pretty positive" Preston gave that order. More importantly, he was standing only four or five feet away from the officer and heard no order given to fire. He didn't see people "striking the guns or bayonets nor pelting them." He was quite positive, though, that the man who gave the order to prime and load was dressed in red, and sash, and carried no arms, although he would not say that man was Preston.

Samuel Quincy brought his witnesses forward in a somewhat hectic manner, their descriptions sometimes contradicting other testimony, but with a consistency about the most pertinent facts. There was disruption in the streets. The sentry at the Custom House, Private White, had been surrounded. He had tried to retreat inside and was unable to do so. Captain Preston and eight soldiers had come to his assistance. Snowballs and ice were thrown. A shot was fired. Then additional shots, rapidly. Men fell, some dead on the spot.

The structure of the trial was loose, and witnesses sometimes were called out of order. At times, the defense was allowed to respond immediately to a claim with its own rebuttal witness.

Alexander Cruikshanks came forward next. Like the other witnesses, he had been permitted to remain in the courtroom during the proceedings. Cruikshanks had tried to stop some boys from quarreling with Private White. "They said you damned rascally scoundrel lobster son-of-a-bitch and desired him to turn out. He told them it was his ground and he would maintain it and would run through any who molested or attempted to drive him off." For that, the witness was struck by the soldiers with tongs (a metal tool consisting of two long arms with clasping fingers or a cup at the end enabling someone to safely hold hot coals) and warned he'd better go home because there would be "the devil to pay in bloodshed."

William Wyat was a coaster, a man who worked aboard the cargo ships that plied the East Coast from port to port. He was a Salem man, but his vessel was stopped in Boston. He said he saw and heard the captain, wearing a cloth-colored long overcoat, a surtout as it was known, ordering the priming, loading and firing of their muskets. It was seemingly damning testimony on the single most important issue in the trial. But under cross-examination his account appeared to fall apart when he admitted that the man wearing that cloth overcoat wasn't actually Preston but had just been speaking to Preston before the men fired. And that afterward Preston had struck up the gun barrels with his sword and cursed his men for firing. With that, Wyat's testimony suddenly became a pivotal moment for the defense.

John Cox, a 53-year-old bricklayer, a man who quite possibly helped build the courthouse in which he was standing and testifying, was far more damning, telling the jury that he'd heard Captain Preston declare after the first round, "Damn their bloods, fire again! And let 'em take the consequences." It was Preston, he was certain of that, but he wore no surtout. Instead he was in "a red coat with a rose on his shoulder."

That epaulette on the right shoulder was the mark of an officer of the 29th Regiment, Preston's regiment.

Prosecutor Paine's notes of Cox's testimony ended more dramatically: "I went down and saw three dead. I said to party it was a cowardly trick to kill men within reach of bayonets and had nothing in their hand." As Cox tried to assist the dead and wounded, Preston made his threat, to which he replied, "Don't kill us who are carrying off the dead."

Most often the court was able to get through five or six cases in a day, and never before had it adjourned during a capital trial. After some discussion, as the clerk noted in his minutes, "The court being unable to go through the trial in one day, the King's attorney and the prisoner consent that the court shall adjourn over night during the trial; the jury being kept together by two keepers . . . besides the officers appointed by the court." It was clear the jurors must remain together until they reached a verdict.

There being no precedent or preparation for such an unusual situation, the jurors were taken to the jail. Under normal circumstances jurors were prohibited from enjoying "food, drink, light and fire" while deliberating, an incentive to push them to reach a verdict, but it was agreed that would not apply. Instead they enjoyed biscuits, cheese and cider, as well as "sperites licker." The total bill from jail keeper, Joseph Otis, for the entire trial was £17 13s. However, the county deducted one pound as an overcharge.

The Boston Gazette and Country Journal, reporting on this unusual adjournment, noted that "our enemies might . . . represent that it was dangerous for the court to sit in the tumultuous town of Boston after dark . . ." but in fact "the judges . . . are all of them stricken in years and one of them labors under infirmities of body." This was a matter of civic pride; the court did not adjourn because the streets were dangerous after dusk, but rather due to the fact that the aging justices could go no further.

The first witness when the trial resumed the next day was Theodore Bliss, who until recently had served on engine #9, a 4-to-6 man pump in Boston's rudimentary volunteer fire fighting society. Bliss responded instantly when he heard the fire bells. He approached Captain Preston, he explained, and asked if the muskets were loaded. Yes, the officer replied. Bliss saw a stick strike a soldier, and saw him fire his weapon in response, although he could not say whether being hit had caused him to fire. Although Bliss was standing close to Preston he did not hear him give an order to fire. Captain Preston was dressed in red and standing before his men when the first gun was fired. But after that first shot, "I thought . . . the Captain did order the men to fire but do not certainly know. I heard the word fire several times but know not whether it came from the Captain, the soldiers or the people."

Next was a giant of a man, both in size and stature, the respected bookseller Henry Knox. He came upon the scene just as a soldier was loading and snapping closed his piece. For a time he said he had stood by Captain Preston, then took hold of him by his coat and warned him that if his men fired, he would die. Preston responded, "He was sensible of that."

Benjamin Burdick, Jr., the constable of the watch for the center part of Boston, heard the order to fire but was not certain who gave it. "The word 'Fire' I took to be a word of command . . . I had not my sword drawn till after the soldier pushed his bayonet at me. I should have cut his head off if he had stepd out of his rank to attack me again . . . After the firing I went up to the soldiers and told them I wanted to see some faces that I might swear to them another day. The sentinel, in a melancholy tone said, 'Perhaps, Sir, you may.' "

Daniel Calef, who previously had such trust in Robert Paine that he had given him his power of attorney, identified Preston as the man who had given the order to fire. "I looked the officer up in the face and saw him mouth 'go' . . . I saw his face plain, the moon shone in it." In his memory the officer "had on a red coat, yellow jacket and silver laced hat, no trimming his coat," the proper dress of an officer of the 29th. "The prisoner is the officer."

Next was Robert Goddard, who became a critical prosecution witness. He testified he had heard Captain Preston warning the crowd, "Go home, lest there be murder done." When the boys did not disband, but

148

instead continued throwing snowballs, Preston went behind his line and, Goddard was certain, had given the order to fire: "Damn your bloods fire [if you] think I'll be treated in this manner . . ." He couldn't be shaken by questions from the defense, replying, "I was so near to the officer when he gave the word fire that I could touch him." In his summation, Adams would deride Goddard as a slow thinker "not capable of making observations."

The blacksmith, Obadiah Winston, watched the guard turn out. He "heard the Captain call the guard and say, 'Damn your blood, why don't you turn out.' They came out, a Corporal leading them to the sentinel."

There was continued confusion about what Captain Preston was wearing, and whether the man who gave the order to shoot was wearing a surtout or a red coat or neither. Twenty-seven-year-old Dimon Morton knew Preston well, and swore he was wearing a cloth-colored surtout, while the rope maker Nathaniel Fosdick swore Preston was "dressed in his regimentals" and "had no surtout on, but was carrying a sword." Unlike so many other witnesses, Fosdick said, "I saw nothing thrown nor any blows given at all."

As the prosecution reached the end of its presentation, Quincy called Jonathan Williams Austin to the stand, a young man who had been clerking for John Adams since the beginning of the previous August. There was no objection to this from the defense, as Austin was going to relate what he had seen in the dim moonlight. The odd fact that he was testifying for the prosecution while working directly for a member of the defense was never considered an issue. He had not seen guns fired, but one of the soldiers, he said, McCauley, had struck at him with his bayonet.

The final three witnesses testified as to what they heard after Governor Hutchinson arrived on the scene. While this might have been excluded as hearsay evidence, which prohibits the admission of most third party conversations, in this situation the judges allowed it as bearing directly on the defendant's claim that the lives of his men were in jeopardy. Isaac Pierce, a tenant farmer, related that he had overheard Hutchinson rebuking Preston for firing on the people without an order from a civil authority, to which Preston had responded, "I was obliged to, to save my sentry."

"Well, then," Pierce said he had replied, "you have murdered three or four men to save your sentry."

Farmer Joseph Belknap, "of good reputation," wrote the *Gazette,* heard Preston say, slightly differently, that he had acted to save his men. After one more bit of essentially the same testimony, the prosecution rested. Quincy had put fifteen men on the stand in his attempt to prove Captain Preston had ordered his men to fire, but much of that testimony turned out to be confusing or contradictory.

Samuel Quincy's case was essentially a more focused version of the long *Horrid Massacre* narrative. The wildest claims in that document, which was riddled with hearsay, exaggerations and inadmissible stories of previous encounters, had been ignored; instead, he had put forth a consistent and plausible version of what happened that night.

There was one other route that the prosecution might have followed but for its own reasons did not: Quincy could have called the soldiers to the stand. The men were not defendants in this trial and so he could have done so, but their answers surely would bear on their own fate. If they testified that their captain had not given them an order to fire, that would have been strong evidence against them in their own forthcoming trial.

151

Most likely they would have refused to answer that question, by citing Blackstone, who had laid the seeds of a right against self-incrimination only a few years earlier, "For at the common law . . . his fault was not to be wrung out of himself, but rather to be discovered by other means, and other men."

While the jury had been stacked with loyalists who might be reluctant to convict the captain of murder, other potential charges could still lead to a manslaughter conviction. And the local citizens were still hoping, expecting, that justice would be served.

At the conclusion of his case Quincy cited several precedents, pointing out the legal difference between murder, manslaughter and accidental death. Murder, he pointed out, requires malice, and according to settled British law, that means, "Circumstances that shew the heart to be perversely wicked, is adjudged to be of malice prepense, and consequently murder."

And he finished by quoting Lord Coke: "The Law doth imply forethought malice."

With that, John Adams stood to begin his defense of Captain Thomas Preston.

CHAPTER FIVE

Although John Adams's voice carried easily to the courtroom walls, his words had to go much further than that; this was a political trial and it was his challenge not only to get Captain Preston acquitted, but to prove to the people of Boston that justice was done. Even more difficult, he had to accomplish this without placing blame on the soldiers that might subsequently be used against them. Almost defiantly, the defense called as its first witness loyalist merchant William "Brazen Head" Jackson, that odd nickname referring to the brass head that decorated the door to his shop. By refusing to honor the nonimportation agreement, Jackson had aroused such anger that an attempt had been made to burn down his store, one of the long string of bitter confrontations that led eventually to the killings. Captain Preston was lodging in the home of Jackson's mother and, as "Brazen Head" told the court, he happened to be present when soldiers arrived and heard them tell Preston that his men were being abused.

The next witness, Edward Hill, was clear in his defense of Preston; he recalled hearing some Boston men saying they were going to attack the Main Guard. When he got to King Street he saw Captain Preston engaged with one of his men when the first bullet was fired. The soldier attempted to fire at a boy. The prisoner took him by the arm and said, "Fire no more, you have done mischief enough."

Merchant Benjamin Davis's testimony was equally powerful: before the guns were fired he was standing near the barracks when a young gentleman clapped him on the shoulder and asked if he would go and fight the soldiers, evidence that some in the town intended to make this fight. He refused, and only later did he hear the shots fired.

The scene set, the court adjourned for a second evening. No one could remember a trial taking this long, but no case before this one had as much potential to disrupt the peace.

Adams's first witness the third morning was Joseph Edwards, a silversmith, who testified he had heard the order given to prime and load by a grenadier dressed in a red coat and holding a musket; it was a corporal, he said — he could see the insignia on the man's arm — who then loaded his own weapon. No one had yet testified that Preston carried a musket. Edwards was sure he did not see Preston give such an order.

Like so many men of the town, young John Frost had answered the fire bells and learned the soldiers and the people were fighting in Dock Square. The soldiers had been driven back into their barracks. The boys "huzza'd up the street. I went up and saw two boys and some men about the sentinel." The sentry retreated and knocked his gun against the Custom House door, but could not get in. The men who came to his aid were led by "a man I took to be the Captain. He had a thing, or plate [an insignia of rank] upon his breast, a sash on, a sword in his hand, and regimentals." Frost did not hear the word to prime and load, but did note Captain Preston was standing third man from the right which would become significant later.

Benjamin Leigh, an apprentice at the Delph Manufactory, where the tin-glazed earthenware popular in the town was made, found himself in the middle of the crowd. He heard one of the barbers' boys shouting, "That's the dog that knocked me down," To which the others responded, "Kill him! Kill him!" As he watched, Captain Preston, dressed in his regimentals, wearing a hat, breast plate and sash, arrived and said he would not fire, upon his honor.

Adams, Quincy and Auchmuty were constructing their defense piece by piece; having built the foundation, they called upon arguably their most important witness, apothecary Richard Palmes, who had been in conversation with Captain Preston when the first shots were fired. For Palmes, and all the defense witnesses, for that matter, there was likely to be a cost for his testimony. The people of the colony had resisted taking a side as long as possible. They were Englishmen. Even when they found fault with the King and Parliament, they were Englishmen. But now people were talking about liberty. As a letter to the *Gazette* from a man who had lived in North America for twenty years said, it was "almost impossible for any people to have a higher regard and affection than these had for their mother country . . . But alas! How altered is the case now, verily altered beyond what I ever thought I should live to see." Almost all of the witnesses were in some way involved in the commerce of the town. Richard Palmes had a shop and there were likely to be patriots who would go elsewhere. And Palmes himself was a patriot, a member of the Sons of Liberty, but that did not deter him from standing in the witness box and speaking his truth for Preston.

On that night he had been brought into the streets by the bells, carrying a cudgel with him for protection; he was confronted by troops and in return he questioned why they were out of their barracks at that hour. "Do you mean to teach us our duty?" demanded one of them. "No," he said curtly, "only to remind you of it." As he reached King Street he saw Theodore Bliss in conversation with Captain Preston as the crowd closed in around the Custom House. He heard Bliss ask, "Why don't you fire?" Preston responded but Palmes did not hear his answer; whatever it was, Bliss responded angrily, "God damn you, why don't you fire!" Palmes stepped between them, placing a calming hand on Captain Preston's shoulder. "I hope you don't intend to fire," he said, and the captain replied, "By no means."

That instant Palmes saw snow or ice strike a soldier, who stepped back and fired. He was standing so close to Preston that the muzzle flash of the first shot scorched his elbow. Then someone shouted "Fire!" It was loud but he did not know who gave that order. It was possible, he admitted, that it was Preston "and I not have heard it." Palmes turned to the soldier who had fired first and "I struck overhand and hit him in his left arm. I knocked his hand from the gun. Upon that I turned . . . and hit Preston. My blow fell short."

Palmes made a narrow escape. A soldier lunged at him with his bayonet. Palmes threw his stick at him and jumped toward the lane. But there was one more bit of information he added: "I had on a cloth-colored surtout." The effect of this testimony was to shower doubt on Bliss's testimony that Captain Preston might well have ordered his men to fire.

In response to Palmes's claim that he was so close to Preston that his clothing was burnt by the firing and yet he did not hear the captain give any order, the prosecution immediately recalled Bliss. This interruption of the defense presentation was quite acceptable at this time. Bliss was a key witness for the prosecution, one of only four of the twenty-three prosecution witnesses who believed they had heard Preston give an order to fire. To refute Palmes, Bliss said that immediately following the event he had told his story in full to John Coffin, though Coffin was not in the courtroom at that moment.

As court attendants searched for Coffin, the defense resumed with Matthew Murray, who was in the street too, standing within two yards of the prisoner. He saw the soldiers load, saw something thrown through the air and hit the soldier, saw the musket go off. But he did not hear an order given, and was certain if Preston had given such an order he would have heard it.

A slave owned by the prosperous merchant and landholder Oliver Wendell was called next to the stand. The laws governing the right of slaves or even free blacks to testify varied among the colonies; in some places they were prohibited, in others their words were to be given less weight, and in places like Boston they were permitted to tell their story, but their testimony was generally considered suspect. His name was Andrew and his story covered a wider period than any other man's, beginning as he encountered an acquaintance who warned him the soldiers were killing everybody and had tried to cut off his arm. He then saw the loyalist justice of the peace James Murray hurrying toward the street, presumably to read the Riot Act, a law that would make this gathering illegal and force the crowd to disperse, but he was chased off by threats and snowballs.

The Riot Act had been passed by Parliament during a time of turmoil in 1714. Officially known as "An Act for preventing tumults and riotous assemblies, and for the more speedy and effectual punishing the rioters," it was simply a legal method of stopping demonstrations. If Murray was prevented from getting to the site, the law could not be enforced.

Andrew described how the crowd closed in tightly on the soldiers, taunting them with threats, waving sticks, throwing snow and ice, daring them to fire; in response the redcoats pushed them away with their bayonets, sticking a few people. He saw "the mulatto," Attucks, grab hold of the bayonet and hold it. Then he heard a voice cry "fire"; it did not come from the officer, of that he was certain, but rather from a soldier.

It was a compelling statement that fit easily with the other pieces. But to ensure the jury gave it full weight, Adams called upon Andrew's master, Oliver Wendell, who acknowledged that his slave was a man of good character, adding that he was able to read and write.

John Coffin had been found and after Andrew's testimony was recalled to add some slight detail. Coffin confirmed that Theodore Bliss had told him of his encounter with Preston, but said that in that conversation, which took place several days after the event, Bliss had been firm that Preston had said he did not intend to fire. "No," Bliss had remembered Preston telling him, "by no means. They could not fire without my leave." The prosecution's attempt to buttress Bliss's testimony had failed, and instead served to weaken their case.

Bliss once again took the witness stand to contest Coffin's testimony. He admitted that he "gave Coffin an account," but claimed, "I do not remember those words." Jack, the slave of the admired Dr. James Lloyd, testified that he had responded to the sound of the bells — and for his trouble was hit on the head by a snowball.

Jane Crothers Whitehouse, who had become the bride of British private Joseph Whitehouse only days after the incident, one of several such unions that resulted from the occupation, was the only woman to testify. Women, unlike slaves, had long been allowed to testify in courtrooms, a tradition that dated back long before the female witnesses in Salem had appeared in the witch trials, In fact, several other women had given depositions to the committee. Jane Crothers Whitehouse said she had seen people badgering the sentinel, throwing snowballs, oyster shells and chunks of wood. After "a space," a brief period of time, the Main Guard, led by Captain Preston, came to assist the sentry. The captain had ordered the sentry to fall in and then tried to return with his men to the guardhouse, but was prevented from doing so by "the riot." It was then that Private White pushed her to safety. He "bid me go away for I should be killed." There was a man walking behind the soldiers, she said, encouraging them to fire, "a man dressed in dark-colored cloaths. I don't remember if he had a surtout or any lace about him." She was standing no more than two yards from the captain and, she said, "I am positive that man was not the Captain."

She had no doubt where the blame lay for the incident: the townspeople. She saw a man take a thick chunk of wood from under his coat and throw it at a soldier, who fell on his face across the gutter.

The freed slave Newton Prince, a West Indian pastry cook who sold food at public entertainments, heard the drums beating to arms and the guns fire — but "heard no orders given to fire," explaining, "Only the people in general cried fire."

There had always been an unsettled question between Adams and Josiah Quincy about how directly the town might be held responsible for the killings. Was it the radicals who caused this to happen, or was it the town more broadly? Quincy wanted to put the blame on the mob. Adams clearly worried about the damage that might be done to the town's reputation and was against this strategy. It appears the issue arose between them during this trial but the more senior Adams overruled his younger associate.

Nautical blockmaker Joseph Helyer was the final man to describe the killings on King Street, and he was certain in his memory, and in his testimony unequivocally blamed the soldiers themselves. No orders were given to fire, he recalled: "The soldiers seemed to act pure nature. I mean they acted and fired by themselves because of being disciplined and fired without orders. I saw no contest between the soldiers and inhabitants that could justify their firing and when I saw men lying in the street I could not believe they were dead."

The final defense witnesses related mostly

to the aftermath; Captain James Gifford, 14th Regiment, said he had spoken with Preston that night; he had sent men to protect his sentinel, Preston told him, but he had given them no orders to fire. Gifford added that Preston was "mild tempered, prudent and discreet."

At that point, jurors had a rare opportunity to hear from the defendant himself. Preston interrupted the witness as was permitted and asked if he had ever known of an officer ordering his men to fire with their bayonets charged, or affixed to their muskets, a position that made it difficult for a man's finger to reach the trigger. The witness replied, "No," he did not, then explained, "Officers never give order to fire from charged bayonet. [If it had been given] They would all have fired together, or most of them." The point was clear, the soldiers were well-trained, and if an order to fire had been given, it certainly would not have been performed in this manner.

After additional testimony that added little new, but reinforced previous witnesses, the defense rested its case. On Saturday morning, October 27th, John Adams began his summation.

John Adams brought to the courtroom a

love of the law and an appreciation for its history, as well as a keen understanding of human foibles and an immense competitive nature. He began by citing Hale's *Pleas of the Crown,* reminding the jury, "What you doubt of, do not do," and "It is always safer to err in acquitting rather than punishing." He guided the jury through a tour of existing law: the natural right of man to respond to provocation, the legal right of self-defense, and the elements of a charge of murder. He then set the scene, reminding them all of the bitterness that existed between soldiers and townspeople. And then artfully dissected the prosecution case, pointing out and perhaps at times, in the way of a clever lawyer, exaggerating all of the flaws in Quincy and Paine's presentation.

Goddard, for example, was easily dismissed. He claimed Captain Preston had threatened "murder," a word that carried such meaning that no one could possibly believe the prisoner would have said it. The testimony of the others were flawed; some had misidentified Preston by claiming he was wearing a surtout; words supposedly were heard from too far a distance to be credible.

These were honest men, good men,

Adams was clear about that, but "circumstances had a tendency to move all the passions." Then, in the middle of his argument, and in the casual way of the court of the time, Adams was permitted to call additional witnesses. Suffolk County sheriff Stephen Greenleaf testified the captain had told him he had not ordered the firing. He was followed into the box by acting governor Hutchinson, who technically — by his position — was the chief justice of this very court. The presence of the most powerful man in the colony in the courtroom was sure to bear on members of the jury, though how depended on their political position. It was an odd pairing, Adams and Hutchinson. Both physically and philosophically they were different as possible; Hutchinson was tall and bone-showing thin, while Adams was shorter and stout. The fifty-nine-year-old governor also was the primary defender of so much that the thirty-five-year-old Adams and other patriots were fighting against. Yet Adams respected the man, once saying he "understood the subject of coin and commerce better than any man I ever knew in this country." It was an odd moment. Whatever their differences, they shared a mutual objective.

Hutchinson admitted his memory of the

night was not perfect. He didn't recall precisely what Preston had said to him in the street, but did remember that when the captain was questioned late that night, he denied giving any orders. Preston was a man of extremely good character, he concluded: "Had I wanted an officer to guard against a precipitate action . . . it would have been him."

That done, the witness was excused and Adams stood and resumed his summation. He referred to carefully prepared notes, reminding the jurors of the case he had presented. Joseph Edwards had told them that a man holding a musket had ordered the soldiers to prime and load.

Henry Knox said the soldiers had primed and loaded their weapons even before Preston got to the head of King Street. Richard Palmes, Adams pointed out, was a resident of the town and therefore not prejudiced in favor of the soldiers, perhaps making him the most important witness in the case: he had heard Bliss cursing Preston for not firing.

And then there were the logical arguments, facts that buttressed the testimony: numerous witnesses for both the prosecution and defense had placed the captain in front of his men. Self-preservation would

Loyalist lieutenant-governor Thomas Hutchinson maneuvered behind the scenes to save the British soldiers. Born in Boston, Hutchinson had advised Parliament against imposing taxes upon the Massachusetts Bay colony, warning, "You will lose more than you gain." But his allegiance to the Crown never wavered and he became the symbol in Boston of British imperialism. COLLECTION OF THE MASSACHUSETTS HISTORICAL SOCIETY

have made Preston stand behind his men when they fired. And as for not preventing additional firing after the first shot, no one had fallen after that shot was fired — and at point-blank range, which might have led him to believe the men had loaded only powder, not shot.

Adams spoke for several hours, taking the necessary bits from the collected wisdom of the philosophers and poets, writers and lawyers who had come before. Adams was not known as an especially theatrical speaker, so rather than flamboyance, he depended on the clarity of his argument, the earnestness of his approach and his command of the law to appeal to the jury.

After Adams was done, Auchmuty finished for the defense with a steady presentation, emphasizing the right of individuals "surrounded by threatening people to defend themselves." Within that context, he explained, citing several cases as precedent, the difference between homicide and manslaughter. In *Rex v. Steadman,* he pointed out, an Old Bailey case from 1704, a soldier who killed a woman who'd struck him in the face with a patten (the raised sole of a shoe) was convicted of manslaughter rather than homicide. "The smart of a man's wound," he explained to the court, "and the effusion of blood might possibly keep his indignation boiling . . ."

It was late in the afternoon, the candles were ready to be lit, when Auchmuty sat down. Rather than prosecutor Robert Paine beginning his final argument, to the dismay of the jurors, court was adjourned. This already was the longest trial in Massachusetts history and the twelve men and their keepers would have to remain together till Monday morning. To mollify them, although they slept at the jail, they were given liberty to roam the courthouse.

That evening a seemingly disgusted Judge Oliver sent a note to Hutchinson, bemoaning the excessive length of the trial. "I know you think you would have finished the cause in half the time and I know it would not have taken half a day at Old Bailey; but we must conform to the times." He added, explaining the early adjournment, that Paine "was so unfit," referring to the ill-health that plagued him, and recognizing the possible repercussions from the town, that "to avoid as much as possible all popular censure we indulged him till Monday morn."

Paine began his closing argument that morning by warning jurors against paying too much heed to Adams's words, thus "mistaking the flowers of rhetoric for reason and argument." Rather than blaming Bostonians for creating the situation, he reminded them that soldiers were patrolling the streets, "brandishing their weapons of death," threatening "bloodshed and slaughter." His words were hard, accusing Preston of "butchering his fellow subjects." As for the evidence, he cited testimony that Preston had been standing before his men, but as he gave the order to fire, he "retired to the rear."

The defense testimony was dismissed as "romantic accounts . . . that may be ornamental in a poet but will never establish the credibility of an historian." The violent attack described by those witnesses "turns out to be nothing more than a few snowballs thrown by a parcel of schoolboys," and that from a distance. As for Preston's position serving as evidence, Paine reminded the jury that Palmes also had stood in front of the men, then wondered why he would stand there if he actually thought the situation was so dire the soldiers might have to defend themselves. "It is impossible that you should seriously believe," he concluded, "that their situation could either justify or excuse their conduct."

Each of the four judges then spoke in turn to the jury. While their speeches involved a recitation of the law to be applied, they also could freely express their own views about the strength of the evidence. Trowbridge went first; after reminding them that in this courtroom an oath given in America has the same meaning as one given in England, he declared that in his opinion there was not sufficient evidence that Preston gave the order to fire, but that the jury had the right to find differently. If they did so, they must then determine what crime had been committed. Based on the law, "If you are satisfied that the sentinel was insulted and assaulted, and that Captain Preston and his party went to assist them, it was doubtless excusable homicide, if not justifiable. Self-defense [is] a law of nature . . ." To which every man is entitled. And if it was not proved to their satisfaction, they must acquit him.

Rather than digging deeper into the law, Judge Peter Oliver took his opportunity to angrily disparage the propaganda campaign that had been waged against the prisoner and the court by patriots, especially Paul Revere's fanciful and insulting print. The bitterness in his words was obvious and it was recorded that he spoke in a "nervous and pathetic manner." He despised the insults and the threats that had been spoken against the court and stated that he would not forgo a moment's peace of conscience for the applause of millions. But he too clearly believed Preston to be innocent. "It turns out to the dishonor of the inhabitants," he wrote to Hutchinson, ". . . he must be acquitted; that the person who gave the orders to fire was not the Captain . . . if it had been he, it at present appears justifiable."

Justices Cushing and Lynde found it disconcerting that their neighbors had become a mob but reminded the jury that the principal question they must answer was whether the prisoner gave the order to fire. Both of them agreed with Trowbridge that Preston had not given the fateful order. Chief Justice Lynde went further, much further than Adams dared, casting blame on Boston for the killings. He was deeply affected, he said, "that this affair turns out so much to the disgrace of every person concerned against him, and so much to the shame of the town in general."

It was dusk when the case went to the jury. Considering their political leanings there seemed little doubt Preston would soon be set free. But should he be convicted, rumors persisted that Governor Hutchinson was holding documents sent from London that would prevent any sentence from being carried out until a pardon arrived. Whether or not that was true, it turned out to be unnecessary. The jury debated only three hours before arriving at its verdict, although it was not announced until the next morning: Captain Preston was found not guilty.

While there was grumbling about the verdict in the town, it was generally agreed that Adams, Quincy and Auchmuty had done a fine job. They had brought out that the prosecution witnesses had given confusing testimony; the two witnesses who swore they had heard Preston giving the order to fire also said he was wearing a surtout, which was not accurate. The defense had successfully countered the most damaging claims and presented a very different story. They had walked the fine line: winning an acquittal for their client while not strongly placing blame on the Bostonians. Preston clearly appreciated the legal acumen of his team and recognized the significance it had played in the proceedings. In a letter to General Thomas Gage after the trial, he wrote: "The Counsel for the Crown or rather the town were but poor and managed poorly . . . my Counsel on the contrary were men of parts, and exerted themselves with great spirit and cleverness . . ."

The Boston newspapers did not spend valuable space reporting the disappointing, and what they believed to be pre-ordained, outcome. Instead, a satirical comment disguised as an ad appeared, perhaps commenting on the defense witnesses, on the front page of the *Boston Gazette and Country Journal* a week later: "Wanted," it read, "To embark for London about the beginning of next month, a person well qualified to give evidence against the colonies at the next sitting of Parliament. He must be a person of bold front, that can tell a story with a good grace. He must also be a man of great duplicity, and a perfect master of dissimulation, thoroughly versed in the various methods of bribery and procuring depositions; if he undertakes cooking them up artfully it will answer the better . . ."

At the end of the month the newspapers did announce the governor had issued a proclamation "for a Thanksgiving, wherein the people are called upon to thank God for the success of the Kings administration for ye year past," which supposedly alluded to Captain Preston's acquittal.

But the legal machine was not yet done. The law in America was still developing its unique character, responding to the needs of a new and growing country, while still retaining both the majesty and quirks of centuries of developed British law. Among those remnants was the medieval right known as an appeal of felony, which did not require a review of the trial, but allowed a close relation of a murder victim to bring a quasi-personal action against the accused killer. In response, the defendant had the option of insisting on trial by battle, literally a fight to surrender or death. As Blackstone explained it, it was based on the belief that "God would always interpose miraculously, to vindicate the guiltless." Some patriots in Boston urged close kin of the victims to bring this appeal against Preston. But, among other things, the specter of fighting a well-trained British officer proved daunting. When that effort failed, it was suggested those wounded that night bring civil actions against Preston for damages. To escape this nuisance, Preston relocated back to the safety of the military fortress at Castle William.

John Adams had won his case, but doing so had made his defense of the eight soldiers that much more difficult. The jury had determined that Captain Preston had not given the order to fire; therefore the soldiers must have done it by themselves, without orders. They were responsible and it put their lives in far greater jeopardy. The penalty upon conviction was death on the gallows.

Making the situation even more precarious, the blood lust in the town had not been satisfied. Blood answers blood, but Preston, the lead officer, had walked away. The soldiers were different. The people knew soldiers from the streets; if they didn't know these particular men, they knew others just like them. They'd had their encounters, and there'd been far more bruises than friendships. Men had been slain for demanding their God-given rights. Would no one pay for that?

Hutchinson was cautious about the soldiers' trial, writing, "For the evidence which appeared upon Captain Preston's trial there is room to expect that, at most, they can be found guilty of manslaughter only, and some of the court seems to think it was justifiable homicide."

Frustrated by the prosecutors' performance in the Preston trial, Samuel Adams and the more radical colonists were determined to be more heavily involved. In a letter from the town clerk William Cooper, it was made clear to Paine that they would be offering more input in this trial. Paine was "directed by the Select men to acquaint you that they depend upon your coming to Town as soon as possible that you may in conjunction with Mr. Quincy prepare for the trial of the

Soldiers, and that they make no doubt of your exerting yourself to the utmost that a fair and impartial inquisition may be made for blood."

Adams also would have several weeks to prepare for this second trial. After Preston's acquittal the session in Boston had adjourned and the court moved to Cambridge and then to Salem. It became clear Adams's courtroom victory had not diminished his position in the town. During this interlude he remained quite busy with his practice, moving forward with several other cases. While the Preston and soldiers' trials remained the most visible, and generated by far the most interest, neither one of them paid especially well. He had been paid a pittance as a retainer and could not expect any great windfall from the trials, no matter how long they lasted. The fee schedule was governed by statute; a trial in superiour court paid 12 shillings (20 shillings were in a pound), and in inferior court it paid 6s. John Adams charged his clients an "attendance fee," slightly more than 1 shilling a day for a court appearance whether or not the case ended in a trial. For his work in court in cases that did not involve a trial he charged an additional 5s "arguing fee." He charged 12s to write writs and the same amount to provide legal advice. On occasion a case might allow him to charge a larger fee, but even then the total usually was calculated by combining fees for each of the small steps. There were civil cases that slogged on through the courts for years and were argued and appealed until the final fee was significant, and he did have wealthy private clients like John Hancock whose businesses required almost continuous legal representation and could be relied upon to generate substantial fees, as well as companies that paid him a flat annual sum. The Kennebec company, for example, which sold land to settlers, paid him £30 annually. While the result was not a princely sum, it provided a fine income; in comparison a carpenter, bricklayer or wallpaper hanger might earn 5 or 6 shillings a day and an unskilled laborer would receive 3s or less. A sailor was paid between £2 and 3 a month; a sea captain might earn twice that.

Among those cases on which he worked while preparing for the soldiers' trial was an attempt by a group of marine insurance underwriters to claw back damages they had paid several years earlier after additional evidence had surfaced; a case in which he had successfully represented the defendant. He also continued preparations for an important civil trial to begin in January in which he represented Hancock (and other creditors) against the loyalist publisher of the *Boston Gazette,* John Mein, in an effort to foreclose on property in payment for substantial debts; on November 2nd he argued an adultery case before Judge Lynde, adultery then being defined as a married woman fornicating with a man, whether he was married or single. He apparently won an acquittal for his clients.

The soldiers' trial was scheduled to begin on November 27th, when the court settled back in Boston. The same four judges would preside and Sam Quincy and Robert Treat Paine would prosecute the case again. From the safety of Castle William, Captain Preston worked with the defense team, passing along the suggestion from Hutchinson that Auchmuty not be retained in this trial. Hutchinson had little regard for Auchmuty and he was replaced by twenty-eight-year-old Sampson Salter Blowers, who had been trained as a lawyer in the governor's office and been admitted to the court only four years earlier. Unlike Adams and twenty-six-year-old Josiah Quincy, Blowers was a loyalist and an admirer of Hutchinson. His primary assignment, Hutchinson admitted, was to help select a favorable jury, making "a very diligent inquiry into the characters and principles of all who are returned."

General Gage, the top military officer in North America, had long advocated that every word of both trials be taken down. Whatever the outcome, these trials would raise passions and influence future relations between England and Massachusetts Bay, if not all of America. In this case, John Hodgson, a bookbinder skilled in shorthand, was engaged to create a word-by-word record. This was quite extraordinary as such verbatim recordings were extremely rare. In Europe, trial reports, which at times included arguments and testimony, first appeared in the midthirteenth century, but historically complete transcripts were not done.

Hodgson was a Scottish immigrant who was not a professional stenographer but had learned shorthand from James Weston's 1743 popular manual *Stenography Compleated; Or, the Art of Shorthand Brought to Perfection: Being the Most Easy, Exact, Speedy, and Legible Method Extant.* He proudly kept samples of his bookbinding and shorthand on display "at his house near the Liberty Tree" and at his printing office on School Street. A transcript of Captain Preston's trial may very well have been sent to England and never made public but all that was left was bits and notes taken down by others including Preston himself, a summary that did not serve the patriot's cause.

In this trial, both the prosecution and the defense would have to employ considerably different strategies than in Preston's trial. Quincy and Paine, having learned a hard lesson, had to do everything possible to prevent another partisan jury from being seated. They would then attempt to prove that after months and years, and in this instance hours, of insults and abuse from the townspeople, the soldiers had chosen to fight back, even to kill. By law, all of them could be convicted if the jurors believed any one of the soldiers had fired with malice and intent. If one soldier was guilty of murder, all of them could hang. Proving the shots were fired with malicious intent would require far greater testimony about the bitterness that led up to the deadly encounter than was heard in Preston's trial.

With it now decided that the soldiers had likely fired without being given an order to do so by their superiour officer, Adams, Josiah Quincy and Blowers had to present sufficient evidence that those men believed their lives were in mortal danger and they had no way to retreat. While Quincy was willing to indict the entire town to make that point, Adams, once again, was not. He would not sacrifice the reputation of the inhabitants to secure an acquittal and that made the defense more difficult. Instead, he would focus specifically on the belligerent actions of the young rabble gathered in front of the Custom House.

By virtue of the fact that many of the same people would be participating and given the close timing, this second trial seemed in many ways to be a repeat or continuation of the captain's trial. It was not. Preston's trial had come down to the single point of whether he had given the order. The issues here were more complex and required a very different legal approach. The two young lawyers assisting Adams had between them a total of six years of experience at the bar, hardly enough to offer any real aid. So it was up to Adams to try to save the lives of those eight men while carefully avoiding implicating the town and its residents. After all, five of Adams's neighbors were dead.

This was to be the most important case in colonial American history. The real Boston Massacre trial was about begin.

... ...

CHAPTER SIX

Acting governor Thomas Hutchinson, the appointed chief justice of the superiour court, had not been trained as a lawyer. But he possessed a keen understanding of how the law worked in practice, and knew that decisions made at the beginning of a case often determined the end of it. While John Adams liked him, even respected him, he also did not trust him, writing once that "the mazy windings of Hutchinson's heart and the serpentine wiles of his head" bore some responsibility for the conflict between England and her colonies. But once again, they had a shared objective.

So perhaps it was not surprising that when jury selection began, the same panel from which nine of the Preston jurors had been selected was once again put before the judges. Whether that simply was an over-sight, an error or an attempt to ensure the same outcome, the judges would not permit it to stand. That panel was released and the trial was delayed for more than a week as an entirely different slate of men was summoned. Each potential juror was asked the same question by the court: Whether he "doth expect to gain or lose by the issue of the cause then depending; whether he is in any way related to [either] party; or hath directly or indirectly given his opinion or is sensible of any prejudice, in the cause." From that new group, nine men eventually were selected, not one of them from Boston. Filling those last three seats proved difficult, as the prosecution remained determined to keep local men out of the jury box. Finally, to the dismay of Samuel Adams, who believed the town had a right to be represented, three talesman, men taken directly from the gallery or even passersby on the street, from the shore town of Hingham were selected.

The trial began with the formalities of English law. The jurors swore to the oath: "You shall well and truly try and true deliverance make between our sovereign lord, the King, and the prisoners at the bar, whom you shall have in charge according to the evidence. So help you God."

The court clerk, Samuel Winthrop, then turned to the eight prisoners and asked each

185

of them to hold up their hand as their name was called: William Wemms, James Hartegan, William McCauley, Hugh White, Matthew Killroy, John Carrol, William Warren and Hugh Montgomery. These were ordinary men, soldiers, sent to America to enforce the wishes of the King and the orders of Parliament. The British army had come ashore in Boston in 1768, primarily to protect the customs commissioners. They had marched into a difficult situation.

If these eight men were typical they had come from poor families and had volunteered for the army as young men, between the ages of seventeen and twenty-five, intending to make it a lifelong career, then retire with the promised pension. Private White, for example, the sentry, was thirty years old and had already served for eleven years. While most of their officers had some formal education, many of the enlisted men did not; some, like Matthew Killroy, were illiterate. Many of them were Irish-Catholic, as William McCauley was believed to be, which made life in Boston even more difficult as the town had an annual celebration with great bonfires and revelry to defame the Pope. Because overseas posting typically lasted for years, a significant number of soldiers had brought their families with them; Edward (Hugh) Montgomery was one of them, having come with his wife, Isabela, and their three children. Single men of necessity often visited prostitutes or took up with local women, and more than forty marriages were recorded in these years.

Living conditions for the soldiers were generally poor. Privates were paid a barely living wage of 8 pence a day (12 pence was worth one shilling), from which deductions were taken for food and uniform. Their rations had often been shipped from England, which sometimes resulted in moldy, rancid, worm-eaten and maggoty bread, biscuits and beef. It was for these reasons that many supplemented their income by taking off-hours jobs in places like John Grey's rope-works — which led to the fight there in which Privates Matthew Killroy and William Warren got involved. Many of the women who had come with them also worked as nursemaids, washer-women or in other suitable occupations.

The officers, many of whom came from the higher social classes and had purchased their commissions, enforced harsh discipline. Whippings were so common the soldiers became known as "bloody-backs," referring to the lashes they received. Desertions were a significant problem and one private was publicly executed for the offense on the Boston Common.

While many of the officers were able to ease into the flow of the town, that was not true of the ordinary soldier. They often drank, committed petty crimes and brawled with townsmen. Bloody confrontations took place so frequently that inhabitants had begun carrying sticks for protection when out at night. The soldiers' continued presence was a daily reminder that Boston was an occupied town.

They did not ask to be there, they were serving their country, and now their fate would be decided in this courtroom. They had been brought into court dressed in their civilian clothes, and shorn of their impressive uniforms so they looked much like ordinary inhabitants of the town. As they stood solemn, Winthrop told the jurors it was their duty to "enquire whether they [the prisoners] or either of them be guilty of the felony and murder whereof they stand indicted, or not guilty . . .

"Good men and true, stand together and harken to your evidence."

There were formalities of dress too. Adams was clad in the traditional black gown and white wig, or "tie wig," of the barrister, while the justices wore robes of scarlet broadcloth, with wide silk bands and large powdered wigs, called "perukes." The tradition of lawyers wearing a robe in court, which later would become a bone of contention between Adams and Thomas Jefferson, was born during the reign of Edward III in the mid-1300s as a demonstration of respect and equality under the law — and to keep judges warm in the chilly, unheated spaces of Westminster Hall. But it was new to Boston, having been introduced within the previous decade by Governor Hutchinson, who desired to dignify the sessions of the superiour court. While comfortable in the drafty courtrooms of late fall, for obvious reasons they were less desirable in the late spring and early summer. Adams thought it haughty, writing of the justices, "They were not seated on ivory chairs but their dress was more solemn and more pompous than that of the Roman Senate when the Gauls broke in upon them."

Wigs were a comparatively recent addition, becoming popular among aristocrats in the mid-1600s as France's seventeen-year-old King Louis XIV began wearing a shoulder-length wig of horsehair to cover his prematurely thinning hair and his British cousin, Charles II, did so to hide his graying mane.

Actually, the presence of so many lawyers in a courtroom was also a recent phenomenon; until early in the eighteenth century the prosecutor, most often the victim of the crime, began a trial by presenting his case. That generally was done through witness accounts. The defendant then responded and could produce his or her own witnesses to the event. Judges, the involved parties, and on occasion jurors, then asked questions. The judges then summarized the evidence for the jurors before allowing them to retire to reach a decision. Lawyers, defense lawyers especially, initially appeared in trials only to answer legal questions, but gradually took a more active role.

Here, two old friends, men who had been admitted to the bar on the same day, would be playing those active roles. Samuel Quincy and Adams had spent many days in the same courtrooms and when necessary had come to rely on each other. In 1764, for example, Adams had written to Quincy, asking him to take over forty legal actions for him in the Suffolk Inferior Court and then, "answer for me in all things once more, and to write to me one line to let me know my fate, as usual." Here, as in Preston's case, they would be on opposing sides.

■ ■ ■ ■

On November 27th the trial began with Quincy reminding the jurors what was at stake, telling them in his opening statement, "The cause is solemn and important; no less than whether eight of your fellow subjects shall live or die! A cause grounded on the most melancholy event that has yet taken place on the continent of America . . ." As to the great pressure put upon these twelve men by the town, "I am aware how difficult, in cases of this sort, it ever is, and more especially in these times, and in this trial, to preserve the mind perfectly indifferent, but I remember we are bound not only by natural obligations towards God and man, but also by an oath to examine into the evidence of fact without partiality or prejudice . . . the object of our enquiry is simply that of truth, and that this enquiry is to be conducted by the wisdom of the laws and constitution." "Constitution" referred to the unwritten British constitution, created over centuries by Acts of Parliament, court judgments and conventions, including the Magna Carta.

His task, Quincy concluded, was to prove the identity of the persons charged, the facts of the killings and the circumstances that led to them. He would have to prove that a specific soldier killed a specific victim, and did so with malice. The first witness he called was nineteen-year-old Jonathan Williams Austin, Adams's law clerk. Using him to open the case was a practical and audacious decision: Who might the jury trust more than the defense counsel's own man, who was an eyewitness to the shooting? Austin admitted that he knew one of the defendants, McCauley, and saw him at the Custom House when he answered the bells. "How many people do you imagine might be there when you got into King Street?"

"There might be twenty or thirty I believe. I saw the sentry at the Custom House door swinging his gun and bayonet, there were a parcel of men and boys round him . . . I walked by the side of them till I came to the sentry box at the Custom House. McCauley then got to the right of the sentry-box; he was loading his piece."

"How near was you to McCauley at that time?"

"I was about four feet off," Austin estimated. "McCauley said, 'Damn you, stand-off,' and pushed his bayonet at me. I did so. Immediately I heard the report of a gun."

Quincy asked several questions about the

number of people in the street, perhaps creating the scene for the jurors, then wondered, "Did you hear any orders given?"

"I did not; either to load or fire." Unlike in the Preston trial, that lack of an order was now an incriminating fact rather than an exculpatory one.

Again, after getting more details, "Did you look round after you heard the guns fired?"

"Yes."

"Did you see McCauley then?"

"Yes."

"Was he loading again?"

"I think he was; it so lies in my mind," he replied, admitting, "I cannot absolutely swear it."

Quincy understood the importance of placing each soldier in position for the jury, asking, "Do you know whether any soldiers stood on the right of McCauley?"

"I took so particular notice of McCauley that I minded no other object."

The merchant Ebenezer Bridgham, a well-known Freemason, a member of the St. John's Grand Lodge, followed Austin to the witness box. Membership in a Masonic lodge was a testament to a man's character and gave his words weight. The very first Freemason lodge in America had been founded in the town in 1733 at the Bunch

Of Grapes tavern, and among the current members were John Hancock and Paul Revere. There appeared to be considerable overlap between the Masons and the Sons of Liberty. When Bridgham was asked if he had seen any of the prisoners in King Street he pointed to Warren and said, "I was well persuaded in my own mind that I saw that tall one, but a few days later, after I saw another man belonging to the same regiment, so very like him, that I doubt whiter I am not mistaken with regard to him." Did he know any of the other prisoners? He indicated William Wemms. "I am well satisfied I saw the Corporal there."

Quincy asked simple, straightforward questions, establishing the facts of the case. "Did you see either of the persons you think you know discharge their guns?"

"Yes. The man I take to be the tall man discharged his piece as it was upon a level." Before the shooting, Bridgham had seen objects he could not identify thrown at the soldiers, who "stood with their pieces before them to defend themselves; and as soon as they had placed themselves, a party, about twelve in number, with sticks in their hands, who stood in the middle of the street, gave three cheers, and immediately surrounded the soldiers, and struck upon their guns with their sticks and passed along the front of the soldiers . . . striking the soldiers' guns as they passed; numbers were continually coming down the street."

"Did you see any person take hold of any guns or bayonets of any of the party?" He did not. Quincy was making it clear the soldiers were not being threatened. "Did you hear any particular words from the party of twelve?"

"I heard no particular words, there was such a noise that I could not distinguish any such words."

And a few questions later, "Did you apprehend the soldiers in danger, from anything you saw?"

"I did not," Bridgham said, "indeed."

It is possible that some in that courtroom perceived this situation as a metaphor for the situation existing between England and Massachusetts: the British held all the guns while the colonists were making noise, making threats, but posed no real danger.

"You said you saw several blows struck upon the guns, I should like you would make it more plain."

"I saw the people near me on the left strike the soldiers' guns, daring them to fire, and called them cowardly rascals for bringing arms against naked men, bid them lay aside their guns, and they were their men." Not a helpful account for the prosecution, but also hardly enough provocation to start shooting.

Quincy finally reached his point. "Did you see any person fall?"

"I saw Gray fall . . . he fell in the middle of the street . . . the gun that killed him must have been nearer to the center."

The prosecutor probed a bit, trying without any success to determine where the shots had come from. Then, "Was you looking at the person who fired the last gun?"

The answer was telling, "Yes. I saw him aim at a lad that was running down the middle of the street, and kept the motion of his gun after him a considerable time, and then fired." The meaning could not be mistaken. The soldier had not fired in passion or without thought. He had tracked his target and fired at him.

"Did the lad fall?"

"He did not. I kept my eye on him for a considerable time."

After another series of questions intended to determine where in the line the shots had come from, Quincy asked, "How many guns were fired?"

"I believe seven."

And the last question, "How many soldiers

were of the party?"

The response was wildly inaccurate: "I did not count them, but I believe twelve."

Samuel Quincy was considered a handsome and urbane man, and respected as a fine lawyer. His questions were brisk and to the point, without the additional comments that many lawyers felt necessary. His next witness was James Dodge, a gentleman from an old Massachusetts family, who had been on King Street but had departed before the guns were fired. The soldiers "were swinging their guns backward and forward and several among the people said 'Fire, damn you fire'; but I think it was Captain Preston who gave the word to fire." Again, this was an account that would have been helpful in Preston's trial, but not so here.

Quincy pressed Dodge for details, desiring to show the crowd posed no real threat to the soldiers. "What had they in their hands?"

"They had nothing in their hands."

Dodge admitted he had seen snowballs and pieces of ice thrown, but could not say they were thrown in anger. "I do not know," he said, but then made a telling point; "I saw the soldiers pushing at the people before any snowballs were thrown."

"Did you see any oyster shells thrown?"

Quincy wondered. Oyster shells, which could be as hard as a stone with a blunted edge and sailed a great distance, were so plentiful in New England that streets might be paved with them. Dodge had not.

Quincy's final question to the witness may have seemed irrelevant at this point. "Was the snow trodden down, or melted away by the Custom House?"

"The street was all covered like a cake," Dodge replied.

John Adams sat quietly at his table, taking his own notes of the testimony with a feather quill. Adams was known for his copious note-taking. Listening to Dodge, he wrote, "I took it the soldiers pushed, to keep the inhabitants off. Saw no oyster shells thrown and believe there were none." And then he added, knowing his adversary so well, "A cake of ice covered the pavement there, and cov(ere)d up all the shells."

Thirty-one-year-old Edward G. Langford had been a town watchman for almost two years when the killings took place. It was a paid position, and his job was to patrol the center of the town, watching for any unusual activity or fires and calling out the hour. When the bells rang he ran into King Street and saw several boys and young men accosting the sentry at the Custom House. "I asked them what was the matter. They said the sentry had knocked down a boy. They crowded in over the gutter; I told them to let the sentry alone . . . I told him not to be afraid, they were only boys and would not hurt him."

"Did you know the sentry?" He did, and pointed to Hugh White. He also knew Matthew Killroy and pointed to him too.

Langford did not believe White was in danger: "The boys were swearing and speaking bad words, but they threw nothing." They pressed closer to the sentry and he retreated up the steps. Langford was speaking with the sentry, he said, trying to calm the situation, when a group of soldiers came down the lane. As Langford drew back, "Samuel Gray, who was shot that night, came and struck me on the shoulder and said, 'Langford, what's to pay here?'

"I said I did not know what was to pay, but I believed something would come of it by and bye. He made no reply. Immediately a gun went off. I was within reach of their guns and bayonets; one of them thrust at me with his bayonet and run it through my jacket and great coat."

The watchman heard orders given to fire, twice, distinctly, although he could not identify the man who gave those orders. Nor did he know who fired the first shot, although it came from his right. Then, he continued, pointing accusingly at Killroy, "I looked this man in the face, and bid him not fire, but he immediately fired, and Samuel Gray fell at my feet. Killroy immediately thrust his bayonet through my coat and jacket; I ran towards the watch-house and stood there."

Quincy had hit a profitable vein and probed deeper: "You spoke to him before he fired, what did you say to him?"

"I said either damn you or God damn you do not fire, and immediately he fired."

"What in particular made you say do not fire?"

"Hearing the other guns go off . . ."

"Did Gray say any thing to Killroy before he fired?"

"He spoke to nobody but me."

"Did he throw any snowballs?"

"No, nor had he any weapon in his hand. He was as naked as I am now . . . His hands were in his bosom and, immediately after Killroy's firing, he fell."

This was Quincy's quest, to prove a certain soldier had killed a victim: "Did you hear any other gun at the time?"

"None, till I got near the watch-house."

After a few more questions about the setting, the prosecutor asked, "Have you any doubt in your own mind, that it was the gun of Killroy's that killed Gray?"

"No manner of doubt," Langford said. "It must have been it, for there was no other gun discharged at that time."

Adams wrote, "I took it Killroys' gun kill'd Gray."

Quincy returned to his point. After ascertaining that his witness did not know Crispus Attucks, "the Indian who was killed," he asked, "After Gray fell, did he [Killroy] thrust at him with his bayonet?"

"No, it was me he pushed."

"Did Gray say anything to Killroy, or Killroy to him?" No, and he was standing right there. "Did you perceive Killroy take aim at Gray?"

"I did not; he was as liable to kill me as him."

With Langford's words hanging in the courtroom air, the session was adjourned for the day, the jury being "kept together in the mean time." They were escorted to the jail to be housed there.

As Adams returned by mostly cobblestone-paved streets to his home on Cold Lane, where Abigail waited with three-year-old John Quincy and their new son, Charles, Boston was enjoying a period of peace. The fears of the summer, that the army was ready to block the harbor and return to the town, had cooled with the coming of the fall. The redcoats were safely out of sight at Castle William and there was no renewed effort being made to strictly enforce the harsh laws. Sam Adams and his Sons of Liberty had cowed the revenue collectors into a less confrontational position. The taverns were still offering the popular British bread and meat puddings in addition to the common chicken, pork, steaks, fresh fish and other potted meats and fish. Those places catering especially to coaches had started offering the newly named Sandwich, which might be enjoyed during the journey. All of those places offered tea and ale, hard cider, hard liquor and wine, as well as coffee and, in some places, pots of chocolate. Most people were suspicious of the water in the town, which was said to have been fouled by the factories. It also was possible to find a few pieces of the new chocolate pieces being offered by John Hannon, who had opened the first chocolate factory in America in Dorchester only five years earlier and had recently set up shop in Boston.

But it was an uneasy calm. Less than a week before this trial began, the *Gazette* reported, "One of the ministerial writers in England tells us that 'It cost the nation more than 40 Million sterling to conquer France in America — that this conquest was made for the protection of the colonies — that forty million equally divided brings each of the colonies in debt to the Mother Country at least two millions, which ought to be repaid by some means or other — and that the poor people of England ought not to be bearers of wood & drawers of water to pay this debt for the colonies.' "

This threat on the eve of the trial to impose new duties or taxes was a reminder, and perhaps a warning, to New Englanders that Parliament still believed the colonists were not to be given their full rights due as British citizens. This was the heart of the matter, the kind of message that served to enrage Americans and heighten tensions. When court resumed, Francis Archibald, a clerk for the wealthy real estate man and head of the local Masons chapter, Henry Price, was called. He had watched the party of soldiers coming out of Murray's barracks; as he did, he recalled, "I saw a soldier and a mean looking fellow with him, with a cutlass in his hand, they came up to me: somebody said, put up your cutlass, it is not right to carry it at this time of night. He said, 'Damn you, ye Yankee bougers, what's your business.' He came up to another that was with me and struck him. We beat him back and seven or eight soldiers came out of the barracks with tongs and other weapons, one aimed a blow at a young fellow, John Hicks, who knocked the soldier down. As he attempted to rise, I struck him down again and broke his wrist, as I heard afterwards. I went to King Street, and when the guns were all fired, I saw several persons dead."

Quincy intended to show that the shootings were not in self-defense, but rather in retaliation for insults and abuses. Through witnesses like Archibald he hoped to prove that there was anger and bitterness in the streets before the soldiers even got to the Custom House. Or as the law might call it, malice.

James Brewer, a laborer working on the docks, began his testimony by identifying Matthew Killroy as one of the soldiers in King Street. As he got there, he said, he saw the sentry surrounded by as many as twenty boys, most of them fourteen or fifteen years old, and called to Killroy, "I don't think anybody was going to do him harm . . . There was no body troubling him." When Captain Preston got there he told him, "Sir, I hope you are not going to fire, for everybody is going to their own homes. He said, 'I hope they are.' I saw no more of him."

Moments later, "I saw Christopher Monk, who was wounded that night. I turned to speak to him and directly they fired, and he seemed to falter. I said, 'Are you wounded?' He said yes. I replied, 'I do not think it, for I then apprehended they fired only powder.' "

It was Killroy, Brewer believed, who had "struck me with his bayonet" for no apparent reason "as no one had done any violence to him." Asked if he had been struck on purpose or by accident, he responded, "I think he did it on purpose, I apprehended it so . . ."

"Said he anything to you?"

"No, nor I to him; he came to form, and I was closer than I wished I was, and he struck me." Brewer was adamant that as Killroy was coming to the Custom House with the other soldiers to form the defensive semicircle, the soldier needlessly struck out at him.

As for what was going on in the street: he saw nothing thrown at the soldiers. He heard no one call them names. And as for threatening speeches he had none of that, "Except that the people cryed fire! Fire! The word fire was in everybody's mouth."

Rather than harmless powder, the bullet that struck seventeen-year-old apprentice shipwright Christopher Monk entered through his groin and passed through his body to exit by his opposite hip. The wound was so grave that artist Henry Pelham's engraving done a few days later referred to young Monk as having been "mortally wounded" on King Street. Instead he survived, though crippled, and lived another decade supported by charitable donations.

The defense had sat silently as Quincy led Brewer through his testimony, but finally had the opportunity to cross-examine him. The right of the accused to face his accuser was firmly established; it was part of the foundation of law, and might be traced back to the Bible. In the book of Daniel, Susanna was falsely accused of promiscuity and based on the testimony of two elders sentenced to death; Daniel interceded and asked, "Are ye so foolish, ye children of Israel, that without examination or knowledge of truth, you have condemned a daughter of Israel?" When questioned, the two elders gave conflicting answers, absolving Susanna, and instead they were condemned.

Throughout the trial there was limited cross-examination and by tradition, the youngest lawyer generally conducted it. In this case that would be Josiah Quincy. Through his questions he suggested quite a different scene. "Did you see any people coming up Quaker Lane with sticks? When you first Saw the molatto [Attucks], did you hear him say anything to the soldiers, or strike them? Did you hear any huzzas or cheers as they are called? Did you hear them call the soldiers any names. Did you hear any body say, 'Kill them. Damn them, knock them over?' Did you hear the whistling about the streets at the time? Did you see any person strike with a club at the soldiers? Did you see them attempt to strike their guns?"

The answer to every question had been "No," Brewer had not seen any of it. But then he was asked, "Did you hear the rattling of guns as though a stick had struck upon them?"

He did not, Brewer said, but then added, "I heard the people around call fire."

Quincy immediately recognized the nuance in the response and followed with, "Did you take that to be the cry of fire, or bidding the soldiers to fire?"

There was no good answer for Brewer, so he deflected it. "I cannot tell now what I thought."

"Did the word 'Fire' proceed from the

people or from the soldiers?"

Brewer answered honestly, an answer that did not serve the prosecution. "From the people."

Sailor James Bailey was next. Most of the witnesses had already testified several times, either in the depositions given in the aftermath of the event or in Preston's trial. While Bailey had not given a deposition to the published Narrative, nor had he been called in the first trial, he had been interviewed by judges at the inquest. He now told the court he had been standing on the Custom House steps, near the sentry, and had seen the soldiers Carrol, Montgomery and White there. There were about twenty boys, teenagers all of them, throwing pieces of ice, "hard and large enough to hurt any man, as big as one's fist . . ."

Bailey knew White and went up to him. "He said very little to me, only that he was afraid, if the boys did not disperse, there would be something very soon. He did not mention what." At that, the boys stopped throwing the ice. The situation had calmed, until the soldiers came down. "Carrol came up to me and clapt his bayonet to my breast, and White said do not hurt him."

"Did you hear the first gun fired?"
"Yes."

"From what quarter?"

"From the right."

"Do you know the man that fired that gun?"

"It was Montgomery, he was the very next person to me, close to me. When White told him not to hurt me, he took his hand and pushed me right behind him."

"Did that first shot kill or wound any person?"

"I do not know." But there was more to his story; before firing "Montgomery was knocked down with a stick, and his gun flew out of his hand, and when he recovered himself he discharged his gun . . . the man that stood the third from the right was Carrol and I believe he was the next that fired." His arm and his gun had been struck by a blow from someone with a stick or club, knocking him down. "His gun flew out of his hand, and as he stooped to take it he fell himself . . ."

"When [Montgomery] took up his gun and fired, which way did he present?"

"Towards Stone's tavern. I imagine he presented towards the Molatto."

"How far distant was he [Attucks] from Montgomery when he fell?"

"About fifteen feet." Quincy had made it clear: Montgomery had fired and presumably hit and killed Attucks. At that distance it would have been difficult to miss him.

When the defense began its cross-examination, Bailey was asked was "the blow Montgomery received, upon the oath you have taken, violent?"

He insisted it was, "Yes, very violent."

While his account had not been heard publicly, Bailey had appeared before the justices during the informal inquest on March 6th to tell his story while it remained fresh in his mind. Josiah Quincy wondered, "Do you remember your saying [in that interview] they were throwing sticks and cakes of ice, in the mob way?"

"No," he replied, adding confusion to his testimony, "not at the soldiers."

Bailey also appeared to damage the prosecution when he said he had seen "a number [of people] going up Cornhill and the Molatto fellow headed them . . . they appeared to be sailors, some had sticks, some had none. The Molatto fellow had a large cordwood stick."

"What did the party with the Molatto do or say?"

"They were huzzaing, whistling and carrying their sticks upright over their heads."

"Did you know their design?"

"I did not . . ."

Adams's personal notes concluded Bailey's testimony: "The man that struck Montgomery down stood at the right of the right hand grenadier. The blow was before the firing."

Samuel Emmons, the prosecution's next witness, lightened a somber day somewhat when asked to point out the soldiers he had seen that night. His answer was that he had seen none of them, because as it turns out he wasn't even in the street that night — it was his brother who had been there. Wrote Adams, the witness Emmon protested: "I don't know any of the prisoners. Nor anything!"

Richard Palmes, the patriot shopkeeper whose testimony had proved so beneficial to Captain Preston, came next. But this time, with different defendants, his testimony would prove to be far more incriminating. Asked simply if he knew any of the prisoners he responded by once again telling his whole story. "I know Montgomery," he began. He had gone into King Street that night, Palmes said, and been told the soldiers were abusing the inhabitants at Murray's barracks. When he arrived he told an officer he was surprised to see his men out at that time of night. "An officer said, 'Do you pretend to teach us our duty, Sir?' I said, 'No, only to remind you of it.' "

When he got to the Custom House he saw Theodore Bliss, who had been a critical witness in the Preston prosecution, in conversation with Captain Preston. He quoted Bliss, demanding of Preston, " 'Why do you not fire? God damn you fire.' " A brief time later Montgomery's gun had been struck by ice, and Montgomery fell back, "whether it sallied him back, or he stept one foot back, I do not know, but he recovered himself and fired immediately." Then "six or seven seconds after that, another soldier on the Captain's right fired, and then the rest, one after another, pretty quick . . . Before the last gun was fired Montgomery made a push at me with his bayonet. I had a stick in my hand, as I generally walk with one, I struck him and hit his left arm and knocked his gun down; before he recovered I aimed another stroke at the nearest to me and hit Captain Preston. I then turned and saw Montgomery pushing at me again, and would have pushed me through, but I threw my stick in his face and the third time he ran after me to push at me again, but fell down, and I had an opportunity to run . . ."

Quincy asked some general questions then came back to Montgomery. "Are you certain that Montgomery was struck and sallied back before he fired?"

"Yes."

"Do you know whether it was with a piece of ice or a club?"

"No."

"Did you see any other violence offered, except that which struck Montgomery and the blows you aimed and gave?"

"No, no other."

Quincy was hitting his mark. It seemed clear from Palmes's testimony that the soldiers were in no immediate danger and had no reason to fear for their lives. He continued, perhaps trying to clear up an apparent contradiction, "Are you sure Montgomery did not fall, just before he discharged his gun?"

"Yes."

"Upon the firing of the first gun, did the people seem to retire?"

"Yes, they all began to run, and when the rest were fired they were a-running." And when the last gun was fired? "They were running promiscuously about every where."

If Palmes was to believed, the crowd was in disarray when the shots were fired, rather than presenting an imminent threat to the soldiers.

To satisfy the discrepancy about when Montgomery fell, the court recalled James

Bailey. He was asked by one of the judges, "Have you heard Mr. Palmes' testimony?" He had. "Are you satisfied, notwithstanding what Mr. Palmes says, that Montgomery was knocked down by a blow given him, immediately before he fired?"

"Yes, I am."

"Did you see any of the prisoners at the rope walks in the affray there, a few days before the 5th March?"

"Yes, I saw Carrol," identifying one of the soldiers, "there with other soldiers in that affray."

The details were like numbers in an equation; by themselves they had little importance, but when added and connected to other such points the result was significant. John Danbrooke came next. He identified two of the prisoners, Hartigan and Carrol, as having been in King Street that night. He had been in the crowd, only a few feet from Preston, close enough to see Montgomery discharge his musket. "I saw a little stick fly over their [the soldiers'] heads but I did not perceive it stuck any of them . . ."

He was looking at Montgomery when he discharged his weapon, Danbrooke remembered, and "I saw two fall, one fell at my elbow, another about three feet from me. I did not hear the sound of another gun before they fell . . . . One was the Molatto, the other I did not know."

"Do you think one gun killed both of these men?" This called for the witness to state his opinion on a critical question. The rules of evidence, governing what is permitted to be asked and answered in a courtroom, were still very much in an embryonic state. It would be at least another half century before they became more formalized. As Justice C. J. Vaughn explained during the 1670 trial of William Penn and William Mead for unlawful assembly, a witness "swears to but what he hath seen or heard; generally or more largely what hath fallen under his senses."

There were exceptions to that though; generally when questions concerning science or skill were to be answered, a jury might be aided by the opinions of people knowledgeable about the subject due to their profession or interest.

While Adams had the right to object to this question he did not. Objections were rarely, if ever, raised. So Danbrooke stated his opinion. "Yes," he said, "for I heard no other gun when they fell."

The prosecution pressed him, "Are you certain the other person was killed?"

"Yes."

"Did you hear any other gun before that man fell?"

"No."

Before the killings, Danbrooke recalled, he had seen as many as thirty men, most of them sailors, going to the Town House. "The biggest part of them had clubs . . . cord wood sticks broken up . . . They were about as thick as one's wrist."

Prosecutor Samuel Quincy also was taking his own notes; Danbrooke, he wrote, "Saw no stick strike him [Montgomery]. Looking at Montgomery when he fired, upon his firing two men fell . . ."

The next witness, forty-nine-year-old Jedediah Bass, could trace his lineage in Massachusetts back 140 years, to the arrival of Samuel Bass in 1630. That settler served as the first deacon of the church in John Adams's hometown of Braintree for fifty years, as well as an elected representative to the Massachusetts General Court, and when he died in 1694 at age ninety-four he was said to be the father, grandfather and great-grandfather of 162 persons, among them John Adams. Jedediah Bass was standing five feet from Montgomery when "I saw a stick knock up his gun . . . He brought it down to the place where it was before, and then he fired."

"Are you certain he did not fall before he fired?"

Yes, he was certain of that.

Quincy made certain the jury understood. "Are you certain he did not fall before he fired?"

"Yes."

"Are you sure if he had fallen you would have seen him?"

"Yes, from my situation I think I must have seen him."

"What sort of stick was it his gun was knocked up with?"

"It looked like a walking stick," he said, echoing Palmes's account.

"Did you see him fall after he fired?"

"Yes," although he did not know what occasioned that fall. He did not see anyone strike him. But he was sure that his gun fell out of his hands "after the firing." Bass could not say that any of the other defendants were there in front of the Custom House.

The next witness, Thomas Wilkinson, had responded to the fire bells, but as he did, "The people out of the chamber windows said, do not go down there, you will be killed. I saw ten or twelve soldiers with naked cutlasses by Boylston's Alley . . . the soldiers were brandishing their swords and sallying up to the people, but I did not tarry there one minute."

"Had the persons the soldiers came up to anything in their hands?"

"No, they had nothing but buckets. I took it [the soldiers] were brandishing their swords at people, but I saw them strike no body." Wilkinson happened to be near the Main Guard when Preston called them out, and he remembered, " 'Turn out,' " the captain ordered, " 'Damn your bloods, turn out.' A party of soldiers turned out . . . They drew up in two files . . . Captain Preston drew his sword and marched down with them." Wilkinson got into King Street as the soldiers did. "I staid there about four minutes when I heard the word given, 'Fire!' There was none fired then. Then I heard, 'Damn your bloods, fire!' Instantly one gun went off, I saw the flash of every gun as they went off, one after another, like the clock striking . . .

"I am positive the firing began at the right and went on to the left . . ."

Quincy, pressing his case that the soldiers' lives were never in jeopardy, asked, "Did you see anything thrown at any of them before the firing?"

"No, I stood all the time they were there, and saw nothing thrown at all."

218

"Did you see anybody knocked down?"

"No."

"You saw no ice nor snowballs?"

"No. I did not."

"Did the people round you seem to be pressing on so as to injure the soldiers?"

"No. Had I seen anything thrown I would have gone away."

"Did you see any blows given by anybody, before or after the firing?"

"No. I did not."

"Did you hear any huzzaing?"

"Yes, before the party marched down there were two or three huzzas, but afterwards none at all."

Adams noted without additional comments, ". . . saw no ice nor snowballs thrown. The People did not press on. I would have departed if I had seen any pressing, or snowballs, or blows . . . 2 or 3 huzzas, before the party marched down, but none after . . ."

Samuel Quincy made his own notes: ". . . Saw no blows given nor snowballs, ice, nor oyster shells thrown, nor pressing in of the people, had he, he should have retir'd. Heard 2 or 3 cheers before the party went down, but none afterwards. (NB: This he says very emphatically!)"

Quincy and Adams had been young men

together, entering the profession and struggling for survival together, and now they stood close to each other in the courtroom but remained so far apart in their politics, making the case against each other in this most important trial in Massachusetts history. And incredibly, each of them taking the side in this case that they opposed in daily life.

The flow of morning witnesses rolled easily into the late November afternoon. Witness after witness came forward, took the oath and earnestly told the jurors and the court what he had seen. The average trial took just an hour, but now they had to figure out a schedule and as Sam Adams wrote: "In the late trials of Preston and the Soldiers, it was observed that the Court constantly from day to day adjourned at noon and at sunset." It became clear on this second day that the trial would take longer than anyone might have imagined.

CHAPTER SEVEN

The soldiers' trial was not the only spectacle being watched by the colonists. According to the loyalist *Boston Gazette and Country Journal,* "A comet of a very uncouth aspect has lately made its appearance in the northern hemisphere. This strange phenomenon was first observed in the latitude of 38; it has been traveling northward for about five weeks past, and has lately been observed by numbers of people between the hours of one and two, with a gloomy pale body from whence issued a long black tail . . .

"Various are the conjectures of old women and other sages upon this remarkable event; Some imagine it to denote a return to the plagues of Egypt, others that it forebodes a restitution of the Stuart family, the poor despised Sons of Liberty look upon it with astonishment, as ambassadors extraordinary from Pandemonium to affect a coalition of the Tory interests upon the continent . . ."

Like an alien visitor, Lexell's comet, which had been discovered the previous June by French astronomer Charles Messier and named after the Scandinavian mathematician Anders Johan Lexell, who computed its orbit, passed closer to the earth than any observed comet in recorded history, then disappeared, never to be seen again.

With a comet hovering and the town recovering from a sudden winter nor'easter that had threatened to blow the town apart, the longest murder trial in the brief history of America continued.

Josiah Simpson followed Wilkinson to the stand. Simpson was a joiner, working to become a cabinetmaker. He readily identified several of the prisoners in the dock. That night he had been right in the thick of it as a crowd gathered around sentry Hugh White. "The soldier repaired to the Custom House door . . . there, with a large brass knocker, gave three loud and remarkable strokes . . . Somebody came to the door and opened it, and spoke to the sentry and shut it again . . . The soldier then turned and loaded his gun, and knocked it twice very loud on the steps . . . I cast my eye up King Street and saw an officer and seven, they came to the west corner of the Custom House."

"Was anything done to molest them?"

"No, nothing at all."

The soldiers formed a kind of circle, he remembered. Then, "I went up to the officer and said, 'For God's sake do not fire on these people;' He made me no answer at all . . . He had on a red coat and laced hat . . ." Corporal Wemms was dressed in that fashion. ". . . I saw no more of him. I went to some of the inhabitants and said, 'Do not trouble these men, they are on duty.' Some said we will neither trouble them nor be driven off by them . . .

"I saw a man going to throw a club, I begged of him not to do it, for I said if he did, the soldiers would certainly fire; he said he would not, and did not. I then saw a white club thrown at some distance from me towards the soldiers, immediately I heard the word, 'Present.' [The command to raise their muskets and prepare to fire.] I stopped down, a little space of time ensued, I heard, 'Damn you, fire!' Two guns were discharged then as I judged . . .

"I believe [the club] hit one of the soldiers' guns, I heard it strike . . . before the firing . . . Three or four more guns were then discharged, which killed Attucks and Gray, I heard and saw them fall; then two more were discharged, one of them killed Mr.

Caldwell, who was about ten feet distance from me, the other struck about five inches over my back."

Simpson delivered his remarkable testimony with assurance; it appeared no other witness had seen the events in such detail. He saw the stick thrown, he saw the guns fired and the men fall. Yet when asked "Did you hear them say to the soldiers, 'Bloody backs, come on you bloody backs'?" he replied, "No, I heard no such thing, but when the two first guns were discharged, someone cryed murder, and by the voice I think it was Maverick. These guns killed nobody, unless Maverick was then shot." Seventeen-year-old apprentice Samuel Maverick, who had been running from the soldiers, was one of the men killed that night.

It is the challenge of each juror to give sufficient weight to each testimony and in the end see how the scale is balanced. There is no magic formula for that, but it appeared Simpson's confident telling may have been too much to have been believed. At the top of Adams's notes of Simpson's testimony, he inserted one word: "Curious." Governor Hutchinson was more critical, writing privately to Lord Hillsborough that Simpson "delivered his evidence as a schoolboy does his lesson," meaning it sounded as if it were memorized, and as a result, he concluded, "no credit was given to it."

The hat maker Nathaniel Fosdick, who'd stood his ground in King Street, forcing Preston's relief column to split around him, came next. He had told his story in the captain's trial but now repeated it for the new jury. He "was pushed from behind me with a bayonet" and when he faced the soldier and demanded to know why he was so poorly treated, "he damn'd my blood and bid me stand out of their way." Minutes later, after the troop had formed, "The word was given fire! Immediately the right hand man fired; after that I pushed in towards them, and they run a bayonet at me and wounded me in my arm." He was "pushed twice in the arm by two different bayonets. I knocked off one of them with my stick and with the other I was wounded in my breast, the wound an inch long, through a double breasted jacket . . . Two different bayonets run into my arm, I can shew the scar now."

Fosdick then displayed the scars of March 5th to the jury.

Following his testimony, the prosecution widened its presentation. Prior to the beginning of the trial the prosecution and defense had reached an agreement. Normally the prosecution would not be permitted to present evidence concerning events that took place before March 5th, at least until the defense introduced such testimony to show the many provocations that led to the final confrontation. But Sam Quincy and Robert Paine wanted the jury to be told about the belligerent attitude of the soldiers in the early days of March. Perhaps surprisingly, Josiah Quincy and Adams agreed to allow this — so long as the defense would have the same opportunity to bring in evidence about the provocative acts committed by Boston men. The court respected the agreement, although the justices gave no assurance they would permit evidence not bearing directly on the event to be part of their charge to the jury.

The first witness to testify about these earlier confrontations was Sheriff Stephen Greenleaf's coachman, Samuel Hemmingway. He knew several of the prisoners, but especially Private Matthew Killroy. Prosecutor Quincy asked him, "Did you ever hear Killroy make use of any threatening expressions against the inhabitants of this town?"

Although Hemmingway was employed by the Crown, he did not hesitate. "Yes, one evening I heard him say he would never miss an opportunity, when he had one, to fire on the inhabitants, and that he wanted to have an opportunity ever since he landed."

"How long was that before the 5th March?"

"A week or fortnight, I cannot say which." There were other people present when he made that statement, Hemmingway testified; he was not "in liquor," there had been no angry words preceding it and he appeared to be serious about it. "I said he was a fool for talking so. He said he did not care."

Joseph Hilyer, who had testified at Preston's trial that the soldiers fired without orders, answered the fire bells and was told there was no fire, but rather "a rumpus betwixt the soldiers and the inhabitants" and that it was dangerous to go into King Street. But when he got there he saw nothing unusual, saying "I saw a few lads, but no great number, I have often seen more collected for their diversion." But when the soldiers began firing, "A little boy run along and cryed, Fire! Fire! Fire! as people generally do when there is fire, a soldier pointed his gun to him and fired, but did not hit him." And then he identified him, ". . . the last but one on the left." That probably was

McCauley.

The consequences of the action did not immediately shock Hilyer; at first he believed the soldiers must be firing powder to frighten the people. It was only after the smoke had blown away that he understood what had happened. There was a sense of disbelief in his words as he said, "I saw them lye in the street but I did not imagine it was anybody killed, but that they had been scared and run away and left their great coats behind them: I saw nothing like an attack that could produce such consequences. I went to look at the Molotto man and heard a noise like the cocking of firelocks, but an officer passed before them and said, 'Do not fire on the inhabitants.'

"The street was in a manner clear, it was as hush as at twelve o'clock at night . . ."

Although the eight soldiers were being tried together, evidence had to be presented against each of them individually. So Quincy made certain to implicate each redcoat individually, asking, "Did the last man on the left fire, or not?"

"He did not fire, his gun seemed to misfire, and he brought it down in a priming position . . ."

The prosecution began reaching back in time, to the fight at Grey's ropeworks three days earlier, calling rope maker Nicholas Ferreter. "I know Warren and Killroy," he began. "They were both at the rope-walks . . . on the Friday before."

There had been a confrontation, he continued, at about noon, "I saw a soldier coming down the outside rope-walk, swearing, and saying he would have satisfaction. Before this, there was one of our hands while I was coiling a cable, said to a soldier, 'Do you want work?'

" 'Yes,' says the soldier, 'I do faith.'

" 'Well,' he said to the soldier, 'go clean my little house.' He damned us and made a blow at, and struck me. When I knocked up his heels, his coat flew open and out dropt a naked cutlass, which I took up and carried off with me. He went away and came back with a dozen soldiers with him, Warren among them: the people that were attacked called to us for help. When they called to us, we came up; then we have several knocks amongst us, at last they went off. They all got armed with clubs, and in the afternoon they were coming again, but Mr. John Grey stopped them."

"When they came the second time was Killroy with them?"

"Yes . . . we had a battle and they went to their barracks. On the 5th of March I went to Quaker Lane and met Samuel Gray." This man, Samuel Gray, was a well-known street fighter, a brawler, who may have been kin to the owner, John Grey — there have been conflicting accounts of the spelling of Samuel Gray's surname. Captain Preston in his deposition confused the two men, stating that one of the victims that night was "Mr. Gray at whose rope-walk the prior quarrels took place."

Ferreter continued, "I said where are you going, he said to the fire . . . When I was walking home I heard the guns go off. I went to King Street and was told several were killed, I then went home . . .

"Samuel Gray, when I saw him that night, was calm as a clock and had no stick."

Adams added details in his notes that the transcriber Hodgson may have missed as his hand tired; Ferreter had said that after the first battle in Dock Square, earlier on the night of March 5th, "The whole barracks came and Killroy and Warren was with them and we had a battle with them and drove 'em off."

Samuel Quincy in his notes wrote that the soldier had come back with "about 30 and had another battle."

By establishing that bad blood existed between the soldiers and the town's inhabitants before that cold night, the prosecution was supplying a motive for the shooting; the bitterness had been growing until it no longer could be checked, and the soldiers could not resist releasing their anger and frustration. It was cold-blooded murder.

Patriot Benjamin Burdick served as the constable of the night watch, as well as working as a "hair-cutter" and peruke [wig]maker. He had felt great dismay as the British troops disembarked two years earlier and several times since then had argued with them about which of them had the right to police the town in the night. Among his duties on the night watch he was to "frequently give the time of the night and what the weather is with a distinct but moderate voice . . . take up all negroes Indian and Molattoe slaves that may be absent from their masters houses after 9 o'clock at night unless they are carrying Lanthorns with light Candles and can give a good and satisfactory account of their business' and endeavor to suppress all routs riots and other disorders that may be committed in the night."

Although he admitted he could not identify any of the soldiers as they were dressed plainly for the court, he said that "When I came to King Street I went immediately up to one of the soldiers, which I take to be that man who is bald on the head . . ." Here he pointed to Private Montgomery. "I asked him if any of the soldiers were loaded; he said yes. I asked him if they were going to fire, he said, 'Yes, by eternal God,' and pushed at me with his bayonet, which I put by with what was in my hand."

"What was it?"

"A Highland broadsword." A broadsword was a basket-hilted weapon with a double-edge blade especially useful for cutting rather than stabbing.

He was carrying it, he explained, because "a young man that boarded with me, and was at the Rope-Works, told me several of them [soldiers] had a spite at him, and that he believed he was in danger. I had seen two soldiers about my house, I saw one of them hearkening at the window, I saw him again near the house and asked him what he was after; he said he was pumping ship [a common term for urinating]. Was it not you, says I, that was hearkening at my window last night? 'What if it was?' he said. I told him to march off and he damned me and I beat him till he had enough of it, and then he went off.

"The reason of carrying the sword was, they spyed the young man in the lane and dogg'd him, for he had been very active in the affray at the rope-works, and they said they would some time or other have satisfaction . . .

"When alarmed by the cry of fire, and I had got below the house, my wife called after me and said it is not fire, it is an affray in King Street; if you are going, take this, so I took it and run down and I asked a soldier what I just now told you. I knocked the bayonet with what I had in my hand; another pushed at me, I struck his gun. My face was now towards the soldiers. I heard the first gun go off and then the second gun went off. As I was looking to see if any body was killed, I saw the tall man standing in a line with me.

"I saw him fall." Most probably he was referring to Attucks.

He was standing in the middle of the group, Burdick continued, and he struck the musket before the firing, struck it as hard as he could, and he "hit the lock of his gun . . ."

The first shot was fired by the right-hand man, he was certain of that. Asked, "Did you see anything extraordinary to induce them to fire that gun?" he replied, "Nothing. But a short stick was thrown, which seemed to go clear over their heads . . ."

When the firing stopped, Burdick saw that Attucks was dead. "I went up and met Dr. Gardner and Mr. Brindley. I asked them to come and see the Molatto and as we stooped to take up the man, the soldiers presented their arms again, as if they had been going to fire. I went to them to see if I could know their faces again; Captain Preston looked out betwixt two of them and spoke to me, which took my attention from them."

Adams's notes added only a few facts to Hodgson's transcript: when Burdick was leaving his house he was carrying a stick and only then took up the broadsword. And when Burdick was collecting the dead he remembered Captain Preston "knocked up the guns and said, 'Don't fire any more.'"

The parade of eyewitnesses continued, each of them adding a detail to the horrific scene. Robert Williams testified that the growing crowd pressed so tightly on the soldiers that he feared they would be pushed into the points of the bayonets, and as the people ran away the soldiers' guns seemed to move after them. Merchant Bartholomew Kneeland was at his own front door when a soldier of the 29th "pointed a naked bayonet at my chest and held it there for some time" before telling him to get inside.

Nathaniel Thayer was a sealer of wood, a town official whose job was to measure cords of fire wood shipped into Boston, and ensure they did not exceed the required dimensions: four-foot lengths of wood stacked four-foot high by eight-foot long; he too had gone to his door when he heard a commotion and saw "seven soldiers from the main guard without any coats on, driving along, swearing, cursing and damning like wild creatures, saying 'Where are they? Cut them to pieces, slay them all.' " When they came to his door he shut it on them. Merchant Nathaniel Appleton also shut his door on the soldiers, then went up to his chamber and looked out the window "and saw people flying here and there like pidgeons, and the soldiers running about like mad men in a fury, till they got to the bottom of the street."

Perhaps the most harrowing story was told by Appleton's son; twelve-year-old John Appleton was on an errand with his younger brother when they encountered soldiers in Jenkins Alley, he told the jury, when "there came out about twenty soldiers with cutlasses in their hands. My brother fell and they ran past him and were going to kill me. I said, 'Soldiers, spare my life,' and one of them said, 'No, damn you, we will kill you all.' He lifted his cutlass and struck at my head, but I dodged and got the blow on my shoulder." Adams heard the young man somewhat differently, writing in his notes, "I dodged or he would have struck me on the head." Either way, the account of a twelve-year-old describing an attack by British soldiers that night was emotional and powerful evidence for the prosecution.

The tailor Thomas Marshall had earned great respect and standing in the community for his service in the Ancient and Honorable Artillery, a paramilitary organization consisting of twelve companies of patriots that might be seen drilling on the Common who were paid only a pittance. John Adams had called the militia an essential part of the foundation of the colony. Equal in importance to the towns, churches and schools, "The virtues and talents of the people are formed there." Most able-bodied white men between the ages of eighteen and sixty were compelled to possess a weapon and serve in their town's defense, primarily to offer protection against Indians. It was a tradition that harked back to 1181, when Henry II's Assize of Arms declared that each man will "bear arms" in the service of the King. The first militia in the western hemisphere, The Military Company of Massachusetts, was chartered by Governor Winthrop in 1638 and had continued to exist as the Ancient and Honorable Artillery Company. Thomas Marshall had served as an officer, a rank that he would carry through his life, and his word was sacrosanct.

Dock Square was quiet when he had come into it a few minutes after nine o'clock, he recalled; he saw the sentry, untroubled; in fact, "I never saw King Street so quiet in my life." Minutes later he had been summoned to his shop when he "heard a cry of murder." He opened his door and just as "a party from the main guard, ten or twelve came rushing out violently. I saw their arms glitter by the moon light, hallowing 'Damn them, where are they, by Jesus let them come!' "

Lieutenant Colonel Marshall remembered to add that he had often seen boys with the sentry "and heard words often," so that part of the night was not unusual. But the presence of the several parties of soldiers caught his attention. He saw their "arms glitter" in the moonlight and wondered about their presence until "I heard a gun go off. I thought it was an accident, but in a little time another gun went off, and a third and fourth, pretty quick, and then the fifth." Even then he had no real concern, but when the smoke blew away, "I saw the people dead on the ground."

With the words of this militia officer still hanging in the air, bringing with them the unforgettable image of the dead of Boston lying under the moonlight, the court adjourned for yet another day. The jurors were escorted to their sparse quarters.

It is possible that as John Adams left the courthouse he passed through King Street on the way to his home. It was a grand lane, among the oldest streets in the town. It had been marked out in 1630 when Puritan settlers, led by John Winthrop, built their houses there. Market Street it was called then, and the Puritans set their meeting house for the First Church in Boston along its broad path. Its name was changed to King Street to honor His Majesty in 1708, and five years later the imposing State House was constructed at the top of the street, where the meeting house had stood. Not long after, the Custom House was built a minute's walk away. Naturally, the taverns followed quickly, including the bustling Bunch of Grapes, and the Marlborough Arms and Queens Head, among others that provided food, drink and lodging for those in need.

King Street had become the most popular

place to shop in the town and "all sorts of goldsmith and jewelry wares . . . women's fine horse-hair and beaver hats" could be found in its stores, along with books and beans and butter, pork and fresh produce. At the foot of the King Street lay the business end of Boston, the docks and warehouses of Long Wharf, where as many as fifty great ships at one time sailed into the city carrying the goods of the Empire, and departed when the winds were right, holds filled with the work and the hopes of farmers and craftsmen. Even on a late November evening there probably were people in King Street, walking briskly past the closed shops, avoiding the damage from the storm yet to be removed or repaired.

The prosecution had built a strong case against the soldiers. When court resumed at 9 a.m. Thursday, November 29th, 1770, Quincy brought on his last few witnesses. Another tailor, Joseph Crosswell, was first that morning; his testimony was brief but telling: "Next morning after the 5th of March, in King Street, before the soldiers were apprehended, I saw Killroy. I have known him by sight almost since he hath been here. I saw his bayonet bloody, the blood was dryed on five or six inches from the point."

"How near were you to the bayonet?" asked Quincy.

"About the same distance I am from the judges, six feet."

The writing schoolmaster, James Carter, said, "I saw the same thing with Mr. Crosswell . . . that's the man." He pointed at Killroy. "His gun was rested on his right arm."

"Did it appear to you to be covered from the point with blood?"

"Yes, I am positive it was blood." The defense offered no objection to this, nor did Adams or Josiah Quincy ask either of the witnesses how they came to be so certain a darkened substance on a knife was dried blood. Instead Adams noted that Carter only was "satisfied it was blood." And in Paine's notes, the teacher saw the bayonet bloody and "called several people to look at it."

"How nigh was you to him?" the prosecution asked.

"As nigh as I am to you, Sir, three feet off."

Jonathan Cary was also a prominent inhabitant of the town. In addition to being a skilled keg maker, he had risen to the rank of captain in the Ancient and Honorable Artillery Company of Massachusetts. His presence on the witness stand was curious

240

as he offered little of substance, stating simply that young Maverick had been eating at his house before responding to the bells. But perhaps in the charged atmosphere of the town, his presence on the stand was as much a political courtesy as a legal necessity.

The same might be true for Justice John Hill, a justice of the peace who had sat in several previous cases involving the soldiers and inhabitants. This time, though, he was a witness. Hill had been near the ropeworks on the day of that brawl and "saw a party of soldiers . . . with clubs." He told them he was "in commission for the peace" and ordered them to disperse. Instead, "they paid no regard to me or my orders, but cut an old man coming by, before my face, and some of them struck at me but did not hit me."

But when asked if he could identify any of the prisoners as being among them, he admitted, "I do not know that they were."

The prosecution's final witness was to be Mary Gardner, who intended to testify that she had been in her home near Green's barracks. A number of soldiers stood across from her gate, and when the shots were heard, she had said in her deposition, the soldiers "clapped their hands and gave a

cheer, saying 'This is all that we want.' "
They went into the barracks and soon re-
appeared, carrying muskets, and ran toward
King Street.

It was innocuous testimony, but the jury
never heard it. Her appearance was "overruled," Paine noted, but failed to provide a
reason.

With that inglorious ending, the prosecution had presented its evidence. Now it was
Sam Quincy's challenge to weave the testimony together for the jurors. The basic
structure of the trial called for the prosecution to make its arguments and present its
evidence followed by the defense's opening,
witnesses and final summation. And while
the court permitted rebuttal witnesses to be
called out of order as part of the opposing
side's case, this was to be Quincy's critical
closing argument.

Quincy promised the jurors he would
present his case "as distinctly as I am able,
without endeavoring to misrepresent or ag-
gravate anything to the prejudice of the
prisoners on the one hand, or on the other
to neglect any thing that [offers] justice to
the deceased sufferers, the laws of my
country, or the preservation of the peace of
society demand."

It is necessary for him to prove, he continued, the identity of the prisoners, that they committed the facts mentioned in the indictments and the circumstances surrounding those felonious acts. Quincy then began sewing his case together, reminding the jurors of the evidence against each soldier. "To Killroy gentlemen, you have Langford, Archibald and Brewer, who swear positively, and further you have the evidence of Ferriter and Hemmingway. The one, of Killroy's being in the affray at the ropeworks and the other to his uttering a number of malicious and threatening expressions in regards to the inhabitants of the town of Boston."

He then proceeded to list each witness that brought evidence against a specific soldier: "To White, gentlemen, you have four more, Simpson, Langford, Bailey and Clark. To Montgomery you have Bailey, Palmes . . ." Quincy then apologized in advance to the jury; he had intended to bring together relevant testimony to make a concise argument, he explained, but due to fatigue and a family issue he was unable to properly prepare his summation. So he would instead review the testimony and explain its meaning in the context of his case.

When Austin came into King Street,

"McCauley pushed at him with his bayonet, damned him and bid him stand off. This was the first instance of their conduct."

Bridgham believed he had seen William Warren in King Street but later saw someone similar, so he could not be certain of it. "My remark upon this, is, it is probable that the first impressions made on his mind were the strongest and therefore you cannot well doubt he was right in judging that Warren was in fact the person he saw . . .

"Mr. Langford comes next, and this witness is perhaps as particular as any one witness on the part of the Crown . . ." It was Langford who was standing with Gray, "talking familiarly, Langford leaning on his stick, Gray standing with his hands folded in his bosom, without a stick in his hand, neither saying or doing anything to the soldiers . . . Langford spoke to Killroy, and after two guns were discharged, seeing him present his piece said to him, 'Damn you, are you going to fire?' Presently upon this Killroy leveled his piece and firing directly at Gray, killed him dead on the spot. The ball passed through his head and he fell on Langford's left foot; upon which, not satisfied with having murdered one of his fellow creatures in that cruel and inhuman manner, he pushed with his bayonet and pierced

Langford through his great coat and jacket; here gentlemen, if any there can be, is evidence. And I think compleat evidence of a heart desperately wicked, and bent upon mischief, the true characteristic of a willful malicious murderer . . .

"If you compare this testimony with Mr. Hemmingway, who swears to Killroy's uttering expressions importing that he would miss no opportunity of firing upon the inhabitant, he had wished for it ever since he landed, you certainly gentlemen can have no doubt in your minds but that he had that intention at heart and took this opportunity to execute it.

"The crime of murder, gentlemen . . . necessarily involves the malice of the heart, and that malice is to be collected from the circumstances attending the action; but it is not necessary to constitute malice, that it should be harbored long in the breast, a distinction is made in the books betwixt malice and hatred and a good distinction it is . . ." Quoting Chief Justice John Kelynge in Mawgridge's case, the murder in the Tower of London, Quincy read that "Malice is a design formed of doing mischief to another.' " Therefore, he continued, "if the act is in its nature wanton and cruel, the law will presume it be malicious . . ."

Adams was silently and dutifully taking notes; his turn would come to refute this presentation.

Quincy continued by reminding the jury that Ferriter testified that Killroy was in the midst of the brawl at the ropeworks, and said that taking "all the circumstances of this testimony together it must remove every sort of difficulty in your minds as to the purpose Killroy had at that time, it seems apart that there were strong marks of malice in his heart, the person you can have no doubt of, nor can you, I think, doubt of the species of crime."

Finished with Killroy, he moved on to the rest of prisoners, taking full advantage of the agreement he had reached with Adams to bring in earlier events. "If you attend to the testimony of several of the witnesses, there were that evening in the streets at all parts of the town a number of soldiers; they sallied out from Murray's barracks and every where with clubs, cutlasses and other weapons of death; this occasioned a general alarm; every man therefore had a right, and very prudent it was to endeavour to defend himself if attacked. This accounts for the reason of Dr. Young or any one inhabitant of the town having a sword that evening."

A key question that had been bandied

about without a firm resolution was which soldier fired the first shot. "Mr. Bailey . . . testifies that there were Montgomery, Carrol and White there," Quincy continued. "He placed himself at a post by the Custom House and stood there all the time . . . He was near the sentinel when the party came down; Carrol pointed at his breast with his bayonet, and White said do not hurt him; that Montgomery discharged his piece first, he thinks it was about half a minute before the second gun went off; the grenadier's gun, he says, was struck out of his hand by some person near him, and that he recovered it, and then fired, that Carrol was the next but one to him; he imagines, gentlemen, that Montgomery killed Attucks; Attucks was about fifteen feet from him . . .

"He did not apprehend himself or the soldiers in danger, from clubs, sticks, snow balls or anything else . . . From this witness you ascertain, gentlemen, that Montgomery fired first, and that he was on the right wing of the party."

"Bailey," wrote Adams. "Thinks Mont kill'd Attucks. That Montgomery fired is clear from this witness."

Quincy continued his presentation like a scholar lecturing able students. Palmes, he said, had ignored advice to stay out of the street, and instead went there to try to make peace. He saw Montgomery hit by a stick, step back and fire. Within seven or eight seconds several others fired. Then, "as the last gun went off, Montgomery pushed at him with his bayonet, and he struck him with his cane and struck the gun down; the bayonet stuck in the snow and the gun fell out of his hand. Mr. Palmes at this time slipt and fell, but quickly recovered himself. Montgomery attempted again to push him with his bayonet, and he threw his cane at him and ran; not satisfied with this, Montgomery attempted to push him a third time and in that attempt he slipt and fell, and thereby gave Palmes an opportunity to get out of his way, or else he would have been run through the body. From the testimony of this witness you have further proof that Montgomery was the person who fired first, that after firing he continued to discover marks of malice and malevolence, by pushing with his bayonet and endeavoring to destroy not only Mr. Palmes but all around him."

Danbrooke saw defendants Hartegan, Montgomery and Carrol. He was standing a short distance from Montgomery and saw him firing, "upon which, the witness thinks, two men fell; if that was the case there was an execution indeed, by the discharge of one gun two persons killed on the spot . . .

"Attucks at that time was near him, at his left, leaning on a stick; that circumstance I would have you keep in your minds Gentlemen, that you may remember it when you have the whole evidence together."

Samuel Adams had been in the courtroom every day listening, and at times even sent prosecutor Paine notes on evidence and suggested trial strategy. He was going to make certain the prosecutors did not hesitate to bring the full might of the law against the redcoats. This carefully woven explanation must have given him confidence that there had been no shilly-shally in Quincy's presentation.

Jedediah Bass saw Montgomery fire and the people beginning to run. Wilkinson ignored warnings that he would be killed if he went into the street; he saw Captain Preston march the guard to King Street. "He saw the flash of each gun; seven went off and one flashed. There, gentlemen, you have evidence of all the party's firing save one." The witness did not see anything thrown by the crowd; "if he had, he should have thought himself in danger and retreated."

Next was the overly confident and descriptive Simpson. And once again John Adams begins his comments with the word, "Curious." Even Quincy was a bit hesitant, cautioning the jury to pay extra heed: "He swears to the discharge of eight guns, which if you give credit to his testimony, will prove to you that the whole party fired . . ."

Next, Fosdick testified to the disposition of the soldiers before and after shots were fired. "When the first gun was fired, the second man from the right pushed his bayonet at him and wounded him in the breast; you saw, Gentlemen, the mark in court; before this two different men pierced him in the arm and elbow quite to the bone; here, Gentlemen were three thrusts given to a person innocently passing down upon the cry of fire! . . ."

In his testimony, Hemmingway quoted Killroy's foul words, that he had wanted to fire on the people of the town ever since he landed. Quincy suggested to the jury, "These expressions . . . are of such a nature as you cannot but draw from them the temper of the man's heart who spoke them . . ."

Witness Hilyer watched as "a little boy ran across the street crying fire — and the soldier on the left followed the boy with his gun; there was nothing passed, he observed,

M.ʳ SAMUEL ADAMS.

Samuel Adams was an astute politician who became a leading force in the revolution and an architect of the resulting republic. He deftly exploited the massacre trial for its propaganda, attending every session, planning strategy, then writing about it under the pseudonym Vindex. After the trial he continued to use it as kindling for the independence movement, staging a commemoration each March 5. COLLECTION OF THE MASSACHUSETTS HISTORICAL SOCIETY

to induce them to apprehend any danger." And yet, Adams writes of the same witness, "A little boy, running and crying fire, the last gun was pointed at him and fired." While transcripts have been known to include errors and dropped or missed words, and later there would be much grumbling about this one, this was a peculiar discrepancy that Adams would have to address in his own case.

Nicholas Ferriter had been at the ropeworks "before this affair happened." He had told the jury about three attacks, the third such fray being "after three-quarters of an hour they came back and went at it again, in this last squabble the soldiers were a third time worsted. From this affair perhaps may be dated a good deal of the proceedings of Monday evening; you have heard from witnesses that the soldiers of that regiment remembered the grudge and discovered [revealed] a malicious disposition, were frequently seen in parties and, when single, with arms, attacking the people passing the streets. Killroy, one of the prisoners, and Warren, are expressly sworn to, that they were in this affray . . ."

The feisty twenty-eight-year-old Benjamin Burdick had struck back and hit a soldier's musket — he thought it was Montgomery but could not testify to that with certainty — when that man thrust his bayonet at him. But moments later, as he was "stooping to take up the dead," the soldiers "cocked their guns and presented at him again; thus you see the same disposition continued . . . after they had killed these persons they were not satisfied with that . . ."

One of the justices then quite suddenly interrupted and wondered if perhaps there might be an argument made that these actions constituted voluntary manslaughter rather than murder. Perhaps he was offering a compromise path for the prosecution to explore. Samuel Quincy would not have it, responding harshly with a devastating indictment: "I readily grant there may; it has also been observed that homicide which includes murder, must be committed with coolness and deliberation. I allow it, and my application of this rule is that it comes within the evidence you have of the particular facts related by the witnesses with regard to Killroy; there is no manner of doubt with me but the fact was done in the manner which the law calls sedato animo, he was doing a deliberate action, with a cool and calm mind. It appears, if you believe Langford, he was not molested, it appears the person he killed, and at whom he aimed, and the person whose clothes he pierced with a bayonet, were standing peacefully, one leaning on a stick, the other with his arms folded."

If Samuel Adams and the Sons of Liberty

had any doubt about the prosecution's commitment to a murder conviction, Quincy had just allayed. it. Quincy resumed by reviewing Lieutenant Colonel Marshall's testimony, which seemed riddled with questions. Marshall's insistence that he had seen bayonets glittering by the light of the moon was troublesome, for example, as the moon was in the wrong part of the sky to enable such acute observation. Quincy dismissed that: "Looking towards the guard-house he saw a number of soldiers issue from thence in an undress, with naked swords, cutlasses and crying out 'Damn them where are they? By Jesus let 'em come.' As to the situation of the moon, whether she was north or south . . . I cannot see it will make much one way or the other, it is sufficient that Colonel Marshall, whose credibility and capacity will not be disputed has sworn" to it. The colonel saw two parties of soldiers armed with cutlasses and other weapons come up Quaker Lane, brandishing their swords and shouting, "Fire."

The evening had erupted with the shouting of "fire" and the ringing of the fire bells. A number of witnesses had testified that they had come running from their homes in response to those cries from the street; others had responded to the bells. The question hung there: What came first, the warning cries or the bells summoning help? In Captain Preston's trial, Marshall had testified that the soldiers had created the false alarm with their shouts, which had been followed by the bells; in this trial he was less certain when the bells were rung. Quincy dismissed that defect too, suggesting a far more nefarious explanation. "The use I would make of it is this," he advised jurors who might question the quality of Marshall's entire testimony, "to compare it with what the other witnesses say of the conduct of the soldiers . . . it appears to me that if we can believe the evidence they had a design of attacking and slaughtering the inhabitants that night, and they could have devised no better method to draw out the inhabitants unarmed than to cry fire!"

This was a serious accusation; Quincy was alleging that rather than a series of unintended events that dissolved into mayhem, this had been planned and carried out efficiently; that the soldiers had lured the inhabitants into the streets by shouting false claims with the intent to do them harm. "Mr. Thayer," he offered, "was sitting at his fire" when he saw soldiers "coming down like wild creatures" and heard a cry of fire, which he believed had come from the town's night watch.

There was one more story to tell and Quincy had saved the heart-rending tale of the twelve-year-old John Appleton for the last. The prosecution's case had been presented without undue drama. The facts needed no illumination. But a trial was a great entertainment, and this act needed a memorable finish. The story told by the "young master . . . with his manner of telling it must strike deep in your minds. I am sure it did in mine. A child of his age, with a younger brother sent on an errand of a few steps and on returning home struck at by a party of soldiers, nay ruffians, with cutlasses . . ."

Quincy's words were colored with his passion.

". . . he innocently crying, 'Soldiers spare my life!'

" 'No, damn you, we will kill you all,' or words to that purpose, attended with a blow, was the answer the little victim received! What can indicate malice if this does not? Cruelty almost equal to that of a Pharaoh or Herod." Here Quincy cited a respected source to prove the power of those words, quoting words spoken only weeks earlier by his adversary, John Adams. "I remember at the last trial, my brother

[John] Adams made this observation, that 'Man is a social creature; that his feelings, his passions, his imagination are contagious.' I am sure if in any instance it is so, here was food enough for such passions, such imaginations to feed upon."

Certainly this horrid incident does not specifically relate to all of the prisoners, Quincy volunteered, but it does suggest "that from the conduct and appearance of the soldiery, in different parts of the town, the inhabitants had reason to be apprehensive they were in danger of their lives; children and parents, husbands and wives, masters and servants had reason to tremble one for another . . ."

Those final words were a chilling reminder to the jury that should this behavior remain unpunished, especially considering the outcome of Preston's trial, the next time might well put them and their families in jeopardy.

To bring his argument to a close, Quincy returned to the law and how it should be applied to the prisoners. His problem, he understood, was that he had been unable to connect each soldier to a killing. But there was provision in the law that addressed this circumstance. "It is a rule of law," he explained, "when the fact of killing is once proved, every circumstance alleviating, excusing or justifying in order to extenuate the crime must be proved by the prisoners, for the law presumes the fact is malicious, until the contrary appears in evidence." The law was clear about that: a defendant claiming he had acted in self-defense was required to prove the underlying facts.

Quincy continued, "There is another rule I shall mention also, and that is, that it is immaterial, where there are a number of persons concerned, who gave the mortal blow. All that are present are in the eye of the law, principals. This is a rule settled by the Judges of England upon solid argument.

"The question therefore then will be, what species of homicide this is, and the decision of that question must be deferred until the defense comes out by evidence on the other side.

"The laws of society, gentlemen, lay a restraint on the passions of men, that no man shall be the avenger of his own cause, unless through absolute necessity, the law giving a remedy for every wrong."

Deftly, he began undermining his opposition's upcoming argument for self-defense. "If a man might at any time execute his own revenge, there would be an end of law.

"A person cannot justify killing, if he can by any means make his escape; he should endeavor to take himself out of the way, before he kills the person attacking him . . ."

Justice Trowbridge stopped him here, and with the support of his colleagues told him it was improper for him to attack an argument the defense had yet to make. There was no legal right for him to anticipate Adams and Quincy's case.

"I was about to make some further remarks," Samuel Quincy told the jury, "but it is thought by the Honorable Court improper to anticipate what may be urged on the other side. I shall therefore rest the case as it is, and doubt not but on the evidence as it now stands, the facts . . . against the prisoners at the bar are fully proved, and until something turns up to remove from your minds, the force of that evidence, you must pronounce them —" and here he slammed down on his final word "— GUILTY."

The prosecution was done.

Adams's last notes were succinct: "J. Trowbridge. You ought to produce all your evidence now."

Chapter Eight

"There is something pleasing and solemn when one enters into a court of law," wrote Samuel Adams under his pseudonym Vindex to the printers of the *Gazette.* (Vindex was the Roman senator who had stood publicly against Emperor Nero.) "Pleasing, as there we expect to see the scale held with an equal hand — to find matters deliberately and calmly weigh'd and decided, and justice administered without any respect to persons or parties, and from no other motive but a sacred regard for the truth."

That was the ideal.

Here was the reality: for Sam Adams and his Sons of Liberty, this trial was a means to an end. Revenge was a sharp tool. The conviction of the soldiers for murder would lay bare the arrogance and brutality of the British government for all the world and might well become the rallying cry for the growing liberty movement.

John Adams clearly understood how useful that outcome might be for the Sam Adams–led movement, but for him there was a greater cause. As he would soon say, "Representative government and trial by jury are the heart and lungs of liberty. Without them we have no other fortification against being ridden like horses, fleeced like sheep, worked like cattle, and fed and clothed like swine and hounds." He was determined that the politics of the town and the desires of Sam Adams and his men would not be allowed to influence the jury. If the legal system could be bent to achieve a desired political outcome, any liberty that came of it would be worthless.

Josiah Quincy, Jr., rose to open for the defense. Quincy was average of appearance; he was a slender man of normal height, with fair hair and a narrow, pleasant face, although he suffered from strabismus, a condition which prevented his eyes from aligning properly. But his voice was considered especially smooth and when necessary could rise to stirring — although even then it was regularly marred with a worrisome cough. It was his task to take the claws out of his older brother's attack, to extinguish the passions that had been inflamed and place the blame where it belonged — even if they would not directly implicate the victims and those men and boys who had battled the soldiers that night. Facing the jury, he began, "The prisoners at the bar stand indicted for the murder of five of his Majesty's liege subjects . . ." They pleaded not guilty and "have put themselves on God and their country; which country you are . . .

"By their plea of not guilty, they throw the burden of proof, as to the fact of killing, upon the Crown . . . the truth of the facts, they may thus alledge, is your sole and undoubted province to determine . . . but upon a supposition that those facts appear to your satisfaction, in the manner we alledge, the grand question then to be determined will be, whether, such matters so proved do in law extenuate, excuse or justify." It was the purview of the jury, he reminded the twelve of them, to determine — by the facts — whether any homicide was committed. If so, who committed it? And were there circumstances that might reduce the offense to manslaughter?

Before addressing those issues, he acknowledged that their decision would reverberate far beyond the courtroom. "Permit me, gentlemen, to remind you of the importance of this trial, as it relates to the prisoners. It is for their lives! If we consider the number of persons now on trial, joined with many other circumstances which might be mentioned, it is by far the most important this country ever saw.

"Remember the ties you are under to the prisoners and even to yourselves: The eyes of all are upon you . . . it is of high importance to your country that nothing should appear on this trial to impeach our justice, or stain our humanity."

Then, addressing directly the passions of the town, he continued, "An opinion has been entertained by many among us that the life of a soldier was of very little value; of much less value than others of the community. The law, gentlemen, knows no such distinction; the life of a soldier is viewed by the equal eye of the law, as estimable as the life of any other citizen . . .

"The reputation of the country depends much on your conduct, gentlemen, and . . . justice calls aloud for candour in hearing and impartiality in deciding this cause which has, perhaps, too much engrossed our affections — and, I speak for one, too much excited our passions."

As Quincy continued, John Adams briefly noted his points in a careful hand: "The criminal law extends itself to every individual of the community. It views man possessed of affections and passions. The law attends to mankind as we find 'em surrounded with all their infirmities and all their passions. Whatever will justify an inhabitant in firing upon an inhabitant will justify a soldier . . ."

Given the great latitude permitted by law in making this opening statement, Quincy directly addressed the political rancor that had affected all of their lives. "About some five or six years ago . . . measures were alternately taken in Great Britain that awakened jealousy, resentment, fortitude and vigilance . . . that our dearest rights were invaded . . . These are concernments . . . we must keep far away from us when in a court of law. It poisons justice when politics tinctures its current."

The soldiers had been sent to Massachusetts to enforce obedience to acts that were believed to be an infringement of the inhabitants' freedom. "Many on this continent viewed their chains as already forged . . . they beheld the soldiers as fastening and riveting for ages the shackles of their bondage . . . Disquisitions of this sort are for statesmen and politicians . . . but we, gentlemen, are confined in our excursions by the rigid rules of the law . . . You are to determine on the facts coming to your knowledge; you are to think, judge and act as *jurymen,* and not as *statesmen.*"

Adams recorded Quincy's words, "You are not sitting here as statesmen or politicians. You have nothing to do with the injuries your country has sustained. The town is not concerned."

Quincy continued, reminding the talesman that the soldiers were only human beings, and therefore susceptible to the natural emotions. "How stinging was it to be stigmatized as the instrument of tyranny and oppression . . ." he wondered. "We must take human nature as we find it, and not vainly imagine that all things are to become new at such a crisis." Quincy then carefully but indirectly placed some of the blame for what happened with Sam Adams and his men. While he did not name them, there could be no doubting his intent: "There are an order of men in every commonwealth who never reason, but act from feelings. That their rights and liberties were filched away one after another they had often been told . . . Each day gave rise to new occurrences which increased animosities . . . Reciprocal insults soured the temper, mutual injuries embittered the passions." But none of that was the fault of the soldiers, who had been sent here by an act of Parliament, ordered "by your Sovereign and mine."

In preparing the defense strategy, John Adams and Quincy had debated how far they might go in holding the inhabitants of the town responsible for provoking the soldiers. Adams had adamantly refused to do so during Preston's trial, but it was known that Quincy felt otherwise. If the soldiers weren't to blame, who was? If the claim was to be self-defense, against whom? It required rhetorical dexterity to thread this needle. In this introduction, at least, it appeared that Adams had prevailed. "Great pains have been taken by different men," Quincy said, "with very different views to involve the character, the conduct and the reputation of the town of Boston . . . The inhabitants of Boston by no rules of law, justice or common sense can be supposed answerable for the unjustifiable conduct of a few individuals hastily assembled in the streets . . ."

To press that point he quoted from esteemed patriot John Dickinson, whose "Letters from a Farmer of Pennsylvania," had been widely published throughout the colonies. These twelve columns argued that Parliament had no right to levy duties and warned that accepting the Townshend Acts would lead to additional taxes. " 'The cause of liberty,' says that great and good writer, 'is a cause of too much dignity to be sullied by turbulence and tumult . . . Those who engage in it should breathe a sedate yet fervent spirit, animating them to actions of prudence, justice, modesty, bravery, humanity and magnanimity.' "

Quincy brought home his point: it was not the inhabitants of Boston as a whole who bore responsibility, but rather the few who had instigated the response. "Was it justice or humanity to attack, insult, ridicule or abuse a single sentinel on his post?" he asked. "Was it either modest, brave or magnanimous to rush upon the points of fixed bayonets and trifle, vapour and provoke at the very mouths of loaded muskets? It may be brutal rage or wanton rashness, but not surely any true magnanimity."

The soldiers were not faultless — he admitted, perhaps a strategic decision — earlier in the evening when they had "acted like barbarians and savages, [but] they had retired and were now confined to their barracks."

As he rounded into the conclusion of his opening remarks, Quincy once again pleaded for the jury to judge the case solely on its merits, separating these men from political policy: "We are to consider the troops, not as the instruments for wresting our rights, but as fellow citizens, who being to be tried by law, extending to every individual claim a part of its benefits — its privileges — its mercy. We must steel ourselves against passions which contaminate the fountain of justice." And then he added a warning that their verdict will have consequences: "We ought to recollect that our present decisions will be scanned, perhaps thro' all Europe. We must not forget that we ourselves will have a reflective hour . . . when the pulse will no longer beat with the tumults of the day, when the conscious pang of having betrayed truth, justice and integrity shall bite like a serpent and sting like an adder."

The defense also had to confront both the natural and the crafted prejudice against the soldiers. The redcoats were outsiders, but in addition to that, the colonists had been subjected to an intense and sophisticated propaganda campaign against the military that had continued for months. After all that rubbish, Quincy seemed to be saying, it would be natural for the jurors to have already formed an opinion. "Let it be borne deep upon our minds that the prisoners are to be condemned by the evidence here in court produced against them, and by nothing else. Matters seen or heard abroad [outside the courtroom] are to have no weight: in general they undermine the pillars of justice and truth." Referring to the colonists' *Short Narrative of the Horrid Massacre* directly, Josiah Quincy continued, ". . . a system of evidence has appeared in the world against us . . . the danger which results from having this publication in the hands of those who are to pass upon our lives ought to be guarded against . . . [We] are not to be denounced guilty upon a new species of evidence, unknown in the English system of criminal law."

As for that completely misleading but extremely popular Paul Revere print, "The Prints exhibited in our houses have added wings to fancy; and in the fervor of our zeal, reason is in hazard of being lost . . . How careful, lest borne away by a current of passion, we make shipwreck of conscience . . ."

If the jurors were already firm in their decision, he acknowledged, there was nothing more that could be done: "I have aimed at securing you against catching flame," but if he has failed at that, "If you are determined in opinion it is vain to say more." He then appealed to their better angels, "but if

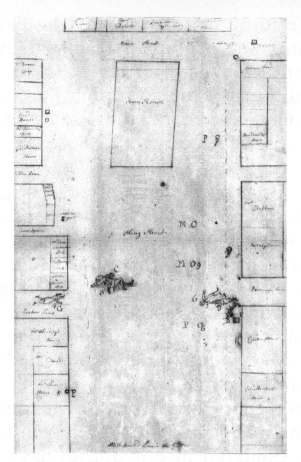

Little physical evidence was presented during the trials. This diagram of the scene indicating the soldiers and where the victims fell was created by Paul Revere and shown to jurors for clarity. Each body is identified by an initial. Not shown is Patrick Carr, who had not yet succumbed to his wounds when this sketch was made. MAP REPRODUCTION COURTESY OF THE NORMAN B. LEVENTHAL MAP & EDUCATION CENTER AT THE BOSTON PUBLIC LIBRARY

you are zealous enquirers after truth; if you are willing to hear with impartiality — to examine and judge for yourselves — enough has been said to apprize you of those avenues at which the enemies of truth and justice are most likely to enter, and most easily to beset you."

Quincy then turned to the prosecution's case, pointing out discrepancies in the testimony. Colonel Marshal's description of the clothes worn by the soldiers did not square with required military dress: ". . . being dressed in short jackets or working coats proves them not to be of the particular party who had mounted guard at this time . . . [and] soldiers of the twenty-ninth are never allowed to wear swords and cutlasses." As for all that testimony detailing the earlier abuses committed by the soldiers, what of it? Ignoring the fact that the defense had agreed that such evidence might be introduced, "Conduct which, if some of the witnesses are not mistaken, seems more like that of madmen and barbarians than like reasonable creatures. If they acted like savages and ruffians, what is that to us? This evidence, therefore not applying to this case, we are injured if it has any influence to our prejudice . . . it ought never to have been introduced, or being introduced it ought to be rejected."

Quincy then dissected his brother's presentation, emphasizing those recollections that supported his contention — which he intended to prove — that the soldiers had been both verbally and physically abused and that the sentry had been attacked that night. As Hodgson recorded, "From the inattention of some and the forgetfulness of others; from the tumult, fright, confusion and passions in the scene, he made such deductions as might account for the contrariety and seeming incompatibility of the evidence." There was such a ruckus, he implied, that no single man or two might tell the entire story. And then he explained that the defense intended to take the same facts and from them tell quite a different story.

Before calling the first witness, Quincy explained some elements of the law to the jury. The side that puts a witness on the stand cannot discredit that witness, his point being that those bits of prosecution testimony favorable to the defense cannot be ignored or dismissed; then he explained that the law states clearly that all else being equal, a witness swearing to a positive must be believed over a witness swearing a negative. Which meant that the jury must be more inclined to believe the testimony of those witnesses who saw snow and ice being thrown and heard taunts, threats and huzzahs than those who did not.

His final admonition, as recorded by John Adams, was that "These persons were upon their duty, and their lives in danger if they moved from their stations."

With the opening remarks behind them, the defense called its first witness, James Crawford, who Adams noted remembered meeting "numbers of people that night as I went home, going down with sticks in their hands . . . They were very great sticks, not common canes for walking with, pretty large cudgels."

After him, the merchant Archibald Gould said, "The streets were as full of commotion as I ever saw in my life . . ." The people were carrying "Uncommon sticks! . . . This was before any bells rang."

Within the first few witnesses the defense had presented a different night. Rather than the soldiers running amok it was the townspeople who were arming for battle. Another merchant, Archibald Wilson, was looking out a window above Dock Square, which was some distance from the Custom House, and "I saw a great number of people assembled there before the bells rung . . . They had sticks and staves . . ."

"What number of persons did you see in

Dock Square?"

"I cannot say, I judge there might be about two hundred in all . . . They also cryed fire. I said it was very odd to come to put out a fire with sticks and bludgeons."

William Hunter, a Scottish vendue master, or auctioneer, went to the balcony of his house "and saw great numbers coming up . . . with large sticks in their hands . . ."

While he could not recall if the bells were ringing he did remember clearly that "a gentleman came up with a red cloak, they gathered round him and he stood in the middle of them, and they were all very quiet . . ."

The reappearance of the mysterious man in a red cloak seemed curious. No one claimed to know who he was or precisely what role he played. There was speculation he proposed going up to the Main Guard. But clearly he was known and respected in the town and appeared to have significant influence. "Was the man who spoke to these people a tall or short man?"

"Pretty tall."

"How was he dressed?"

"He had a white wig and red cloak, and instantly after his talking a few minutes to them, [they] made huzzahs for the main guard."

David Mitchelson, the seal cutter, a carver of official seals, saw the man in the red cape too. He had been at the bottom of Royal-exchange Lane, near to Dock Square, when a group of town men, routed by the soldiers, came rushing toward him. He went into Hunter's auction house to avoid them and joined several men on the balcony. "Fire was called several times and then the bells were set a ringing. This drew a great concourse of people . . . the greatest part had sticks of various sorts; they made several attempts to get up a lane leading to Murray's barracks, but I suppose meeting with opposition there they came down as if they had been pursued."

There were about two hundred of them, he suggested, then was asked, "Did you see a man with a red cloak and a white wig?"

"Yes. He made a considerable figure there."

"Was he in the attitude of speaking and they of attention?"

"Yes."

"Could you hear what he said to them?"

"No, but after he had harangued them about three minutes, they huzza'd for the Main Guard."

Prosecutor Samuel Quincy heard Mitchelson's testimony a bit differently. In his version some "Cried out let's attack the Main-Guard, huzza'd and executed that proposal." And then noted, Mitchelson also "Saw the gentlemen in a red cloak."

The unanswered question was, who was that gentleman? The rumors began spreading. If it could be shown that the chaos had been instigated by this disguised figure, rather than being a spontaneous uprising, the soldiers' defense would be strengthened significantly. Surely those men who spoke with him could describe him in detail, or perhaps even identify him, but they were not being called upon to do so. The relative silence from both the prosecution and the defense was puzzling, as if it were better for the town not to know more about him or his role in the night.

Merchant Benjamin Davis repeated much of the testimony he had given previously during Captain Preston's trial. He had stood on the south side of the Town House and watched the troops gather, which caused him to believe "Col. Marshall, I think, must be mistaken in what he says relative to the shade of the moon being on the north side, for I remember well, I went to the south-side on purpose that I might be in the shade and see more clearly what was doing on the opposite side of the way . . ."

"Was the sentry in the shade?" Quincy asked.

"No, I saw him very plain standing on the custom-house steps. I heard a considerable noise, the boys were laughing and saying fire! And 'Why do you not fire?' I saw the sentinel bring his piece upon a level as if to fire, and the people gave back, and he put it up again . . . While I was standing there two men without hats on came up to the Main Guard and said, 'You must send assistance directly, or the sentry will be murdered.' " Adams finished the story in his notes, "By and by out guard. About 7 came out, their guns not shouldered and walked across the street to the box. A great noise. There I stood until the guns were all fired. 5, 6, or 7 guns."

Candle maker Shubal Hughes was called. As with other witnesses, in keeping with the tradition of courtroom procedure, he was asked simply, "Give the court and jury an account of what you saw in the streets on the 5th of March last."

"That night I spent the evening with an acquaintance near the town-dock, sitting in the room," he replied. When the fire bells rang, "as I belonged to the engine, I was the first out of the door . . ." After learning there was no fire, but rather "a dispute betwixt the inhabitants and soldiers," he walked on. "The street," he remembered, "was middling full, as generally when fire is cryed; at last I saw a number of young people get foul of the stalls in the market, pulling out the legs of them . . ."

The next witness was the merchant James Selkrig, a Scotsman who had landed in Boston with his brother Robert only a few years earlier. The Selkrig brothers had raised the ire of Sam Adams with their refusal to adhere to the Non-Importation Agreement of August, 1768, in which Boston's merchants and traders agreed not to import or export items to Britain. Subsequently their offer to finance the building of two ships had been turned down by the town's Body of Trade, and James Selkrig had been assaulted by unknown assailants. Hence their willingness to take the stand in defense of the soldiers surprised no one. James Selkrig had been one of the men at Hunter's house and had gone with him to the balcony after hearing the great noise in the street. He saw "considerable numbers of people coming from the North-end, all armed, or the greatest part of them, in the same manner, with white sticks. They made attacks on the barracks and were always drove back . . . there were about five or six different attacks made. In the middle of the street I saw a large man, with a red cloak and white wig, they gathered round him, and he spoke two or three minutes . . ."

There were as many as three hundred men in the street, he testified, a great number of them threatening "to do for the soldiers."

Auctioneer Archibald Bowman also was at Hunter's at the foot of Royal-exchange Lane and he too "observed a gentleman with a red cloak and white wig. The crowd gathered round him, they staid a little while with him and then drew off and huzzaed for the Main Guard . . . I cannot say how many there were, there was a great number . . ."

The next few witnesses described essentially the same scene. William Dixon was certain the large numbers had huzzaed for the Main Guard. John Gillespie, who advertised he imported "A Genteel Assortment of English Goods," said in the street he had met "a good many people with sticks and bags and some other things." Thomas Knight, who sold everything in his shop from sugar and snuff to sets of enameled glass and stoneware, was at home (in Cornhill, in the center of the town) reading his newspaper when he heard the bells and "run to the door; when I came there people were passing pretty thick . . . one company consisting of eight or ten had white sticks or clubs in their hands, one of the hallowed out, 'Damn their bloods, let's go and attack the Main Guard and knock them to hell first.' There was one in the same company made a stop, and either said 'I will go back and get my gun,' or 'Let us go back and get our guns.' I cannot tell which."

He was asked by the defense, "Was this before the firing?"

"Yes, this stopt my curiosity from going to King Street . . . I was apprehensive there would be blood shed from what I heard. I tarried about two or three minutes in the room . . . About a minute or two I heard one gun fired, in two seconds I heard another and so on."

The defense had begun strong, drawing a clear picture of riotous inhabitants aroused to action by rumors and lies and a strange man in a red cloak; mobs running through the streets carrying sticks and shouting threats. As the dusk settled, the Custom House clerk William Strong was the last witness of the day's session. In his words it was possible to hear the fear in the mind of the sentinel, standing lonely in front of the Custom House. Strong had been at Marston's when he heard the cry of fire. He went out and "asked what the matter was; they said a soldier had killed a boy. I was answered in that manner by another, some people said we will go back again and get our sticks . . . I then went into King Street . . . when I heard a huzza and a number of feet behind me, and I stood to let them pass, there might have been about ninety . . . when they came opposite the Custom House they stopped and some said that is the fellow that used the inhabitants ill; another contradicted them and said it was not him; upon that the people encroached on the sentinel . . . I saw him go on the steps of the Custom House and they went closer, and he set his back to the door and loaded. I heard the [musket] ball go down distinctly . . .

"He presented his gun and said, 'Keep off or I will fire upon you.' The reply was, 'Fire, God damn you fire, fire and be damn'd.' . . . There was a man standing by me, he had the butt end of a bat in his hand and said he would throw it at the Sentinel; I said, 'Do not, for he will fire at whatever place it comes from.' Whether he threw it or not I do not know, for I left him . . . I walked to the Custom House steps, curiosity led me to see if they were so prudent as to fasten the Custom House door. I tryed the latch and it was fast. A fellow said to one of the soldiers, 'Why do you turn your bayonet this way? Turn it the other way.' I thought I was not safe there, but went to my old place and stood there a few minutes . . ."

"Did you see anything hit the Sentinel?"

"I believe there were snowballs thrown but they fell short of him."

"These people that were round the sentinel, had they clubs?"

"Yes. Some of them."

With that, the candles were snuffed and court was adjourned until nine o'clock the following morning.

The day had gone well for the defense, but to John Adams his younger colleague had come perilously close to defaming the town. The rift that had surfaced first during Preston's trial once again caused friction between the two men. Adams remained adamant that the town not be put on trial. Governor Hutchinson later informed General Gage that Adams had gone so far as to threaten to resign the case should the town's reputation be soiled, writing that Adams "declared he would leave the cause if such witnesses must be produced as served only to set the town in a bad light."

Although the pages of the *Short Narrative* had been filled with first person accounts of what had transpired, the witnesses presented thus far had been the observers, the men who had seen the doings of the mob rather than participants. The streets were filled with "boys" and "young people," while most of the others had come out of their homes to serve the town by answering the fire bells. They had come out of their homes to see the mob, the crowd, however they referred to them, stream past; the witnesses had been the peacemakers, urging others not to throw their sticks or telling them to go home. It was, at worst, a handful of instigators who had caused the soldiers to be backed against the wall, not the town.

The question to be answered was how much further the defense would go to convince the jurors that the soldiers' lives were truly in jeopardy.

The first witness on the morning of November 30th was Dr. Richard Hirons, the physician who cut the bullet out of Sam Maverick. Like the many others, he had heard the disturbance in the street and "went out to know what it was." Having learned it was a disturbance between soldiers and inhabitants, he went back inside and shut his door. Soon after he heard a man shouting out, "Town born turn out," a shout that was repeated twenty or thirty times. But rather than so doing, Dr. Hirons stayed inside. "The noise of the clubs induced me to lock my door, put out my light in the fore part of my house and go upstairs into the chamber fronting the barracks . . .

"About that time there came a little man, who he was I do not know, he said [to an officer], 'Why do you not keep your soldiers in their barracks?' They said they had done everything they possibly could and would do everything in their power to keep them in their barracks. On which he said, 'Are the inhabitants to be knocked down in the street? Are they to be murdered in this manner?' The officers still insisted they had done their utmost, and would do it, to keep the soldiers in their barracks. The same person then said, 'You know the country has been used ill. We did not send for you, we will not have you here, we will get rid of you,' or, 'We will drive you away.' Which of the last expressions I cannot say, but it was one or the other."

The officers repeated their claim that they had done all that was possible to control their men, "and begged the person to use his interest to disperse the people that no mischief might happen. Whether he did address the people or not I cannot say, for the

confusion was so great I could not distinguish."

In the confusion, Dr. Hirons continued, a
considerable number of people went up
Boylston's Alley toward the Town House,
and then "A little boy came down the alley,
clapping his hand to his head and cried he
was killed, he was killed. On which one of
the officers took hold of him and damned
him for being a little rascal, asking him what
business he had out of doors.

"Some little time after that I saw a soldier
come out of the barrack gate with his
musket; he went directly facing the alley, in
the middle of the street, and kneeled down
on one knee and said, 'Now damn your
bloods, I will make a lane through you all.'
While he was presenting [an officer] laid
hold of him and took the musket from him
and shoved him towards the barrack, and I
think gave him the musket again and
charged him at his peril to come out again."

As the confusion continued, townsmen
made an effort to stop it. Dr. Hirons described another man whom he did not know
requesting "the soldiers might be kept in
their barracks and that the officers would
do everything in their power to keep them
there, and the officers said they had and
they would do so. And as the soldiers were

in their barracks [he] begged the people might go away. This little man said to the people, 'Gentlemen, you hear what the officers say, that the soldiers are all in their barracks, and you had better go home.' On which the cry was, home, home, home . . .

"While he was talking I heard the report of a musket . . ."

Some time after the shooting, the doctor was sent for to tend to the wounded Maverick. Now he was asked, "Did he say anything to you?"

"Yes. About two hours before his death I asked him concerning the affair. He went, he said, up the lane and just as he got to the corner he heard a gun. He did not retreat back but went to the town house, as he was going along, he was shot. It seems strange by the direction of the ball how he could be killed by the firing at the Custom House; it wounded a portion of the liver, stomach and intestines, and lodged betwixt the lower ribs where I cut it out. The ball must have struck some wall or something else before it struck him."

It was an odd shot and if the doctor was right, it had not been aimed at Maverick, which would be an enormously helpful fact for the defense. Adams noted that Dr. Hirons testified, "I was call'd to Maverick and

286

he told me he was running away from the soldiers, and yet the ball went into his breast . . ." The town coroner, a thirty-one-year-old decorative painter and a leader of the Sons of Liberty named Thomas Crafts, Jr., had brought the fatal ball into the courtroom. After examining it, Adams wrote, "The ball was bruised as if it struck some object before him." The implication was clear; Adams felt sure Maverick was the unfortunate victim of a ricochet rather than being shot directly.

Captain Lieutenant John Goldfinch of the 14th Regiment, a man who had played a significant role in the night's events, was next to tell his story. He was the officer Dr. Hirons had seen near the barracks. "I was passing over Cornhill, I saw a number collected by the passage to the barracks. I went towards it and two or three people called me by name and begged me to endeavor to send the soldiers to their barracks or else there would be murder. With difficulty I got to the entrance of the passage, the people were pelting the soldiers with snowballs, the soldiers were defending themselves at the entrance." The soldiers were not armed, he continued: "I think one of them had a fire shovel . . . I saw some officers of the 29th, I told those officers I suspected there would be a riot and as I was the oldest officer I ordered the men to the barracks . . .

"The mob followed me . . . and abused the men very much indeed, with bad language, so that the men must have been enraged very much, but by the vigilance and activity of the officers the men were kept within bounds." The mob heaped insults upon the boxed-in soldiers, until finally Captain Goldfinch continued, "A little man came up and spoke to the people and desired them to go home . . . Immediately the best part made towards the passage at Cornhill . . . in a quarter of an hour or twenty minutes after the people had moved off I heard some guns fire and the Main-Guard drum beat to arms."

Almost as an aside, he explained the confrontation that may have lit the fuse. "That same evening, about half an hour before this affair happened, I was in King Street and was accosted by the barber's boy, who said, 'There goes the fellow who hath not paid my master for dressing his hair.' Fortunately for me, I had his receipt in my pocket. The Sentinel said, 'He is a gentleman, and if he owes you anything he will pay it.' I passed on without taking any notice of what the boy said."

Robert Paine heard more in the words

than Hodgson recorded, adding that the captain indicated, "It appeared to me it was a premeditated plan, and designed as an affront on the military in Gen'ral."

Adams had his own impression of that testimony, writing that Goldfinch said basically, "I had conducted myself with that propriety, that I thought I was the last person to be insulted. But I found that any man that wore the K(ing)'s Com(missio)n was lyable to be insulted any hour of the night."

Benjamin Davis, Jr., a young boy whose father had testified previously in both trials, came upon the barber's boy after the encounter with Captain Goldfinch. He was crying "and said the sentry had struck him and asked him what business he had to do with it." Young Davis then went home and eventually encountered Samuel Gray, who soon was to be shot and killed, and Gray "asked where the fire was. I said there was no fire, it was the soldiers fighting. He said, 'Damn it, I am glad of it. I will knock some of them in the head.' He ran off, I said to him, 'Take heed you do not get killed in the affray yourself.' He said, 'Do not fear, damn their bloods.' "

"He had a stick in his hand?"

"He had one under his arm . . . I do not

suppose he could have got into King Street two minutes before the firing." This was critical testimony for the defense, not just that Gray was carrying a stick, but that he was heading out to King Street to use it.

Sailor James Thompson seemed to support the growing impression that much of the night's terrors had been plotted. After leaving the Green Dragon tavern, he was on his way to the wharf when he passed a group of about fifteen persons with sticks in their hands. "They seemed to be pretty large sticks, rather too large for walking sticks, just as they passed I turned about and heard them say, 'We are rather too soon.' " On board his ship he told others he believed there would be mischief that night. After the bells rang he heard a woman say at a distance, "It is no fire. Good God there will be murder committed this night." Then the guns fired.

Adams quoted him in his notes: "I am afraid there will be mischief tonight, for I met a number of people and they seemed to hint that they were about something."

Jeweler Alexander Cruckshanks came upon a group of lads abusing the sentinel "with a fresh repetition of oaths. They said to him, 'Damn you, you son of a bitch.' Called him lobster and rascal . . . wished he was in hell's flames . . . I never heard nor saw the Sentinel do anything to them, only said it was his post and he would maintain it, and if they offered to molest him he would run them through. Upon saying this, two boys made up some snow balls and threw them at the Sentinel."

In response to this, the sentinel, Private White, called out the guard, Cruckshanks testified. Seven or eight men responded: "Some had bayonets, some swords, others sticks in their hands, one had a large kitchen tongs in his hand." Cruckshanks walked away and was confronted by several soldiers he did not know. "I was going home peacefully," he told them, "and interfered with neither one side or another. One of them with a bayonet or light sword gave me a light stroke over my shoulder and said, 'Friend, you had better go home, for by all I can fore-see there will be the devil to pay or blood shed this night." The stroke, he replied when asked, "was not in anger. It was very light."

Josiah Quincy continued his deft balancing act, placing on the mob blame that several witnesses had tried to escape, and finally on specific individuals. While Samuel Gray had been carrying a stick he had been in the back of the crowd. But the man then known as Michael Johnson, who was to be revealed to be Crispus Attucks, was at the front and appeared to pose a real danger. Witness Patrick Keaton followed the noise to King Street. "I went up to the foot of Jenkin's Lane and there I saw a tall Molatto fellow, the same that was killed, he had two clubs in his hand, and he said, 'Here, take one of them.' So I did . . . They were cord wood sticks." Standing by the Custom House, Keaton saw nothing thrown, but agreed that the crowd, about two hundred, appeared to be pressing on the soldiers.

Sergeant Major William Davis of the 14th Regiment saw the mob in the street. He stepped aside and heard them saying, " 'Damn the dogs, knock them down. We will knock down the first officer or bloody-backed rascal we shall meet this night.' Some of them then said they would go to the southward and join some of their friends there and attack the damn scoundrels, and drive them out of town for they had no business here." Now knowing the danger, Davis changed out of his regimentals and returned to Dock Square. "I came near the market place," he said, repeating the story he had told previously, "and saw a great number of people there, knocking against the posts, tearing up the stalls, saying, 'Damn the lobsters, where are they now?' I heard several voices, some said, 'Let us kill that damned scoundrel of a sentry then attack the Main Guard.' "

He continued walking through the town. Then, he said, he saw a man loading his piece by Oliver's dock, "he said he would do for some of these scoundrels that night. The people were using threats against the soldiers and commissioners, 'Damn the villain that first sent them to Boston and they shall not be here two nights longer.' " Sergeant Davis then returned to his barracks to find all his men present.

He stepped down from the stand and was replaced there by Nathaniel Russell, a chair maker. He had arrived in King Street a minute before the shooting. On his way there he had seen men and boys with clubs and heard their threats. "They would destroy them, and sink them, and they would have revenge for something or other . . . that they would drive them before them." In King Street, "I was looking over the Molatto's shoulder. I saw Samuel Gray there. Upon these things being thrown I intended to retreat as fast as I could. I had not got three yards before the guns were fired." He described the scene; the crowd was making a great noise. He heard something strike the guns, the crowd pressed on the soldiers so closely "that I think you could not get your hat betwixt them and the bayonets."

"Did the soldiers say anything to the people?" he was asked.

"They never opened their lips; they stood in a trembling manner, as if they expected nothing but death . . ."

On a rare cross-examination he was asked, "Might not their trembling proceed from rage as well as fear?"

He could not dismiss that possibility. "It might proceed from both," he admitted.

The prosecution interceded to put bricklayer John Cox on the stand to refute Russell's story. He had met the previous witness at the Town House, where he saw three soldiers — none of them belonging to the 14th or 29th — by the Liberty Tree. "One said to the other, bring half your guard and we will bring half ours, and we will blow up this damned pole. I said, 'So sure as you offer ye scoundrels to blow up that pole, you will have your brains blown out.'"

The defense resumed, calling the young bookseller and military historian Henry Knox, who had testified for the prosecution in the Preston trial. He told essentially the same story: he came into King Street to see the sentinel "waving his piece about and held in the position that they call charged bayonets. I told him if he fired he must die for it. He said, 'Damn them,' if they molested him he would fire; the boys were hallowing fire and be damned."

"How old were these boys?"

"Seventeen or eighteen years old. I endeavored to keep one fellow off the Sentinel. I either struck him or pushed him away." More evidence the troubles were caused by rabble, not by the majority in the town. Under cross-examination he admitted the party of soldiers had come down in a threatening manner, "At least their countenances looked so, they said, 'Make way, damn you, make way,' and they pricked some of the people."

Asked if he had seen Corporal Wemms, he said he felt sure he had, and confirmed he was wearing a surtout. That was an interesting point made by the prosecution. Several witnesses had testified the man who gave the order to shoot had been wearing a surtout, and as became clear in the Preston trial, the man wearing the surtout may have been Palmes, who had said he was wearing one while standing right there with the soldiers.

Coincidentally, just as Adams's law clerk

had testified for the prosecution, now so did John Bulkely, clerk to Josiah Quincy, except for the defense. He had been at work in the legal office when he heard "a prodigious noise." The Officer of the Guard, twenty-year-old lieutenant James Basset, inexperienced and visibly nervous, plainly did not know what to do. Bulkely "pitied his situation." Asked by Quincy what he expected might happen to the sentinel, he replied, "I did not know what would be the consequence. I thought if he came off with his life he would do very well."

The young clerk had done his job, for the impression was clear: Private White's life must have been in jeopardy. Then apprentice Benjamin Lee confirmed the threat was a real one. He was standing by the sentinel when the barber's boy pointed at the soldier and said, "There is the son of a bitch that knocked me down." As a result, Lee testified, "The people immediately cried out, 'Kill him, kill him, knock him down.' " The sentinel primed and loaded his weapon, then called for help.

Under further questioning, however, Lee admitted that among the people surrounding the sentinel, "I saw no clubs, some had sticks, such as people generally walk with."

"Did you see anything thrown at the

Sentinel?" he was asked.

"No."

Another apprentice, John Frost, was there too, and guessed the crowd consisted of "fifty or sixty young men and boys."

And how old were those young men? "About twenty or twenty-two." And about the boys? "Such as myself, about eighteen."

While Frost saw nothing thrown at the sentinel, sailor James Waddel saw "the soldiers very much molested by the people of the town throwing snow balls, sticks and more rubbish than I can mention . . . I saw a soldier knocked down . . ."

One thing was clear, the evidence was conflicting. So how were the jurors to assess the credibility of the accounts? There was not much precedent on which to rely. Sam Adams, as Vindex, wrote in the *Gazette,* "Witnesses, who are brought into a court of justice, while their veracity is not im-peached, stand equal in the eye of the judge." Then, harkening back to the earliest days of trial by jury, when jurors were selected from the close community of the accused, he continued, "The jury, who are taken from the vicinity, are supposed to know the credibility of the witnesses." In Preston's trial, he reminded readers, the witnesses were from the town, while the jurors were from the country, so the jurors could not possibly know the characters of the witnesses. Here, "It is the duty of the jurors, who are sovereign in regard to facts, to determine in their own minds the credibility of those who are sworn to relate the facts."

The strategy of the defense, it appeared, was to bludgeon the jurors into accepting its version of events by bringing forth a seemingly endless stream of witnesses who testified to essentially the same facts. Daniel Cornwall, a barber, saw about thirty or forty people "throwing oyster shells and snow balls at the sentry at the Custom House door . . . Some were hollowing out, 'Let us burn the sentry box, let us heave it overboard,' but they did neither."

John Ruddock, a justice of the peace and a town selectman, was called. In contrast to the young apprentices or the transient seamen, Ruddock was a notable Bostonian; he had run the lottery to raise money for repair of Faneuil Hall and served as a monitor of the public schools and a fire official, before being elected in '65. He was a man whose character was known and could be attested to by the jurors. His testimony was short: "As I went home that evening," he said, "I met a number of boys with clubs." This did not surprise him: "They went so for several months before, they chused to do so because they had been so often knocked down by the soldiers. Some said the soldiers were going to fight with the people."

"What number did you meet?" he was asked.

"They were in two's and three's, three's or four's in a bunch, in the whole there might be about twenty."

The next witness, Newton Prince, was a free black man who prepared and sold food at most public entertainments and who had testified previously. Prince, being free, did not need a white person to attest to his character. "When the bells rung I was at my own house," he began. The bells brought him to his door, where he was told, "It was something better than a fire." At the Town House he heard some people say, " 'Let's go attack the Main Guard.' Some said, 'For God's sake do not meddle with them.' They said, 'By God, we will go.' Others again said do not go. After awhile they huzzaed and went down King Street."

When Prince got near the Custom House door, "There were people all round the soldiers."

"How near were the people to the soldiers?"

"About three or four feet from the point of their bayonets . . . When I got to the corner I saw people with sticks striking on the guns at the right wing. I apprehended danger and that the guns might go off accidentally. I went to get to the upper end towards the Town house. I had not got to the center of the party before the guns went off. As they went off I run, and did not stop till I got to the upper end of the Town house."

He was asked, "Did you hear at the time they were striking, the cry of 'Fire! Fire!'?"

"Yes, they said, 'Fire, damn you fire. Fire, you lobsters. Fire, you dare not fire.' "

"Did you see anything thrown at the soldiers?"

"Nothing but snow balls, flung by some youngsters."

He stepped down, and minutes later was replaced in the box by another black man. But this man was in a very different situation and told a very different story. He had been part of the mob.

CHAPTER NINE

On the day the soldiers' trial began, this advertisement had appeared in the *Gazette:* "To Be Sold, a hearty, likely strong Negro fellow of about 28 years old, he has some good qualifications, he is sober and good natu'd, but is a runaway, a thief and a liar. If such a Negro will suit any person to send out of the Province, they may hear of him if they apply soon to Edes and Gill."

The irony was large: as the Massachusetts colony led the fight for freedom from Parliament's dictates, it also allowed human beings to be bought, sold and held in bondage. There were several thousand black men in the colony at that time, most of them free. In fact, among the people living on King Street was eighteen-year-old Phillis Wheatley, a slave from Senegal who had published the first of her many poems three years earlier and three years later would publish a celebrated book of her work.

There was no need for slaves in the local economy and the inhabitants generally were against it as an institution. But still, wealthy people kept them. For a time, to discourage the slave trade, a £4 duty was levied on every Negro brought into the colony. John Adams personally detested slavery, and years later would write, "I have throughout my whole life, held the practice of slavery in such abhorrence." Neither he nor Abigail ever owned a slave, but like his neighbors he accepted the law as it existed, choosing to make his stand over other, broader issues.

His one-time close friend and associate, Samuel Quincy, now his opponent here, felt differently. In fact, during the trial the *Gazette* reported, "A Negro lad belonging to Samuel Quincy, Esq. going into a cellar, drop't instantly dead." Offering no additional details.

The defense had waited till very late in the day to call Andrew, Oliver Wendell's slave. The testimony of Andrew at the captain's trial had been long and compelling, but here there would be an added fact. "On the evening of March 5th I was at home," he began, telling his story. In response to the bells he went to the street and there "saw another acquaintance coming up holding his arm. I asked him what's the matter, he said the soldiers were fighting, had got cutlasses and were killing everybody, and that one of them had struck him on the arm and almost cut it off. He told me I had best not go down. I said a good club was better than a cutlass, and he had better go down and see if he could not cut some too."

Andrew went into King Street and saw "a number of people picking up pieces of sea coal that had been thrown out thereabout, and snow balls and throwing them over at the Sentinel . . . two or three boys run out from among the people and cried, 'We have got his gun away, and now we will have him.' "

He stood watching as the guard turned out, he continued. Someone said that James Murray was coming to read the Riot Act, but he was chased away. "I turned back and went through the people until I got to the head of Royal-exchange Lane, right against the soldiers. The first word I heard was a Grenadier say to a man by me, 'Damn you, stand back.' "

"How near was he to him?"

"He was so near that the Grenadier might have run him through if he had stept one step forward. While I stopt to look at him, a person came to get through betwixt the Grenadier and me, and the soldier had like to have pricked him. He turned about and said, 'You damn'd lobster, bloody back, are you going to stab me?' The soldier said, 'By God will I.' Presently somebody took hold of me by the shoulder and told me to go home or I should be hurt . . . I turned about and saw the officer standing before the men, and one or two persons engaged in talk with him. A number were jumping on the backs of those who were talking with the officer, to get as near as they could."

"Did you hear what they said?"

"No . . . One of the persons who was talking with the officer turned about quick to the people, and said, 'Damn him, he is going to fire.' Upon that they gave a shout and cryed out 'Fire' and 'Be damned, who cares, damn you, you dare not fire,' and began to throw snow balls, and other things, which then flew pretty thick."

"Did they hit any of them?"

"Yes. I saw two or three of them hit. One struck a Grenadier on the hat, and the people who were right before them had sticks, and as the soldiers were pushing with their guns back and forth, they struck their guns, and one hit a Grenadier on the finger . . ." But as the crowd seemed to be dispersing, he continued, "A number of people came down from Jackson's corner, huzzaing and crying, 'Damn them they dare not fire. We are not afraid of them.' One of these people, a stout man with a long cordwood stick, threw himself in, and made a blow at the officer. I saw the officer try to fend off the stroke. Whether he struck him or not I do not know. The stout man then turned round and struck the Grenadier's gun at the Captain's right hand and immediately fell in with his club and knocked his gun away and struck him over the head. The blow came either on the soldier's cheek or hat. This stout man held the bayonet with his left hand and twitched it and cried, 'Kill the dogs. Knock them over.' This was the general cry, the people then crowded in and upon that the Grenadier gave a twitch back and relieved [broke free] his gun, and he up with it and began to pay away [to move a leveled musket right and left in a continuous motion] on the people.

"I was then betwixt the officer and this Grenadier. I turned to go off, when I had got away about the length of a gun I turned to look towards the officer and I heard the word, fire; At the word fire I thought I heard the report of a gun, and upon my hearing the report, I saw the same Grenadier swing his gun and immediately he discharged it."

The questioning was quite straight-forward, simply to lead the man through the pertinent details. "Do you know who this stout man was, that fell in and struck the Grenadier?"

"I thought, and still think, that it was the Molatto, who was shot."

"Do you know the Grenadier who was thus assaulted and fired?"

"I thought then it was Killroy . . . I now think it was he from my best observation, but I can't positively swear to it."

"Did the soldiers of that party, or any of them, step or move out of the rank in which they stood to push the people?"

"No, and if they had they might have killed me and many others with their bayo-nets."

Then came a question asked for the first time: "Did you . . . see a number of people take up any and everything they could find in the street and throw them at the sol-diers?"

"Yes, I saw ten or fifteen round me do it."

"Did you yourself pick up every thing you could find and throw at them?"

"Yes, I did."

Perhaps there was more meaning to this testimony than recorded by Hodgson. The only man the defense put forth who admitted joining the mob and throwing at the soldiers was a slave. Andrew, a man so easily dismissed he did not require a last name, and whose testimony was to be believed only if a white man confirmed that he was trustworthy. It would not have been difficult for the defense to find others who had joined the mob and thrown snowballs or more. Several of them had said so in depositions months earlier. But they did not. This seemed like a strategic choice, an effort to implicate a mob consisting of rabble rather than the respected inhabitants of the town.

But his testimony contained claims no one else had made; he appeared to have seen chaos that no one else had seen. He was the only witness to put Crispus Attucks, "the molatto," at the front of the assembly. No other man had seen him, or anyone, take hold of a bayonet and pull at a musket. There was much to put the quality of his testimony in doubt. But as before, the respected merchant Oliver Wendell followed his man Andrew to the stand. It was necessary that a person in good standing support a slave's testimony. "Is the witness last examined your servant?" he was asked. Indeed. "How long has he lived in your family?"

"Above ten years."

"What is his general character for truth?"

"It is good. I have heard his testimony and believe it to be true. He gave the same relation to this matter to me on the same evening . . . I then asked him if our people [the Americans] were to blame; he said they were."

"Can Andrew read and write?"

"Yes, very well; he has been well educated."

The prosecution could not allow this damning account to stand unchallenged. Although who asked the next question was not noted, it might well have come from the prosecution, a juror or even a justice, any of whom were permitted to do so under the trial rules. But clearly this was someone who knew the slave's reputation was not as shining as Wendell put forth. "Pray Sir," he was asked, "is it not usual for Andrew to amplify and embellish a story?"

"He is a fellow of a lively imagination," Wendell agreed, with a smile in his voice, "and will sometimes amuse the servants in the kitchen; but I never knew him to tell a serious lye."

This was the dramatic end to the day that served the defense. Jurors retired with Wendell's words still in their minds: "I then asked if our people were to blame; he said they were."

Not surprisingly other observers were quite distraught by Andrew's melodramatic testimony. Samuel Adams later wrote bitterly in the *Gazette* that "Andrew, a Negro . . . is remarkable for telling romantick stories in the circles of his acquaintance, and whether his fancy had beguil'd his own judgement, or whether he had a mind to try his success at painting upon so serious an occasion, or lastly, whether he was resolv'd to do his utmost to save the prisoners I pretend not to say . . .

"His character . . . has been on this occasion wrought to so high a pitch that I am loath even to hint anything that may tend to depreciate it; otherwise, I should say, that there are some whose kitchens Andrew has frequented who will not give him quite so exalted a character as others, who had not known him, thought he deserved."

The trial resumed on Saturday morning, which was not unusual even during a wildly unusual trial, as Saturday was kept only as a half-day holiday. William Whitington was at the Guard House when "some person in the crowd fronting the soldiers cried out to the guard, 'Will you stand there and see the Sentinel murdered at the Custom

House?' . . . Said Preston [to another officer, Basset] 'Take out six or seven of the men and let them go down to the assistance of the Sentry . . ." When they reached the Sentry, "I heard Captain Preston use many entreaties to the populace, begging they would disperse and go home . . . Captain Preston desired them to go home many times . . ."

Harrison Grey, Jr., the loyalist son of the wealthy receiver-general of the Massachusetts colony, estimated that he saw seventy to a hundred boys and men around the sentinel White, "making use of opprobrious language and threatenings. I desired them to go off," he said, warning them "the consequences would be fatal if they did not. Some few snow balls were thrown and the abusive language continued. They said, 'Damn him, let him fire, he can fire but one gun . . .' When I could not prevail to take them off I went to Mr. Payne's . . . soon after I heard the guns fired and Mr. Payne was wounded with one of them."

The witnesses came fast now, telling their stories, filling in small details. Matthew Murray saw a boy who said the sentry had knocked him down, then saw the grenadier on the right side struck by a thrown object, and soon after, he fired.

Victualler Thomas Symmonds kept the tavern at which Crispus Attucks and several other sailors had been drinking when they'd walked out to join the uproar. Symmonds heard people near Murray's barracks declare, "If the soldiers did not come out and fight them, they would set fire to the four corners of the barracks and burn every damned soul of them." Before that, "I saw a good number of towns people had cutlasses, clubs and swords. There was knocking down, riot and disturbance, and this declaration of theirs was after that, and before the bells rung."

An odd witness was seaman John Williams, who was called to repeat a story he had been told by rope maker Richard Kibbey concerning the earlier confrontations at Grey's ropeworks three days before the killings. The prosecution immediately objected to this as hearsay evidence; the rules concerning the admissibility of such evidence were still being forged. By the 1500s witness testimony had become the primary evidence introduced in a trial and the courts had begun placing limits on second- or even third-hand "tales of a tale" or "stories from another man's mouth." In 1603 Sir Walter Raleigh was convicted of treason based primarily on hearsay evidence; he was executed without being given the opportunity to directly confront or question his accuser. Gradually, hearsay evidence came to be excluded with certain exceptions.

It became obvious as John Williams spoke that he had no direct knowledge of this story; he simply was repeating it as it had been told to him and there was no way of knowing the truth of it. Sam Adams dismissed it as "hearsay of an hearsay; the story which one man told another at sea, and months after the facts were committed." The prosecution objected to his appearance, the objection was overruled by the bench, but then something unexpected occurred. The defense acknowledged such testimony was not proper and should not be considered by the jury. "To the honor of one of the prisoners' counsel was by him interrupted and stopped," praised Sam Adams. "This worthy gentleman declared in open court that it was not legal, and that it ought not to have the least weight in the minds of the jurors; upon which it was ruled, that the witness should proceed no further, and he was dismiss'd." Hodgson made no record of Williams's appearance in his transcript.

Next called was the merchant John Gridley, who a year earlier had endeared himself to John Adams and other patriots with his spirited and bruising defense of the aging and doddering once great attorney James Otis in a coffee shop brawl, suffering a broken arm as he fought off "an onslaught of cutlasses, canes and other weapons," according to the *Gazette*.

On the night of the massacre, Gridley had been with several gentlemen at the Bunch of Grapes tavern and was drawn outside by the tumult and saw about twenty-five men and boys outside the Custom House. "Little trifling boys," he called them. He then went to the Town House, where men were gathering. "I asked them what was the matter? They told me that the soldiers had rushed from Murray's barracks and had cut several of the inhabitants with their cutlasses; several people were running about the streets, and the cry was 'God damn the rascals.' Some said this will never do, the readiest way to get rid of these people is to attack the Main guard. Strike at the root, there is the nest."

Upon returning to the tavern he was asked to give an account of what he had seen. "Mr. Davis asked me what was the collection of people before the Custom House, who did they consist of; 'They are nothing,' said he, 'but a parcel of boys.' I hastily replied, 'Yes, Mother Tapley's boys.' "

"What did you mean by that?"

"I meant boys as big as I am." Minutes later he heard a "general noise and cry, 'Why do you not fire, damn you? You dare not fire. Fire and be damned!' These words were spoken very loud, they might be heard to the Long Wharf. The noise was very great indeed . . ."

A delicate thrust came next, as the defense set out to show that the victims were not innocent men, but rather participants in the events. There had been great funerals for the victims. Their names had become revered, so it required a deft touch to suggest otherwise. The defense called Catherine Field, with whom Patrick Carr had been boarding. Carr also worked with her husband at a shop on Queen Street making leather breeches. Carr had been home that evening, she said. She was asked, "Did you hear anything he said when he was told there was an affray with the soldiers?"

"When the bells rung he went upstairs and put his surtout on, and got a hanger [a cutlass] and put it betwixt his coat and surtout. My husband coming at that time gave him a push and felt the sword. He wanted to take it from him, but he [Carr] was unwilling to let it go. My husband told him he should not take it with him. I do not know what he said, but one of the neighbors was in the house and coaxed the sword out of his hand, and he went without it."

Then she added some hearsay evidence to which there appeared to be no objection. "He said on his death bed he saw a parcel of boys and negros throwing snow balls at the guard. He thought the first or second man from the Sentinel box was the man that shot him."

John Mansfield apparently boarded in that house too, and confirmed much of Mrs. Field's story, but then he too was allowed to give hearsay testimony, telling the jurors, "I was often at his [Carr's] bedside, and all that I heard him say was that he thought he knew the man that shot him, but he never made it known to me."

Dr. John Jeffries, a loyalist who had tended to some of the wounded, was sworn. Dr. Jeffries was another Harvard man, coincidentally a classmate of both defense lawyers Quincy and Blowers, although he had gotten his medical degree only a year earlier from Scotland's University of Aberdeen. With the first question, "Was you Patrick Carr's surgeon?" it became apparent Carr was going to speak to the court from his grave.

"I was," he acknowledged, "in company with others. I was called that evening about eleven o'clock to him. I was engaged with Mr. Payne and could not go. Next morning I went. After dressing his wounds I advised him never to go again into quarrels and riots. He said he was very sorry he did go. Dr. Lloyd, who was present, turned round to me and said, 'Jeffries, I believe this man will be able to tell us how the affair was. We had better ask him.'

"I asked him then how long he had been in King Street when they fired? He said he went from Mr. Field's when the bells rung. When he got to Walker's corner he saw many persons coming from Cornhill, who he was told had been quarreling with the soldiers down there, that he went with them as far as the stocks, that he stopped there, but they passed on. While he was standing there he saw many things thrown at the sentry. I asked him if he knew what was thrown? He said he heard things strike against the guns, and they sounded hard. He believed they were oyster shells and ice . . ."

As he continued relating his conversation with the wounded Carr, the prosecution sat silent, raising no objection to this critical hearsay evidence.

"He heard the people huzza every time they heard any thing strike that sounded hard: that he saw some soldiers going down towards the Custom House, that he saw the people pelt them as they went along. After they had got down there he crossed over towards Warden and Vernon's shop, in order to see what they would do. That as he was passing he was shot. That he was taken up and carried to Mr. Field's by some of his friends. I asked him whether he thought the soldiers would fire? He told me he thought the soldiers would have fired long before.

"I then asked him if he thought the soldiers were abused a great deal, after they went down there? He said he thought they were.

"I asked him whether he thought the soldiers would have been hurt if they had not fired? He said he really thought they would, for he heard many voices cry out, 'Kill them.'

"I asked him then, meaning to close all, whether he thought they fired in self-defense, or on purpose to destroy the people? He said, he really thought they did fire to defend themselves; that he did not blame the man whoever he was, that shot him. This conversation was on Wednesday [7 March]. He always gave the same answers to the same questions, every time I visited him."

This testimony potentially was devastating to the prosecution. According to Dr. Jeffries, the victim had forgiven his killers. More than that, while he lay dying he admitted that the defense argument was correct: the soldiers' lives had been in danger and they had fired to save themselves.

Dr. Jeffries was asked if Carr was apprehensive of his danger. Did he know when he made these statements how precarious was his condition? His answer was vital. More than five hundred years earlier, during the reign of Richard the Lionhearted, English courts had accepted the doctrine of *Nemo moriturus praesumitur mentiri:* a dying person is presumed to not be lying. The belief was that a dying person would not risk meeting the Lord with lying words still warm on his lips. There was no record of this exception to the hearsay rule being applied in an American courtroom. Even so, the prosecution and judges let this testimony proceed.

"He was told of it," Dr. Jeffries responded, inferring that Patrick Carr knew and understood his fate. Jeffries continued, "He told me also, he was a native of Ireland, that he had frequently seen mobs, and soldiers called upon to quell them. Whenever he mentioned that, he always called himself a fool, that he might have known better, that he had seen soldiers often fire on the people in Ireland, but had never seen them bear half so much before they fired in his life."

"How often did he repeat this conversation?"

"Almost every day I saw him, though he was more particular the day, but one, after he was shot."

"How long did he live after he received his wound?"

"Ten days."

"When had you the last conversation with him?"

"About four o'clock in the afternoon, preceding the night on which he died. And then he particularly said he forgave the man whoever it was that shot him, he was satisfied there was no malice, but fired to defend himself."

Sam Adams recognized the significance of the testimony and later tried to minimize it, saying publicly that Carr "probably died in the faith of a Roman Catholic" to suggest Boston's Protestants should not trust him.

Having gotten that testimony before the

jury, the defense questioned the witness about his own experience on that night, asking him what he had seen. He was with his father, he responded, when a neighbor came in and said, " 'Pray sir, come out. There will be murder. The soldiers and people are fighting.'

"I saw several soldiers towards Mr. Greenleaf's. I think there were three, one of them had a pair of tongs in his hand . . . behind them were several officers driving the soldiers towards the barrack gate, ordering them to go in. I saw them strike them, they turned them into the gate, they then shut the barrack gate entirely. I think the officers did that themselves; as they were putting them in there were a great many snow balls thrown at them; they were called cowards, cowardly rascals and that they were afraid to fight."

There were a great many people crowding the alley leading to the barracks. A gentleman, perhaps Palmes, was speaking with an officer, "who promised the gentleman . . . that if any body had been injured, enquiry should be made the next day and the persons should be punished. I heard this repeated four or five different times. [The officers] begged the people would go away. They said they would not. The officers said they had done all they could, they had turned the soldiers in and shut the gate, that no soldiers should come out that evening. Somebody replied, 'You mean they dare not come out, you dare not let them out.'

"Many persons cried, 'Let us go home.' Others said no, 'We shall find some soldiers in King Street . . .' "

The crowd was already in a high state, he continued, "As they went up several of them struck against Jackson's shop-windows and said, 'Damn it, here lives an importer.' Others ran towards the town house and took up pieces of ice and threw them at Jackson's windows and broke four panes of glass. I stood and counted them. At that time Mr. Cazneau came up and said, 'Do not meddle with Mr. Jackson. Let him alone. Do not break his windows,' and they left off throwing . . .

"I had been but a little while in the house, I had just took off my cloak when the girl ran in from the kitchen and said, 'There is a gun fired.' I replied to the company I did not believe it, for I had seen the officers put the soldiers in and shut the gate."

To blunt Dr. Jeffries's remarkable testimony the prosecution put Thomas Hall on the stand; the purpose of this might well have been to remind jurors that others who were present remembered a different scene as much as to simply change the beat of the case. Hall was friendly with several of the prisoners, he said, among them the sentry, Hugh White. And White warned him earlier in the night that there was to be trouble. "When I went down King Street just after the bells began to ring, and he said, 'Hall, I am molested and imposed [up]on on my post; I cannot keep my post clear. Hall, take care of yourself, there will be something done by and bye.' I moved away to the corner of Stone's house and stood there." White, he continued, was being harassed by about twenty people. "He said he could not keep his post clear. They said he dared not fire. He cocked his gun on the steps, then he presented his gun and they drew off again."

He saw snowballs and oyster shells thrown at the guard. None of them struck him, but "I saw them hit his gun two or three times. Then he hollowed for the guard and the guard came down . . . As soon as they came down the people pressed in on them and they pushed with their bayonets to keep them off, but did not move out of their ranks." According to Hall the soldiers acted responsibly. The soldiers told them to keep away, "but they still pressed on. Then one man fired, and I run down Royal-exchange Lane as fast as I could . . ."

The defense put a few more men in front of the jury to clear up some technical points. Captain Barbason O'Hara of the 14th said that Private Carrol was "a discreet sober orderly man." Then they called their final witness, carpenter Theodore Bliss, who also had been a critical witness in Preston's trial. An earlier witness, Richard Palmes, testified that he had heard Bliss asking Captain Preston, "Why do you not fire?" and "God damn you fire." Now Bliss, who was in the thick of it, would speak on his own behalf. He confirmed that he had answered the fire bells and saw the soldiers and an officer on King Street. His recollection of the event often conflicted with other witnesses; Captain Preston, he said, was standing in front of the guns. He stood right next to him, but when asked, he could not remember if Preston was wearing a surtout. "I went to the officer and asked him if his men were loaded; he said they were. I asked him if they were loaded with ball; he made me no answer. I asked if they were going to fire; he said they could not fire without his orders. Directly I saw a snow ball and stick come from behind me which struck the grenadier on the right, which I took to be Warren. He fended it off with his musket as well as he could, and immediately he fired."

The question of who had fired that first shot still had not been settled. "Where did he stand?" Bliss was asked.

"He was the first man on the right," Bliss replied, which would have been Montgomery, not Warren, "and the third man from the officer. Immediately after the first gun the officer turned to the right and I turned to the left and went down the lane. I heard the word 'Fire' given, but whether it was the town's people or the officer, I do not know."

Rather than bolstering the defense case, his story added to the confusion and some of his answers were surprising: "Were any blows given to the soldiers before the firing?"

"I saw none."

"Were any blows given after the first and before the second gun fired?"

"No."

"Did you, or did you not, after the first gun was fired see a blow aimed?"

"I did not."

Then, "Did you not aim a blow yourself?"

"Yes," he then admitted, "when I was going away." He did not instigate the firing; he said he responded to it.

After a few more questions, "Directly on the first gun's going off, did any close in upon the soldiers and aim a blow or blows at them?"

"I did it myself. Whether anyone else did or not I cannot tell . . ."

Finally, "Are you sure it was the man nighest to the Custom house that fired first, and that the stick struck?"

"Yes. I think I am certain of it."

As a rebuttal witness, the prosecution called merchant Henry Bass, a cousin of Sam Adams and one of the Loyal Nine, the founding members of the Sons of Liberty. He told an adventurous story, a story of his narrow escape that might have come from the pen of the late popular novelist and political activist Daniel Defoe: on the night of the 5th he was on his way to visit a friend when he saw "a number of boys and children from twelve to fifteen years old . . . some of them had walking canes." Suddenly four soldiers came out of an alley. "They fell on these boys, and everybody else that came in their way; they struck them. They followed me and almost overtook me, I had the advantage of them and run as far as Col. Jackson's. There I made a stand, they came down as far as the stone shop."

"Did you see that their cutlasses were drawn?"

"Yes. It was a very bright night; these lads came down, some of them came to Market Square, one got a stave, others pieces of pine. They were very small. I do not know whether any of the lads were cut. I turned and then saw an oyster-man, who said to me, 'Damn it. Here is what I have got by going up.'" He showed Bass his slashed shoulder. "I put my finger into the wound and blooded it very much . . ."

"Was it before the bells rung as for fire or after?" The bells had played a significant role in the evening, yet the question of who rang the bells, or precisely when, remained unanswered. Bells had been a primary means of communication for centuries; the Egyptians and the Romans had rung bells to honor their Gods; medieval towns had rung them to chase away evil spirits, vanquish storms and ease the passage of souls of the recently departed. In Boston the bells rang in celebration, to warn of danger and to call people to sabbath services or funerals. Each bell was unique and people learned to recognize the peal of their own church bells. But on the night of the 5th there had been a cacophony of bells, warning of fire, bringing men running into the street. Was that the purpose, to create the situation, or rather were they rung in response to the chaos? No one seemed able to settle that, including the witness.

"It was some time before . . ." Bass then took a roundabout way to return home. "In a little time I imagine about twenty gathered . . ."

"Did the bells ring then?"

"No, I went up from Royal-exchange lane to the north-side of the Town house, and when I came there the Old Brick meeting house bell began to ring."

"Did this gather a great many?"

"Yes. I proceeded towards home, I met several of my acquaintance and told them there was no fire, but there had been a quarrel with the soldiers and inhabitants, but that it was over. In particular I met Mr. Chase, presently after another bell rung."

"What bell was that?"

"Dr. Cooper's . . ."

"Did you know previous to the Old Brick bell's ringing that it was to ring to alarm the inhabitants?"

He did not, "But after it had rung I knew it."

The final witness also was "produced on the part of the Crown," meaning he was a witness for the prosecution. This was Edward Payne, a successful and skillful merchant like John Hancock, known to be trading both in the sunlight and shadows. But far more important, Payne was the only person wounded by the soldiers' shot to testify. He was at Amory's when the bell rang, he said. "I was going out to enquire where the fire was; Mr. Taylor came in, he said there was no fire, but he understood the soldiers were coming up to cut down Liberty-tree. I then went out to make inquiry; when I came out of the door . . . I met Mr. Walker, the ship carpenter . . . He said the soldiers had sallied out from Smith's barracks and had fell on the inhabitants, and had cut and wounded a number of them, but that they were drove into the barracks . . .

"When I came into the street there was nobody in the street at all. The Sentry at the Custom House was walking by himself as usual, nobody near him . . . Presently I heard a noise of some people coming up Silsby's alley; at first I imagined it was soldiers coming up that alley and had some thoughts of retiring up the Town House steps, but soon found they were inhabitants . . .

"I believe there were as many with sticks as without; they made a considerable noise and cried, 'Where are they?' At this time there came up a barber's boy and said the Sentry at the Custom House had knocked down a boy belonging to their shop. The people then turned about and went down to the Sentry. I then was left as it were alone: I proceeded towards my own house, when I got about half way I met Mr. Spear, the cooper. He said, 'Mr. Payne do not go away, I am afraid the Main guard will come down.' I told him I was more afraid of those people who had surrounded the Sentry and desired if he had any influence over them to endeavor to take them off . . . I then retired to my own house and stood on the sill of my door."

"Was there noise by the sentry?"

"Yes, a confused noise; five or six were upon the steps. I remained at my door and Mr. Harrison Grey came up and stood there talking with me; the people were crying out, 'Fire! Damn you, why do you not fire?' "

"Was this before the soldiers came down?"

"Yes. Mr. Grey and I were talking on the foolishness of the people in calling the Sentry to fire on them. In about a minute after I saw a number of soldiers come down from the Main guard and it appeared to me they had their muskets in a horizontal posture. They went towards the Custom

House and shoved the people from the house. I did not see in what manner they drew up: At this time Mr. Bethune joined us on the steps at the door, and the noise in the street continued much the same as before, 'Fire! Fire! Damn you, fire! Why do you not fire?'

"Soon after this I thought I heard a gun snap. I said to Mr. Grey, 'There is a gun snapped. Did you not hear it?' He said yes; immediately a gun went off. I reached to see whether it was loaded with powder, or any body lying dead. I heard three more, then there was a pause and I heard the iron rammers going into their guns and then there was three more discharged, one after another. It appeared to me there were seven in all. As soon as the last gun was discharged I perceived I was wounded and went into the house."

"Was it the last gun wounded you?"

"I do not know. I did not feel it before the last gun went off."

And then the same questions that had been asked so many times previously, "Did you see any body throw any thing at the soldiers?"

"No, I was not near enough to see whether the people struck or threw any thing at the soldiers."

"How many people were there?"

"From fifty to a hundred."

"Were they near to them?"

"Pretty nigh."

"Could you see all the soldiers?"

"Yes."

It had been a full Saturday in the court. As the justices prepared to adjourn, the prosecution offered to produce additional witnesses to provide evidence bearing on the threats and behavior of the soldiers. Rather than extending this trial even further the defense agreed to stipulate, meaning it would accept as fact, that "there was a reason for going armed and coming out that night." With that, the testimony ended. Court adjourned for the Sabbath, to resume Monday morning at nine o'clock.

There had been nearly fifty witnesses called and questioned, the result being a stew of supporting and conflicting testimony about what was called either a massacre and an incident.

This was hardly a totally straightforward case. In addition to various eyewitnesses recalling a very different set of events leading up to the shooting, there were also questions of intent. Even if jurors did not fully embrace self-defense, would they really convict the soldiers of murder? The closing arguments would be critical and John Adams would be presenting the primary one. To shape the evidence into a compelling argument, he had prepared diligently and divided it into categories, listing those witnesses that might be fit into each of them. He wrote, for example, "Evidence of Commotions that Evening," and beneath that included such as "James Crawford . . . very great sticks, pretty large cudgels, not common walking canes." And among several others, Thomas Knight, who heard inhabitants boasting they would attack the Main Guard and "Went in and told his wife he believed there would be bloodshed."

He listed each of the prisoners and those witnesses who had specifically named them. Montgomery had been mentioned by five witnesses, from J. Bailey to Thomas Wilkinson. Killroy too had been named by five men.

Under "Attack, Assault and Insult," he had listed the "Crown Witnesses," including "E. Bridgman: A number of things, ice or snow, thrown. Sticks struck the guns . . . Call'd em cowardly rascals. Dared em to fire. All the bells rung"

J. Bailey saw "The boys have pieces of ice at the sentry as big as your fist, hard and large enough to hurt a man . . ."

"Assault upon the Sentry . . ." While Adams's notes were cursory, they provided an outline that would enable him to bring together his final argument that the lives of the prisoners should be spared, an argument that would become a defining moment of his early career, and one that would be quoted for decades.

CHAPTER TEN

Years earlier professional theater had been banned from the province. The Massachusetts Act of 1750 had cautioned inhabitants to be wary of "the many and great mischiefs which arise from public stage plays, interludes and other theatrical entertainments, which not only occasion great and unnecessary expenses, and discourage industry and frugality, but likewise tend generally to increase immorality, impiety and contempt of religion." To foreclose the possibility that such an enterprise might still take root — and perhaps be used by the British for political propaganda — stage performances were outlawed by the Massachusetts Assembly in 1767. By law, "If an audience exceeded 20 people, actors and the owners of the premises might be fined."

In its place, street theater took hold; demonstrations, celebrations, orations and even funerals were enacted with great flair.

But real theatrics took place in the court-room where the stakes were highest. Trials were a popular form of entertainment, and these trials especially were a welcome diversion from the economic troubles caused by the various Parliamentary acts and the terrible damage done by the recent storm. The soldiers' trial had thus far presented all the elements of great theater: it was a murder, five men had died and eight lives were at stake, the story included the audience and would impact all of them, the script was being written as it was performed and the outcome remained a mystery. Every member of the audience had an interest, although the protagonists and antagonists differed depending on the spectator's political beliefs; but that stopped no one in the town from admiring the performances of the main players, nor from having an opinion about it.

The final act began with Josiah Quincy's summation for the defense. This was the prelude to John Adams taking center stage. "May it please your honours, and you gentlemen of the jury," Quincy said, standing. "We have at length gone through the evidence in behalf of the prisoners. The witnesses have now placed before you that state of facts from which results our defense." He apologized to the jurors for the great length of the trial, but reminded them that eight lives were in their hands. And sitting in judgment was their duty to the town; in words that might resonate through the centuries, "You are paying a debt you owe the community for your own protection and safety: by the same mode of trial are your own rights to receive a determination; and in your turn, a time may come, when you will expect and claim a similar return from some other jury of your fellow subjects."

Quincy then asked them once again, as he had at the beginning of the trial, not to allow their political beliefs to color their examination of the evidence, saying, "I appeal to you Gentlemen, what cause there is now to alter our sentiments. Will any sober, prudent man countenance the proceedings of the people in King Street? Can any one justify their conduct? Is there any one man, or any body of men who are interested and espouse their conduct? Surely no. But our enquiry must be confined to the legality of their conduct: and here can be no difficulty . . .

"To the *facts,* Gentlemen, apply yourselves . . . and then according to your oaths, 'Make true deliverance according to your evidence.' " Quincy then attempted to draw a clear delineation between the actions of the soldiers in the streets and those that took place by the Custom House, admitting that the inhabitants may have become enraged by the soldiers cutting and wounding the peaceful inhabitants, suggesting, "The reasoning or rather ferment seems to be, the soldiers have committed an outrage, we have an equal right to inflict punishment — or rather revenge, which they had to make an assault . . . These are sentiments natural enough to persons in this state of mind, we can easily suppose even good men thinking and acting thus . . ."

His words had been carefully chosen, offering understanding and even an excuse for the reactions of the inhabitants, then getting to the gist of it: "What says the law? . . . What is natural to the man, what are his feelings are one thing: What is the duty of the citizen is quite another . . ."

The courts had been struggling with the legal boundaries of self-defense for centuries. The concept, Quincy explained, was that "Early in the history of jurisprudence, we find the sword taken from the party injured and put into the hands of the magistrate." Establishing the law, paying obedience to the law is the price paid by all citizens for protection and security.

The law also laid out the difference between murder and manslaughter, it being "Whenever the party injuring has escaped by flight, and time sufficient for the passions to cool, in judgement of the law, hath escaped; however great the injury, the injured party must have recourse to law for his redress. Such is the wisdom of the law; of that law, than which we are none of us to presume ourselves wiser; of that law which is founded in the experience of ages . . . For 'No man,' says the learned Judge Foster, 'under the protection of the law is to be the avenger of his own wrongs. If they are of such a nature for which the laws of society will give him adequate remedy, thither he ought to resort. But be they of what nature soever, he ought to bear his lot with patience, and remember, that vengeance belongth to the Most High.' "

Quincy was quoting Sir Michael Foster from his treatise *Crown Law*, which was both a review of the 1746 trials of Jacobite rebels and a textbook, published in 1762 and already a pillar of jurisprudence.

It remained vital to the defense that the jury's deliberations not be limited to King Street, but that they included the circumstances throughout the town earlier that night that culminated a few minutes after nine o'clock in front of the Custom House. "To get regular and right ideas," he urged, "we must consider all the commotions of the season . . ."

Faced with having to explain away the threats uttered by the prisoners, the young lawyer made a claim that hence became a staple of lawyers faced with foul words uttered by their client: "Words are often misrepresented, whether through ignorance, inattention or malice . . . for the tone of voice, the gesture, all that proceeds, accompanies and follows the different ideas which men annex to the same word, may so alter or modify a man's discourse that it is almost impossible to repeat them precisely in the manner in which they were spoken. Besides, violent and uncommon actions . . . leave a trace in the multitude of circumstances that attend them, but words remain only in the memory of the hearers, who are commonly negligent or prejudiced."

Having attempted to present a logical prism through which the jurors might view the evidence, he then began a discussion of how the law dictated that evidence should be viewed. The law, he explained, takes into consideration the "feelings, passions and infirmities" of human beings, rather than relying "upon the absurd supposition that men are stocks and stones, or that in the fervor of the blood, a man can act with the deliberation and judgment of a philosopher." The law strikes a balance between the excesses of passion and "the wisdom, good order and the very being of government."

As Quincy painted a word-picture of the verbal abuses being heaped upon the prisoners, Robert Paine took notes quoting him, " 'Place yourself in King Street and consider how the soldiers view'd 'em. Consider the exasperating circumstances!' "

"Would you not spurn at that spiritless institution of society?" Quincy railed, "which tells you to be a subject at the expense of your manhood?

"But does the soldier step out of his ranks to seek his revenge? Not a witness pretends it: Did the people repeatedly come within the points of their bayonets, and strike on the muzzles of the guns? You have heard the witnesses. Does the law allow one member of the community to behave in this manner towards his fellow citizen, then bid the injured party be calm and moderate?"

Accusatory words, vile words, were shouted by both sides in the streets that night, he argued. "Was anything done on the part of the assailants similar to the conduct, warnings and declarations of the prisoners? Answer for yourselves, gentlemen. The words reiterated, stabbed to the heart . . . to awaken every passion of which the human breast is capable. Fear, anger, pride, resentment, revenge alternately take possession of the whole man. To expect . . . that such words would assuage the tempest, that such actions would allay the flames, you might, as rationally expect the inundations of a torrent would suppress a deluge, or rather that the flames of Etna would extinguish a conflagration!"

It was a bravura performance; a fine entertainment within a neatly structured legal argument. But there still was one important argument that needed to be addressed. The church was the center of intellectual life in the town, and even those who might question doctrine understood the role religion played in the everyday lives, as well as in the minds, of the people. The influence of church leaders like Cotton Mather, a leader of the Salem Witch trials who had warned, "The New-Englanders are a People of God settled in those, which were once the Devil's Territories," was still quite prevalent. Ingrained religious beliefs, as well as superstitions and traditions, continued to play an important role in secular life. Some buildings in Boston still showed witches seats, stones protruding from a chimney where a passing witch might rest, rather than coming into the house.

The law still being settled, juries often looked to the Biblical virtues for guidance. The concept that blood requires blood, an eye for an eye, had been quoted in the newspapers. That would not serve the defense here, but it had to be addressed in a manner respectful of the belief while dismissing it. "We have heard it publicly said of late, oftener than formerly," he said, " 'Whoever shedeth man's blood, by man shall his blood be shed.' This is plainly, Gentlemen, a general rule which, like all others of the kind must have its exceptions. A rule, which if taken in its strict literal latitude would imply that a man killing another in self-defense would incur the pains of death. A doctrine which no man in his senses would embrace: a doctrine that certainly never prevailed under the Mosaical institutions. For we find the Jews had their six cities of refuge to which a manslayer might flee from the avenger of blood.

"And so, that 'the murderer shall flee to the pit,' comes under the same consideration. And when we hear it asked, as it very lately has been, 'Who shall slay him?' I answer, if the laws of our country slay him, you ought to do likewise . . ." But the real question to be considered is whether the prisoners are murderers "in the sense of our laws, for you recollect that what is murder and what is not is a question of law . . ."

It was a very long and complex legal presentation during which he cited numerous cases and experts that might bear on the jury's deliberations. These were the blocks on which the law in the colonies had been built. And those in the practice of law had made themselves familiar with them. John Adams noted each of Quincy's authorities in preparation for his own argument, although to those outside the law those notes would remain as incomprehensible as an exotic code:

"Foster 257. 4. Blac 180 2. Foster 298 3 Inst. 56. I. H.H.P.C. 482 (discusses killing *se defendendo*) I Hawk. 72. Dangerous Rioters. Foster 273. Repell Force by Force. Foster 274. Any other person may interpose.

"Key. 128 Not fit to be trusted with dangerous weapons.

"Excusable. Foster 278.

"Manslaughter. Foster 198 (298?) Foster 292. Stedmans case. Keyling 51. The room in the tavern. Justifiable. Quaeried by Holt.

Bacons Elements 25."

When he had concluded presenting the case law, Quincy faced the jury and explained, "I have gone thro' those authorities in law which I thought pertinent to this trial. I have been thus lengthy, not for the information of the Court, but to satisfy you, Gentlemen, and all who may chance to hear me, of that law, which is well known to those of us who are conversant in courts, but not so generally known . . . by many as it ought to be.

"A law which extends to each of us, as well as to any of the prisoners, for it knows no distinction of persons."

The applicable law stated firmly, his pleas for justice made, Quincy then made an effort to rise above the mundane facts of the law and remind the jurors of its majesty; to remind them once more of their duty and their obligation to history. "The doctrines that have been thus laid down are for the safeguard of us all. Doctrines which are founded in the wisdom and policy of ages; which the greatest men who ever lived have adopted and contended for . . . That you may not think the purport of the authorities read are the rigid notions of a dry system, and the contracted decision of municipal law, I beg leave to read to you a passage from a very great, theoretic writer, a man whose praises have resounded through all the known world, and probably will, through all ages; whose sentiments are as free air, and who has done as much for learning, liberty and mankind as any of the Sons of Adam. I mean the sagacious Mr. Locke . . ."

The concepts of philosopher John Locke, dead for six decades, had formed the basis of liberal political thought, in which every person was said to be born with a natural right to defend his "life, health, liberty or possessions."

"He will tell you, Gentlemen . . . 'That all manner of force without right puts man in a state of war with the aggressor, and of consequence that, being in such a state of war, he may *lawfully kill* him, who put him under this unnatural restraint.' According to this doctrine we should have nothing to do but enquire, whether here was force without right. If so, we were in such a state as rendered it lawful to kill the aggressor . . .' We cite this author to show the world, that the greatest friends to their country, to universal liberty, and the immutable rights of all men, have held tenets and advanced maxims favorable to the prisoners at the bar . . .

"There is a spirit which pervades the

whole system of English jurisprudence, which inspires a freedom of thought, speech and behavior . . . From our happy constitution there results its very natural effects — an impatience of injuries, and a strong resentment of insults: (And a very wise man has said, 'He who *tamely* bear-eth insults *invite-th* injuries.' . . .)"

Although Quincy failed to identify the source of this quote, there is reason to believe it was an ancient Jewish proverb.

With that Biblical reference he reached his conclusion. "Gentlemen of the Jury, this cause has taken up so much of your time . . . indeed I should not have troubled you by being thus lengthy, but from a sense of duty to the prisoners . . . I trust you Gentlemen will do the like, that you will examine and judge with a becoming temper of mind: remembering that they who are *under oath* to declare the *whole truth,* think and act very differently from by-standers, who, being under no ties of this kind, take a latitude, which is by no means admissible in a court of law.

"I cannot close the cause better, than by desiring you to consider well the genius and spirit of the law . . . and to govern yourselves by this great standard of truth."

And at the end he relied, as often was the

case among lawyers, on the wisdom of Shakespeare: " 'The quality of mercy is not strained,' " he read, quoting from *The Merchant of Venice*. " 'It drop-peth like the gentle rain from heaven — It is twice blessed; It blesses him that gives, and him that takes' . . .

"I leave you, Gentlemen, hoping you will be directed in your enquiry and judgement; to a right discharge of your duty . . . May the blessing of those, who were in jeopardy of life, come upon you — may the blessing of him who is 'not faulty to die' descend and rest upon you and your posterity."

He sat.

John Adams collected his notes and stood. Quincy had prepared the court for him; he had delivered a fine, if lengthy, statement. The task facing Adams was considerable.

Only a few years earlier, an engraver and cartographer in London named John Spilsbury had created a new diversion. In 1767 he had affixed his map of the world to hardwood, then carefully cut it into pieces along national boundaries. By putting the pieces back together in their proper places, the children of King George III and Queen Charlotte learned geography. This "dissected map," as it became known, was later considered the first "jigsaw" puzzle, loosely named after the tool used to cut out the pieces.

Adams faced a similar challenge: the days of testimony had provided for him all the dissected pieces of the night, and it now had become his duty to put them together to form a complete picture for the jury, a picture that would show clearly that the soldiers were not guilty. He had been a practicing lawyer for more than a decade, and this would require all that he had learned in that time. Quincy had done a fine job laying down the applicable law and focusing on the big picture, but more was required. Adams had to specifically defend each of his clients while not impugning the reputation of the town; he had to use the testimony of witnesses without casting blame on anyone.

He was well aware he would not win his argument with his grace or natural charm that might entice the jury. Unlike the roguishly handsome Josiah Quincy, or his perfectly presentable older brother, Adams was more pear-shaped. Standing at full height he was about five-foot-seven and stocky leaning to plump, so much so that years later he would be called behind his back, "His Rotundity." His features were ordinary; he was balding on top, his nose was thin

John Adams would eventually take his place as a towering figure in American history. It has been said the young nation was shaped as a reflection of his values and humanity. But at the time of these trials he was still a young lawyer well-aware that defending the British troops would impact his future. It was his unshakable belief that the rule of law must be respected if individual rights were to be protected that caused him to accept these cases. COLLECTION OF

THE MASSACHUSETTS HISTORICAL SOCIETY

and his lips puckered. Only his sparkling blue eyes hinted at the lively mind behind them. He would once describe himself, quite contentedly, as the image of a short, thick Archbishop of Canterbury.

His personality was hardly any more naturally appealing. Many years later he would decline a suggestion from Thomas Jefferson that he draft the declaration of independence, explaining, "Reason one: You're a Virginian and a Virginian ought to appear at the head of this business. Reason two: I am obnoxious, suspected and unpopular." He also was known for his quick temper, his feistiness, his overly mannered attitude and great mood changes that swung easily from great joy and generosity to deep depression and despair. When it suited him, he was a great companion, a devoted and loyal friend and always a loving husband to Abigail. He was, to many who knew him, an enigma.

Perhaps it was Ben Franklin who described him best; "Always an honest man, often a great man," he said, then added, "but sometimes absolutely mad."

It was his extraordinary intellect that had gained him his position; John Adams was a brilliant man and everyone knew it; he read incessantly, retained the knowledge, and when it was needed he could recall all of it and shape it to fit his purpose. In the streets he was no match for Sam Adams and the like, but on the battlefield of ideas he was a warrior. Words poured out of him with wit and passion, endearing honesty and an appreciation for the beauty of the English language. The prospect of John Adams making his case for the soldiers would fill the courtroom.

"I am for the prisoners at the bar," he began, "and shall apologize for it only in the words of the Marquis Beccaria, 'If I can but be the instrument of preserving one life, his blessing and tears of transport, shall be a sufficient consolation to me, for the contempt of all mankind.' " Beccaria's treatise *On Crimes and Punishment* had been published in Italy only six years earlier but already had gained respect around the world for his enlightened views, especially his condemnation of capital punishment.

The task of an attorney is to capture the attention of the jury. Adams did this, so much so that years later his son, John Quincy Adams, would write that he had "often heard, from individuals who had been present among the crowd of spectators at the trial, the electrical effect produced upon the immense and excited auditory, by the first sentence with which he opened his defense."

Adams set the stage for his argument, drawing on the words of the eminent British justice Sir Matthew Hale, "whose character as a lawyer, a man of learning and philosophy, and as a Christian, will be disputed by nobody living; one of the greatest and best characters the English nation ever produced." In Preston's trial jurors had been instructed that if they had doubt that the captain had given his men the order to load their muskets, they could not charge him with doing so. The doctrine, "reasonable doubt," had not yet gained traction in the courts; jurors were expected to make their judgment if the evidence satisfied them of his guilt. But Adams wanted more than that, telling them that if in their minds they were not certain of the prisoner's guilt, they were justified in acquittal. Adams quoted Hale, "It is always safer to err in acquitting, than punishing, on the part of mercy, than the part of justice . . . the best rule in doubtful cases, is, rather to incline to acquittal than conviction . . . Where you are doubtful never act; that is, if you doubt of the prisoner's guilt, never declare him guilty; this is always the rule, especially in cases of life.

"Another rule from the same author, where he says, 'In some cases, presumptive [circumstantial] evidence go far to prove a person guilty; though there is no express proof of the fact, to be committed by him;

but then it must be warily pressed, for it is better, five guilty persons should escape unpunished, then one innocent person should die . . .' Indeed, this rule is not peculiar to English law, there never was a system of laws in the world in which this rule did not prevail; it prevailed in the ancient Roman law, even the judges in the Courts of Inquisition, who with racks, burnings and scourges, examine criminals; even there they preserve it as a maxim, that it is better the guilty should escape punishment than the innocent suffer. This is the temper we ought to set out with, and these the rules we are to be governed by. And I shall take it for granted, as a first principle, that the eight prisoners at the bar had better be all acquitted — though we shall admit them all to be guilty, than, that any one of them should by your verdict be found guilty, being innocent."

Having introduced the argument supporting the concept of reasonable doubt, Adams now had to raise that doubt. He began to do so by diving far more deeply into the nuances of murder than Quincy had done. "The killing of one man by another, the law calls it homicide; but it is not criminal in all cases for one man to slay another. Had the prisoners been on the Plains of Abraham and slain a hundred Frenchmen apiece, the English law would have considered it a commendable action, virtuous and praiseworthy: so that every instance of killing a man is not a crime in the eye of the law . . . much less a crime to be punished with death."

Like a professor in front of his class, he went further, reminding them of the natural right of all men to defend their own life. He said, "The law divides homicide into three branches; the first is justifiable, the second excusable and the third felonious; felonious homicide is subdivided into two branches: the first is murder, which is killing with malice aforethought, the second is manslaughter, which is killing a man on a sudden provocation. Here, Gentlemen are four sorts of homicide . . . One of these four it must be . . .

"If an officer, a sheriff, executes a man on the gallows, draws and quarters him, as in case of high treason, and cuts off his head, this is justifiable homicide, it is his duty. So also, Gentlemen, the law has planted fences and barriers around every individual; it is a castle round every man's person, as well as his house . . . That precept of our holy religion which commands us to love our neighbor as ourselves does not command us to love our neighbor better than ourselves . . . A man is authorized therefore by common sense, and the laws of England, as well as those of nature, to love himself better than his fellow subject: If two persons are cast away at sea, and get on a plank — a case put by Sir Francis Bacon — and the plank is insufficient to hold them both, the one hath the right to push the other off to save himself. The rules of the common law therefore, which authorize a man to preserve his own life at the expense of another's, are not contradicted by any divine or moral law . . ."

And then he issued a chilling warning to the jurors that their verdict would not be limited to the eight men on trial, but rather would reverberate through history, becoming part of the developing law and bearing upon countless lives in the years to come. It was a statement of extraordinary magnitude, pointing out to them the power of precedent to change lives. Reminding them of their responsibility, he continued, ". . . for whatsoever the law pronounces in the case of these eight soldiers will be the law, to other persons and after ages, all the persons that have slain mankind in this country, from the beginning to this day, had better have been acquitted, than a wrong rule and precedent shall be established."

Adams then introduced the existing precedent on which his claim of self-defense had been based, reading directly from law books, which also was permissible. Foster had written, " 'The injured party may repell force with force in defense of his person, habitation or property, against one who manifestly intendeth and endeavoureth with violence, or surprise, to commit a known felony upon either.' " Then, paraphrasing the seventeenth century chief justice of the King's Bench, Sir John Kelynge, Adams continued, "In these cases he is not obliged to retreat, but may pursue his adversary till he findeth himself out of danger, and if in a conflict between them he happeneth to kill, such killing is justifiable." Thus, he summed up, ". . . the injured person may repell force with force against any who endeavors to commit any kind of felony on him or his; here the rule is, I have a right to stand on my own defense, if you intend to commit felony. If any of the persons made an attack on these soldiers, with an intention to rob there, if it was but to take their hats feloniously, they had a right to kill them on the spot, and had no business to retreat." Then, explaining it in simple language, he continued, "If a robber meets me on the street and commands me to surrender my purse, I have the right to kill him without asking questions; if a person commits a bare assault on me, this will not justify killing, but if he assaults me in such a manner, as to discover an intention to kill me, I have a right to destroy him, that I may put it out of his power to kill me . . ."

In this sense, the law of self-defense was primal and straightforward. A man can use deadly force to avoid getting killed himself. "If any reasonable man, in the situation of one of these soldiers, would have had reason to believe in the time of it, that the people came with an intention to kill him . . . they were justifiable, at least excusable in firing . . . You must place yourselves in the situation of Wemms or Killroy, consider yourselves, as knowing that the prejudices of the world about you, were against you; that the people about you thought you came to dragoon them into obedience to statues, instructions, mandates and edicts, which they thoroughly detested; that many of these people were thoughtless and inconsiderate, old and young, sailors and landmen, negroes and molattos, that they, the soldiers, had no friends about them; The rest were in opposition to them . . . with all the bells ringing to call the town together to assist the people in King Street . . . the people shouting, huzzaing and making the mob whistle . . . a most hideous shriek . . . the people crying Kill them! Kill them! Knock them over. Heaving snow balls, oyster shells, clubs, white birch sticks three inches and a half in diameter. Consider yourselves in this situation and then judge whether a reasonable man in the soldiers' situation would not have concluded they were going to kill him . . . the law does not oblige us to bear insults to the danger of our lives, to stand still with such a number of people round us, throwing such things at us, and threatening our lives, until we are unable to defend ourselves."

Adams admitted to the jury that he was not such an authority on the law that he might quote it from his own memory, so he diligently continued quoting those men who had first laid down the law, citing Foster to remind the jury that if one man is in jeopardy others may come to his assistance without themselves being threatened; if one soldier was threatened, all of them might legally aid him, "Where a known felony is attempted upon the person, be it to rob or murder, here the party assaulted may repel force with force, and even his own servant then attendant on him, or any other person present, may interpose for preventing mischief, and if death ensues, the party so interposing will be justified . . ."

After Foster came William Hawkins's *Pleas of the Crown,* in which the terms were laid out under which self-defense is justifiable, "And not only he who on an assault retreats to the wall or some such straight, beyond which he can go no further, before he kills another, is judged by the law to act upon unavoidable necessity, but also he who is being assaulted in such a manner, and in such a place that he cannot go back without manifestly endangering his life, kills the other without retreating at all . . . And an officer who kills one that insults him in the execution of his office, and where a private person, that kills one who feloniously assaults him in the high way, may justify the fact without ever giving back at all."

The attorney Adams was playing to a considerably larger audience than just the jury. The courtroom was packed and these spectators would spread their impressions of what happened in there to the town. And from these impressions the inhabitants would determine whether justice was done. In those troubled times that interpretation was vital, as it might well generate its own response, which could easily lead to additional conflict and blood. The people in the streets had every right to arm themselves, he said, but for their own defense, "not for offence, and that distinction is material" and must be considered.

But the result of that placed the prisoners in a precarious position. ". . . these soldiers were in such a situation that they could not help themselves; people were coming from Royal-exchange lane and other parts of the town, with clubs and cord-wood sticks. The soldiers were planted by a wall of the Custom House; they could not retreat, they were surrounded on all sides, for there were people behind them, as well as before them, there were a number of people in Royal-exchange lane; the soldiers were so near to the Custom House that they could not retreat, unless they had gone into the brick wall of it.

"I shall shew you presently that all the party [civilians] concerned in this unlawful design were guilty of what any one of them did; if any body threw a snow-ball, or threw a club, and the club had killed any body, the whole party would have been guilty of murder in law."

While still laying out his pieces, Adams began fitting some of them together. ". . . take Montgomery, if you please, when he was attacked by the stout man with the stick, who aimed it at his head, with a number of people around him crying out, 'Kill them! Kill them!' had he not a right to kill the man? If all the party were guilty of the assault made by the stout man, and all of them had discovered [revealed] malice in their hearts, had not Montgomery a right, according to Chief Justice Holt, to put it out of their power to wreak their malice upon him?"

Adams's strategy, as he later explained, was to make certain the jurors understood the right of a man to defend himself. "It appeared to me," he later said, "that the greatest service which could be rendered to the people of the town was to lay before them the law as it stood, that they might be fully apprized of the dangers of various kinds which must arise from the intemperate heats and irregular commotions."

To accomplish that meant treading on dangerous ground: if the soldier's lives truly were in jeopardy then the mob, and individuals within it, must have been the aggressors. And if that was so, the town would bear responsibility — precisely the conclusion Adams sought to avoid.

But perhaps not all of the mob. Perhaps some of the inhabitants were fine men caught in an untenable situation. The doctrine of collective responsibility was far from finished law. Essentially it was interpreted to mean that any member of a group that commits an unlawful act is equally guilty of that act because they have abetted it, or tolerated it by their very participation, even if they themselves did not commit the act. But it was useful to Adams in this situation: "In the case of unlawful assembly," he continued, "all and every one of the assembly is guilty of all and every unlawful act, committed by any one of the assembly, in prosecution of the unlawful design they set out upon . . ." Later in his argument he would cite a case in which a group of men went into a park to steal a lord's deer. One member of that company went off by himself and killed the lord in the park. But all the men in the park, even though separated, were found equally guilty of murder and executed. Adams did not offer his opinion of the concept of universal guilt; rather he simply made certain the jury understood the law.

"Rules of law should be universally known," he continued, "whereever there is an unlawful assembly, let it consist of many persons or a few, every man in it is as guilty of every unlawful act committed by any one of the whole party . . ." That had been the law for centuries, its purpose "to discourage and prevent riots, insurrection, turbulence and tumults."

There were other men who could find their way through the wickets of law as well as Adams, and certainly there were men who made a far more impressive appearance in the courtroom than he did, but few were his equal in the use of the English language in a courtroom. It was grand, filled with flourishes, each word chosen to catch the ear of the listener. This was what the people came to see and hear and he did not disappoint. "In the continual vicissitudes of human things," he explained, "amidst the shocks of fortune and the whirls of passion, that take place at certain critical seasons, even in the mildest government, the people are liable to run into riots and tumults. There are Churchquakes and state-quakes in the moral and political world, as well as earthquakes, storms and tempests in the physical . . ."

And slowly he came round to fixing the blame. ". . . the aptitude of the people to mutinies, seditions, tumults and insurrections is in direct proportion to the despotism of the government . . . The virtue and wisdom of the administration may generally be measured by the peace and order that are seen among the people . . ."

These laws that discourage unlawful assemblies are necessary, he continued, for the safety of the people as well as the security of the government, "because once they begin there is a danger of running to such excesses as will overturn the whole system of government." He then quoted Hale once again: " 'All present, aiding and assisting are equally principal with him that gave the stroke, whereof the party died. For tho' one gave the stroke, yet in interpretation of law, it is the stroke of every person that was present aiding and assisting . . .' "

If it is true, Adams continued, that all who participate in an unlawful assembly are equally guilty of any felony committed by one of them, so the reverse must also be true; in a lawful assembly each man is responsible only for his own actions. "If you are satisfied that these soldiers were there on a lawful design, and it should be proved any of them shot without provocation and killed any body, he only is answerable for it." Hale's *Pleas* once again became his sourcebook. " 'If many be together upon a lawful account, and one of the company kill another of an adverse party . . . they are not all guilty that are of the company, but only those that gave the stroke or actually abetted him to do it.' "

The law had been settled by Foster, and Hale and the other great men who gave America the foundation for its legal system; wrote Foster, " 'It was sufficient that at the instant the facts were committed, they were of the same party and upon the same pursuit, and under the same engagements and expectations of mutual defense and support, with those who did the facts." And, added Adams, the inhabitants in the streets that night should have known that "whatever mischief happens in the prosecution of the design they set out upon, all are answerable for it."

But for these laws to apply, the assembly had to be considered unlawful. Once again, he referred to the sages; quoting William Hawkins in *Pleas of the Crown,* " 'Wheresoever more than three persons use force or violence for the accomplishment of any design whatever, all concerned are rioters.' "

Hawkins was giving the common law definition of "rioters." It did not depend on a magistrate's "reading the Riot Act." Three people acting together, using force or violence, constituted a riot — and each participant a rioter. This is why Adams rhetorically asked: "Were there not more than three persons in Dock-square? Did they not agree to go to King Street and attack the Main guard? Where then is the reason for hesitation at calling it a riot?

"If we cannot speak the law as it is, where is our liberty?"

There is an exception to that law, he continued; it is legal to "assemble a competent number of people, in order with force, to oppose rebels, or enemies, or rioters, and afterwards with such force, actually suppress them." He then carefully noted he did not mean to imply than any Bostonian was a rebel, at least not the natives of the country. And noted that if the prisoners were not soldiers, but rather simply neighbors who were attacked in King Street, "they had a right to collect together to suppress this riot . . ."

Adams in his legal arguments liked to use familiar metaphors as a means of bringing his point home to the jury and spectators; in this case he wondered how the inhabitants would respond if a British press gang without a warrant took hold of a sailor on shore, a recognizable threat; "Would not the inhabitants think themselves warranted by law to impose in behalf of their fellow citizens? . . . I believe that it would be lawful to go into King Street and help an honest man there, against a press master."

Then, he reminded them all that in the courtroom the law protects the soldier, the sailor and the citizen equally, and the law that applied to the inhabitants applied in every way the same to the soldiers.

But now he began a discussion of degree; suppose, he wondered, that the inhabitants did not intend to jeopardize the sentry's life? Suppose they simply wanted to take him off his post, or maybe go further and tar and feather him? It didn't matter, he explained. If he could not preserve his liberty "without hazard to his own life, he would be warranted in depriving those of life who were endeavoring to deprive him of his . . . surely the officer and soldiers had a right to go to his relief, and therefore they set out upon a lawful errand, and they were therefore a lawful assembly . . .

". . . according to the evidence, some imprudent people before the sentry proposed to take him off his post, others threatened his life, and intelligence of this was carried to the main guard before any of the prisoners turned out: They were ordered out to relieve the sentry, and any of our fellow citizens might lawfully have gone on the same errand; they were therefore a lawful assembly."

The concept of a lengthy trial being new

to the colony, it remained important to maintain a steady course while keeping the attention of the jury. Adams was not known for his histrionics in the courtroom — few cases called for broad displays of emotion, and it was considered by most to be unprofessional — but he had it in him. Here that was not necessary but he did still need to make a critical point about blame. He told the jurors that there were some lawyers who believed it necessary to demonize the other side in a case. Not here, here that would not do. "I do not pretend to prove that every one of the unhappy persons slain were concerned in the riot . . . I believe it but justice, to say, some were perfectly innocent of the occasion . . . Mr. Maverick, he was a very worthy young man, as he has been represented to me, and had no concern in the riotous proceedings of that night and, I believe, the same may be said in favour of one more, at least, Mr. Caldwell, who was slain; and therefore many people may think, that as he, and perhaps another was innocent, therefore innocent blood having been shed, that must be expiated by the death of somebody or other. I take notice of this because one gentleman nominated by the Sheriff for a Juryman upon this trial, because he said, he believed Captain Preston was innocent, but innocent blood had been shed and therefore somebody ought to be hanged for it . . .

"I am afraid many other persons have formed such an opinion. I do not take it as a rule, that where innocent blood is shed, the person must die." Imagine a father who killed his son in a hunting accident. Innocent blood was shed but nobody would argue the father should die for it. If a man is attacked by two men and strikes back, killing a third man, that killing is excusable because it happened by accident. In the heat of passion if a blow aimed at one man strikes another, that is but manslaughter. Here Adams cited Foster again: "If an action unlawful in itself is done deliberately and with intention of mischief or great bodily harm to particulars . . . fall where it may and death ensues against or beside the original intention of the party, it will be murder.

"But if such mischievous intention doth not appear, which is a matter of fact and is to be collected from circumstances, and the act was done heedlessly and inconsiderately, it will be manslaughter."

Manslaughter. He was presenting the jury with a potential compromise verdict other than murder. "Supposing in this case the

Molatto man was the person made an assault; suppose he was concerned in an unlawful assembly, and this party of soldiers endeavoring to defend themselves against him happened to kill another person who was innocent . . . I say, if on firing on these who were guilty they accidently killed an innocent person, it was not their faults; They were obliged to defend themselves against those who were pressing upon them, they are not answerable for it with their lives, for upon supposition it is justifiable or excusable to kill Attucks or any other person, it will be equally justifiable or excusable if in firing at him they killed another who was innocent . . ."

Once again, Adams cited cases supporting this contention. "If a third person accidentally happen to be killed by one engaged in a combat with another upon a sudden quarrel, it seems that he who kills him is guilty of manslaughter only."

He proceeded diligently, laying it out in workmanlike manner that said clearly, this is the law that applies and it is our duty here to abide by it. His final point about the law, he said, was provocation: "how far persons might go in defending themselves against aggressors, even by taking away their lives, and now [I] proceed to consider such provocations as the law allows to mitigate or extenuate the guilt of killing, where it is not justifiable or excusable."

What remedy did the law offer for those defending themselves against an attack that did not rise to life-threatening? The law stated that "an assault and battery committed upon a man in such a manner as not to endanger his life is such provocation as the law allows to reduce killing down to the crime of manslaughter . . . The law considers a man as capable of bearing any thing and every thing, but blows. I may reproach a man as much as I please, I may call him a thief, robber, traitor, scoundrel, coward, lobster, bloody back, etc, and if he kills me it will be murder — if nothing else but words precede; but if from giving such kind of language I proceed to take him by the nose, or fillip him on the forehead, that is an assault! That is a blow; the law will not oblige a man to stand still and bear it.

"There is the distinction: hands off, touch me not, as soon as you touch me if I run you thro' the heart it is but manslaughter."

Adams then artfully extended that difference, adding, "It is an assault whenever a blow is struck, let it be ever so slight, and sometimes even without a blow."

Adams proceeded to read several definitions of assault that fit his need, quoting Hawkins, " 'Neither can he be thought guilty of a greater crime (than manslaughter) who finding a man in bed with his wife, or being actually struck by him, or pulled by the nose, or filliped upon the forehead, immediately kills him . . .' Every snow-ball, oyster shell, cake of ice or bit of cinder that was thrown that night at the sentinel was an assault upon him, every one that was thrown at the party of soldiers was an assault upon them, whether it hit them or not . . ." Quoting Hawkins once again, he buttressed his contention, " 'That the blood, already too much heated, kindleth afresh at every pass or blow. And in the tumult of passions, in which mere instinct self-preservation had no inconsiderable share, the voice of reason is not heard. And therefore, the law, in condescension to the infirmities of flesh and blood doth extenuate the offence.' Insolent, scurrilous or slanderous language, when it proceeds an assault, aggravates it." While words alone are not sufficient provocation, in the law, "the assault in this case, was aggravated by the scurrilous language which preceded it. Such words of reproach stimulate in the veins and exasperate the mind . . . killing under such a provocation is softened to manslaughter but killing without such provocation makes it murder."

It was a good place to end the day. Adams had laid out the bones of his defense, and beginning the next morning, Tuesday the 4th of December, he would put flesh on it.

CHAPTER ELEVEN

John Adams was a well-known figure in the town now, a man to be talked about. The dismay at the verdict freeing Captain Preston had not yet had time to settle, and there were some who blamed him for it. Now, once again he was defending the Crown, which did not sit well with many inhabitants.

It had been an unusually long day in the courtroom. His lengthy summation may well have taxed his voice. And his voice would need to be even stronger for the conclusion of his argument, when dramatics might be expected.

Fortunately, there were many popular remedies for a stressed throat. Among them, which was included in Elizabeth Jenner's 1706 recipe book, was "a stiff paste of sugar, herbal oils and powders and rose water, with small rounds punched out with a thimble, then dried in an oven." Also recommended for a cold or hoarseness was several large spoonfuls of a brew made from two ounces of kidney suet from a wether sheep, shredded finely and mixed into a pint of cold milk, then brought to a boil and strained. And always there were mugs of cooling cider and home-brewed beer or even boiled tea to sooth the rawness.

By the time court convened again at 9 a.m. the following morning, a fire already was warming the courtroom. The small room was brightened by shafts of winter light streaming through the tall windows. The sound of chairs sliding and leather-heeled shoes and boots reverberated on the rough-planked wooden floor. Adams stood once again and resumed his argument, making it clear to all that there was only one logical way to square the law, "which must govern all cases of homicide" and the evidence. With that, he launched into his understanding of that evidence. "The witnesses are confident they know the prisoners at the bar, and that they were present that night and of the party; However . . ." and one can imagine Adams raising a cautionary finger ". . . witnesses are liable to make mistakes, by a single example before you. Mr. Bass, who is a very honest man and of good character, swears positively that the tall man, Warren, stood on the right that night and was the first that fired, and I am sure you are satisfied by this time, by many circumstances that he is totally mistaken . . ."

As for Bridgham, a man even Sam Adams admitted in the *Gazette* was above reproach, "he says he saw the tall man, Warren, but saw another man belonging to the same regiment soon after, so [much] like him as to make him doubt whether it was Warren or not. He thinks he saw the Corporal, but is not certain, he says he was at the corner of the Custom House . . . other witnesses swear he was the remotest man of all from him who fired first, and there are other evidences who swear the left man did not fire at all. If Wemms did not discharge his gun at all, he could not kill any of the persons, therefore he must be acquitted on the fact of killing; for an intention to kill is not murder nor manslaughter, if not carried into execution.

"The witness saw numbers of things thrown, and he saw plainly sticks strike the guns, about a dozen persons with sticks gave three cheers and surrounded the party and struck their guns with the sticks several blows. This is a witness for the crown and his testimony is of great weight for the prisoners; he gives his testimony very sensibly and impartially. He [Bridgham] swears positively that he not only saw ice or snow thrown but saw the guns struck several times . . ." He was only one of several who testified to those circumstances, reminding the jury, "There were dozens of persons with clubs surrounding the party; twelve sailors with clubs were by much an overmatch to eight soldiers . . . Clubs they had not and they could not defend themselves with bayonets against so many people; It was within the power of the sailors to kill one-half or the whole of the party if they had been so disposed . . ."

Not just inhabitants, Adams emphasized, but sailors. Sailors, who were thought to be rough men, and with whom there already existed such animosity that sailors and soldiers "fight as naturally when they meet as the elephant and rhinoceros." And sailors, of course, were generally not true inhabitants of the town, but rather men who landed there for a period of time.

He wondered if anyone in that situation would "have stood still to see if the sailors would knock their brains out . . . Their clubs were as capable of killing as a ball, an hedge stake [a thick club] is known in the law books as a weapon of death as much as a sword, bayonet or musket . . ." They had come out of Dock Square, he continued, where they had attacked Murray's barracks, armed now with "sticks from the butcher's stalls and cord wood piles . . . Some witnesses swear a club struck a soldier's gun, Bailey swears a man struck a soldier and knocked him down before he fired." Here Adams quoted the witness, " 'The last man that fired, leveled at a lad and moved his gun as the lad ran.' You will consider that an intention to kill is not murder . . . Suppose that soldier had malice in his heart and was determined to murder that boy if he could, yet the evidence clears him of killing the boy, I say admit he had malice in his heart, yet it is plain he did not kill him or anybody else . . . that malice was ineffectual . . ."

As any fine lawyer would do, he pointed out conflicting testimony. For example, "The next witness is Dodge, he says there were fifty people near the soldiers, pushing at them; now the witness before says there were twelve sailors with clubs, but now here are fifty more aiding and abetting of them, ready to relieve them in case of need. Now what could the people expect? It was their business to have taken themselves out of the way, some prudent people by the Town house told them not to meddle with the guard, but you hear nothing of this from these fifty people; No, instead they were huzzaing and whistling, crying 'Damn you! Fire! Why don't you fire!' So that they were actually assisting these twelve sailors that made the attack . . ."

The testimony had most clearly implicated the soldier Killroy, so defending him presented a more difficult challenge than for most of the other men. Adams faced it directly, drawing bits from scattered testimony; "Mr. Langford, the watchman, is more particular with his testimony and deserves very particular consideration because it is intended by the counsel for the Crown, that his testimony shall distinguish Killroy from the rest of the prisoners and exempt him from those pleas of justification, excuse or extenuation, which we rely on for the whole party because he had previous malice, and they would from hence conclude he aimed at a particular person . . . Hemmingway, the Sheriff's coachman, swears he knew Killroy and that he heard him say he would never miss an opportunity of firing upon the inhabitants. This is to prove that Killroy had preconceived malice in his heart, not indeed against the unhappy persons who were killed but against the inhabitants in general, that he had the spirit not only of a Turk or an Arab, but of the devil — but admitting that this testimony is literally true, and that he had all the malice they would wish to prove; yet, if he was assaulted that night, and his life in danger, he had a right to defend himself as well as another man. If he had malice before, it does not take away from him the right of defending himself against any unjust aggressor." Adams speculated how those words were said, perhaps in anger, perhaps when Killroy was in his cups, or perhaps those words were misunderstood; perhaps those words were "uttered at a kitchen fire, before a man and a coachman, where he might think himself at liberty to talk as much like a bully, a fool and a madman as he pleased, and that no evil would come of it." None of that mattered; what mattered amounted to nothing more than " 'I will bear no more than what I am obliged by law to bear.' "

Adams then suggested that Killroy's outburst was sparked by a series of events, including the Liberty Tree rioting in New York, that bore hard upon the soldiers: "No doubt it was under the fret of his spirits, the indignation, mortification, grief and shame that he had suffered a defeat at the Ropewalks . . . There was a little before the 5th of March much noise in this town and a pompous account in the newspapers of a victory obtained by the inhabitants [in New York] over the soldiers . . . the defeat of the soldiers at the Rope-walks was about that time too, and if he did, after that, use such expressions, it ought not to weigh too much in this case . . ." There also was testimony that Killroy harbored a special enmity for one of the victims, Samuel Gray, that both men had been active in the battle at the Rope-walks and that on the night of March 5th he had taken the opportunity to "gratify his preconceived malice; but if all this is true . . . the rule of law is, if there has been malice between the two and at a distant time afterwards they meet, and one of them assaults the other's life, or only assaults him, and he kills in consequence of it, the law presumes the killing was in self-defense, or on account of the provocation, not on account of the antecedent malice . . . However, it does not appear that he knew Mr. Gray, none of the witnesses pretend to say he knew him or that he ever saw him. It is true they were both at the Rope-walks at one time, but there were so many combatants on each side that it is not even probable Mr. Killroy should know them all and no witnesses say there was any rencounter there between them two. Indeed, to return to Mr. Langford's testimony . . . he says expressly he did not aim at Gray. Langford says, 'Gray had no stick, was standing with his arms folded up.' "

Adams had been careful to this point not to challenge the honesty of the witnesses against the prisoners. Even when it became necessary to refute their testimony he did so with a light hand. He continued, "This witness is however most probably mistaken in this matter, and confounds one time with another, a mistake which has been made by many witnesses in this case, and considering the confusion and terror of the scene it is not to be wondered at."

The most gruesome claim by the prosecution was that the substance seen on Killroy's bayonet the next morning was blood that had come from attacking an inhabitant. Adams railed, "It would be doing violence to every rule of law and evidence, as well as common sense and the feelings of humanity, to infer from the blood on the bayonet that it had been stabbed into the brains of Mr. Gray after he was dead, and that by Killroy himself who had killed him.

"Young Mr. Davis swears he saw Gray that evening, a little before the firing, that he had a stick under his arm and said he would go to the riot, 'I am glad of it [that there was a rumpus] I will go and have a slap at them, if I lose my life.' And when he was upon the spot, some witnesses swear, he did not act that peaceable inoffensive part, which Langford thinks he did. They swear, they thought him in liquor — that he run about clapping several people on the shoulders saying, 'Don't run away. They dare not fire.' Langford goes on, 'I saw twenty or five and twenty boys about the Sentinel, and I spoke to him and bid him not be afraid.'

"How does the Watchman Langford tell him not to be afraid? Does this circumstance prove that he thought there was danger, or at least that the sentinel in fact was terrified and did think himself in danger?

"Langford goes on, 'I saw about twenty or five-and-twenty boys that is young shavers.' We have been entertained with a great variety of phrases to avoid calling this sort of people a mob. Some call them shavers, some call them geniuses. The plain English is, gentlemen, most probably a motley rabble of saucy boys, negroes and molattoes, Irish teagues and outlandish [non-Bostonians] jack tarrs." ("Teagues" was a somewhat derogatory slang term for Irish ruffians, and "Jack Tarrs" were seamen.) Previously Adams had made clear that the inhabitants of the city had mostly retreated to their houses, leaving the streets to the rabble, but now he named them. They were the low sort, troublemakers, "and why we should scruple to call such a set of people a mob I can't conceive, unless the name is too respectable for them: The sun is not about to stand still or go out, nor the rivers to dry up because there was a mob in Boston on the 5th of March that attacked a party of soldiers. Such things are not new in the world, nor in the British dominions, though they are comparative rarities and novelties in this town."

As Adams dug into his presentation, jurymen shifted in their hard wooden chairs searching for comfort while spectators — led by Samuel Adams, who was busy making his own notes — standing in the gallery moved their weight from foot to foot. Outside, life continued noisily; horse-drawn wagons rolled by, hawkers shouted their wares, and from time to time a dog made its presence known. Shafts of the dull winter light moved slowly across the room, perhaps illuminating Adams as he continued describing a raucous scene, drawing on testimony to show the chaos of the night, ". . . when so many things were thrown and so many hit their guns, to suppose that none struck their persons is incredible."

Adams focused on those small details that seemed exculpatory. Langford testified a bayonet had been thrust through his great coat and jacket, while the soldier had remained in his place. "This looks as if Langford was nearer the party than became a watchman." His meaning was clear: if the soldier had maintained his position, Langford must have been pressing close.

Brewer was in Royal-exchange Lane and he told the people to go home. "It was excellent advice," said Adams. "Happy for some of them had they followed it, but it seems all advice was lost on these persons. They would harken to none that was given them in Dock-square, Royal exchange-lane or King Street." His accusation was strong, "They were bent on making this assault, and on their own destruction."

The witness James Bailey identified soldiers Carrol, Montgomery and White. "He saw some round the sentry heaving pieces of ice, large and hard enough to hurt any man, as big as one's fist . . ." He may well have displayed a clenched fist for the jury. "If you want evidence of an attack upon [the sentry] there is enough of it; here is a witness an inhabitant of the town, surely no friend to the soldiers for he was engaged against them at the Rope-walks; . . . certainly cakes of ice of this size may kill a man . . ."

The sentry, he reminded them, had fulfilled his legal obligation: "He retreated as far as he could, he attempted to get into the Custom House but could not; then he called to the guard . . ."

Bailey swore that Montgomery had fired the first shot. This witness, Adams said, "certainly is not prejudice in favor of the soldiers; he swears he saw a man come up to Montgomery with a club, and knock him down before he fired, and that he not only fell himself, but his gun flew out of his hand and as soon as he rose he took it up and fired . . . If he was knocked down on his station," Adams argued, "had he not reason to think his life was in danger? Or did it not raise his passions and put him off his guard? So that it cannot be more than manslaughter."

Once again he described the chaos, a mob screeching and threatening, bells ringing. People coming out of the streets throwing every species of rubbish while others threw clubs. "Montgomery in particular, smote with a club and knocked down . . . what could he do? Do you expect he should behave like a stoic philosopher lost in apathy? Patient as Epictatus while his master was breaking his legs with a cudgel? It is impossible you should find him guilty of murder. You must suppose him divested of all human passions if you don't think him at least provoked, thrown off his guard and into the furor brevis, by such treatment as this."

Decades later "the Molatto," the hulking Crispus Attucks, would become a significant historic figure, but in this courtroom Adams cut him down; rather than a victim he was portrayed as an instigator. "Bailey saw the Molatto seven or eight minutes before the firing at the head of twenty or thirty sailors . . . and he had a large cordwood stick. So that this Attucks, by this testimony . . . appears to have undertaken to be the hero of the night, and to lead this army with banners, to form them in the first place in Dock Square and march them up King Street with their clubs . . . If this was not an unlawful assembly there never was one in the world . . ."

Adams repeated this cry: " 'Kill them. Knock them over!' And he tried to knock their brains out . . . He had the hardiness enough to fall in upon them, and with one hand took hold of a bayonet and with the other knocked the man down: This was the behavior of Attucks, to whose mad behavior, in all probability the dreadful carnage of the night is chiefly to be ascribed."

These weren't regular Boston men causing such terror that night; Adams was careful to make that point. "It is in this manner this town has often been treated; a Carr from Ireland and an Attucks from Framingham, happening to be here, shall sally out upon their thoughtless entertainment, at the head of such a rabble . . . as they can collect together . . ."

Adams continued, probing the testimony of each witness to show again and again as Hodgson recorded, "that the assault upon the party was sufficiently dangerous to justify the prisoners; at least, that it was sufficiently provoking to reduce to manslaughter the crime — even of the two who were supposed to be proved to have killed."

He had begun his argument a full day earlier with a thorough explanation of the applicable law: what it meant, how it had developed and how it must be seen in this case. Now he was tucking his prisoners under its shelter, showing repeatedly that they had been threatened, physically assaulted, they had been provoked and had good reason to believe their lives were in jeopardy. And if some of those men had reason for malice, it made no difference. The law, always the law; at most, he admitted, there might be reason to find two of the men had committed manslaughter.

That hard work done, he reached for passion and common sense, finding words that would echo through courtrooms for centuries: "I will enlarge no more on the evidence, but submit it to you. Facts," he said, "are stubborn things; and whatever may be our wishes, our inclinations or the dictates of our passions, they cannot alter the state of facts and evidence. Nor is the law less stable than the fact: If an assault was made to endanger their lives, the law is clear, they had a right to kill in their own defense. If it was not so severe as to endanger their lives, yet if they were assaulted at all, struck and abused by blows of any sort, by snow-balls, oyster shells, cinders, clubs or sticks of any kind, this was a provocation for which the law reduces the offense of killing down to manslaughter, in consideration of those passions of our nature, which cannot be eradicated. To your candor and justice I submit the prisoners and their cause."

His final charge to them was a reminder that they had been called to do a noble thing; honor the law. "The law, in all vicissitudes of government, fluctuations of the passions or flights of enthusiasm, will preserve a steady undeviating course; it will not bend to the uncertain wishes, imaginations and wanton tempers of men." As he had in the Preston trial, he reminded the courtroom of the words of British politician and political theorist Algernon Sidney, who was executed for treason for challenging the divine right of kings. "To use the words of a great and worthy man, a patriot and a hero and enlightened friend of mankind, and a martyr to liberty, I mean Algernon Sidney, who from his earliest infancy sought a tranquil retirement under the shadow under the tree of liberty, with his tongue, his pen and his sword, 'The law,' says he, 'no passion can disturb. 'Tis void of desire and fear, lust and anger. 'Tis *mens sine affectu* [thought without emotion], written reason, retaining some measure of the divine perfection. It does not enjoin that which pleases a weak, frail man, but without any regard to persons, commands that which is good, and punishes evil in all, whether rich or poor, high or low — 'Tis deaf, inexorable, inflexible.' On the one hand it is inexorable to the cries and lamentations of the prisoners, on the other it is deaf, deaf as an adder to the clamours of the populace."

The defense rested.

As had been the way a trial has been conducted throughout legal history, the prosecution got the final word. Paine made the last closing. He had not been well for some time and it was supposed by some that his illness hampered his argument. He set out to take the same pieces Adams had used but attempted to put them together in a different way, to create quite a different picture.

He began by apologizing to the jurymen for the great length of the trial, but noted that it served to demonstrate the desire of English law to secure justice. "Justice, strict justice is the ultimate object of our law." He cited Lord Coke's "observation on our Law in general that it is *ultima ratio,* the last improvement of reason which in the nature of it will not admit any proposition to be true of which it has not evidence, nor determine that to be certain of which there remains a doubt; if therefore in the examination of this cause the evidence is not sufficient to convince beyond a reasonable doubt of guilt of all or any of the prisoners by the benignity and reason of the law you will acquit them, but if the evidence be sufficient to convince you of their guilt beyond reasonable doubt the justice of the law will require you to declare them guilty . . ."

As the task of the jury to deliberate and reach a consensus had developed there had been little instruction advising them how to assess "reasonable doubt." How far the courts had come in the centuries since trial by ordeal was an accepted test: that method had left to God to determine innocence or guilt, but now that grave decision was being put solely in the hands of twelve men. This was an appeal to each man in the jury box to look deep into his own conscience. Neither side offered any guidance or suggested where exactly that might be, but rather left it to each man to find it.

Paine continued, acknowledging the task facing him was to argue "against the lives of eight of our fellow subjects, the very thought of which is enough to excite your compassion." That "human side," as he referred to it, gave an advantage to the defense, as "appeals to the passions in favor of life as might be grating to your humanity should I attempt the like against life."

There was another thing quite unusual about this trial, he said. The great length of time between the "unhappy homicide" and the beginning of the trial had allowed for depositions to be printed and be eventually dispersed to the public. Although Paine admittedly was "at a loss to determine whether this unexpected and undesigned event has tended more to the advantage or disadvantage of the prisoners," he said it did make known to the defense the strength of the evidence against them and allowed them to prepare to counter it. Unfairly, he suggested, the counsel for the Crown "were surprised with a great part of the evidence" produced in favor of the prisoners and "had not the same opportunity to prepare evidence to oppose it." His only recourse in that event was to appeal to the jurymen, who he was confident "are not prejudiced in the cause nor have formed any judgement respecting it," and he would "endeavor to address myself to your cool and candid reason."

The first defense claim he would contest is that "the disorders of the evening" had been the result of a design, or plan to attack the soldiers, which had begun with inhabitants coming from all parts of town armed with clubs and sticks and some of them with guns. That was not true, he said: "If we recollect the evidence we shall find previous to all this collection a number of soldiers had come out of their barracks armed with clubs, bayonets, cutlasses, tongs and instruments of diverse kind and in the most disorderly and outrageous manner were ravaging the streets, assaulting every one they met . . . [they] even vented their inhumanity on a little boy of 12 years old. That some of them were conspiring to blow up the Liberty Tree in the manner as had been done in New York, the account of which had then just come among us . . . Consider also the testimony of those who give an account of the affray at Murray's barracks where by the testimony of Mr. Archibald 18 or 20 soldiers had rushed out with cutlasses, tongs etc., attacking all that came in their way, struck him and another person . . . Consider also the testimony of Mr. Wilkinson and Helyer to the behavior of the soldiers and inhabitants . . . and it will represent to you the true light in which that affair ought to be viewed."

Many inhabitants carried sticks, he continued, because they were aware of the "ill disposition and abusive behavior" of the soldiers; in fact, they often so armed themselves and this was little more than might be seen on any other night. Paine's view of the night was remarkably different from Adams's. Rather than the poorly lit night, in which armed men set on mayhem angrily moved through the shadows as described by the defense, "it appears it was a bright moon light evening," he said, adding, "the pleasantness of which increased by a new fall'n snow . . ." The inhabitants had come out of their houses by the ringing of the fire bells, and some of them pulled legs out of butcher's stalls only after learning that the soldiers were abusing townsmen. It should not be surprising, he continued, "that among a number of people collected on such an occasion there should be some who should rashly and without design express themselves in such a manner; and must the disposition and intention of the whole be collected from such expressions heard only by a few."

Paine emphasized that it was not the inhabitants that raged that night, but only a few men who acted "rashly" and without any plan. "How many sailors and foreigners of the lower class may we well suppose there is in so populous a sea port who are fond of mingling with such commotions and pushing on a disorder of which they feel not the slightest consequence?"

The number of men was confusing too, he said. Some said two hundred men were collected in Dock Square, and there also was a large number of men near Murray's barracks, all of whom appeared to "run several ways to King Street," but "we find but a very few that ever got into King Street, for by the best account we don't find above 70 or 80, there are some credible witnesses of good judgement say 50 or 60 and some say about 100 and as many boys as men, and of these it is clear from the current of the evidence that many came from else where and but a small proportion had sticks . . ."

As for the actual attack, "The prisoners would have you believe that a number of men armed with clubs rush'd down into King Street, first assaulted their sentry there and then surrounded and assaulted them when they came to support him and endangered their lives in such a manner as that they were obliged to fire on them for their own preservation . . . Such a coloring to the appearance and behavior of the people in King Street as may render them a riotous and unlawful assembly and the objects of fear and resentment to the party."

An effective summation shapes the evidence in the most favorable manner to that side, while also attacking the scenario put forward by the other side. Robert Paine seemed incredulous at the defense claims, wondering "Can any person living, from the history of this affair as it turns up in evidence, suppose these persons were such dangerous rioters as to bring them within those rules of law which have been read to you that it is lawful to kill them? Shall the innocent and peaceable, who by mere casualty are mixt with the ruder sort, be liable to be shot down by a party of soldiers merely because they please to call 'em dangerous rioters?"

Perhaps there might not be complete truth to these claims either, he suggested, while not directly challenging any individual witness. "Great pains has been taken to satisfye you that this collection of people actually assaulted and endangered the lives of the party . . . Numbers of the most impartial and judicious and who stood in the best situation of observation saw nothing of such transactions as are testified by others which one would think could not escape notice. The showers of snow balls, oyster shells and multitude of sticks; the frequent and loud huzzaing and threatening cries . . . were totally unobserved by a very great number of the best witnesses, many of whom were produced by the prisoners and whose credibility, judgement and situation were equally good as those who relate it . . . Is it possible to conceive that such facts should exist as have been asserted and escape the notice of so great numbers of such witnesses? If the facts did exist it must have been in such a degree as only to be observed accidently by a few and not in such manner as to engage the notice of the whole."

The testimony that Paine was compelled to challenge was the alleged words of the victim, Patrick Carr, who it was claimed had taken responsibility for his fate. Paine moved deftly around the edges: "To me, gentlemen, it seems unaccountable that any stress should be laid on this evidence. Carr, it seems, was for taking a sword when he went out, whether to fight for or against the soldiers is very uncertain . . . [He] had been there but a very short space of time and was going from them when he was shot, and I can't conceive why his judgment of the matter whose character and disposition we know not, without the obligation of an oath, and so situated tho a dying man should weigh more than the testimony of numbers of judicious reputable witnesses who were in the midst of it and told you they saw nothing that should occasion them to fire and wondered at the reason for it. And that if they had suspected any such thing they should have gone away . . ."

Adams had deftly laid down the law and then fit the evidence into it; after attacking the reliability of the evidence, Paine questioned that fit. "It is proved to you gentlemen that all the prisoners at the bar were present in King Street at the firing. It appears by the current of the testimony that seven guns were fired, and it appears pretty certain that Wemms, the corporal, was the one who did not fire. It is certain that five men were killed by the firing of which Montgomery killed Attucks and Killroy killed Gray. But which of the other five prisoners killed the other three of the deceased appears very uncertain." He then turned Adams's legal authorities round on him: "But this operates nothing in their favour if it appears to you that they were an unlawful assembly, for it has been abundantly proved to you by the numerous authorities produced by the counsel for the prisoners that every individual of an unlawful assembly is answerable for the doings of the rest. They are all considered as principals, and all that are present aiding, assisting and abetting to the doing an unlawful act as is charged . . . are also considered as principals. The counsel aware of this have endeavored to make it appear they were a lawful assembly . . . but it must be remembered that no man or body of men have a right to do a lawful action in an unlawful manner; if they do they become an unlawful assembly . . .

". . . even tho they were lawfully assembled when they got there . . . the moment they turned their arms on the people without just cause they became an unlawful assembly . . . The Kings troops have undoubtedly a right to march thro' the streets and as such are a lawful assembly. But if in such marching without just cause they fire on the inhabitants and but one man is kill'd they surely are all answerable; tho it can't be proved who did the execution."

Lawful assembly, unlawful assembly, Paine clearly wondered why such argument was even necessary. "If there is just cause for firing they will be acquitted on that plea and there will be no occasion to determine the legality of their assembling. If there is no just cause of firing how will you excuse them all of the guilt, tho it is not proved who were the actual perpetrators. When you recollect further, the account given you by many witnesses that on firing the first gun the people dispersed and were in a manner withdrawn to a distance at the firing of the last guns; that the last gun was fired at a boy at a distance running down street; that they presented their firelocks again at the few people who came . . . to pick up the dead, it appears to me you must be satisfy'd they were possessed of that wicked depraved malignant spirit which constitutes malice, that from the whole evidence taken together no just cause appears for such outrageous conduct and therefore they must be considered aiding and assisting each other in this unlawful act which the lawfulness of their assembling will not excuse . . .

"Will not the reason of law impute guilt to all of them tho at first lawfully assembled, seeing they joined in doing an unlawful action?"

Finally, as Paine began his conclusion, he reminded the jurors that the case came down to one basic question: "Does there appear sufficient evidence to justify or excuse the killing in order for which it must appear to be done to prevent the commission of a known felony?" Was it truly a matter of self-defense? On that question their decision must be made. Then he explained why it was not: "It seems Montgomery was not knock'd down, if at all, till he pushed with his bayonet and the blow was not followed.

"Had the people intended any more than to resent the insolence of the party who were pushing and wounding them they certainly would have executed their design on the discharge of the guns. But nothing of that kind appears."

Paraphrasing the authorities, in this instance Foster, he told them, "The plea of self-defense . . . must inevitably fail unless you can be satisfied there was no other possible way of saving their lives but by killing. No one who recollects that till the firing the first gun Captain Preston stood talking with a witness can believe this to be the case, and if so it was an unlawful act to kill, and as they were all combined in the firing they are all answerable."

This was murder, Paine insisted, cold-blooded murder. "Neither doth it seem by taking the evidence all together it will alleviate their crime to manslaughter. Shall throwing a snow ball from a distance alleviate the crime of firing a ball amidst a number of people who at first stood so thick they could not throw . . . Shall this be likened to the filliping a man on the forehead as has been read to you?" Referring to the Tower of London precedent, Paine continued, "Is it not manifest that in that case the very assailant was killed, but here it appears that none of the persons killed were assailants. Attucks 15-feet off leaning on his stick, Gray 12-feet off with his hand in his bosom, and the other three just run into the street and scarce knew of the affair before they were shot down. Tis to human frailty and that only [that the law permits reducing a charge of murder to manslaughter], and not to such brutal rage and diabolical malignity as must have impelled the prisoners to fire as they did . . .

"Indeed, if you believe that Montgomery was knock'd down in the manner asserted, his crime I acknowledge can amount no higher than manslaughter — but what evidence is there that any of the rest receiving such a provocation before firing as will alleviate their crime? The left wing of the party was uncovered by the people, the crowd was chiefly at the right. [The witness] Andrew indeed supposes Killroy was struck, but when we consider he looked about and saw Attucks fall he must have confounded this fact, as in my opinion he has many others.

"The witness who testifies of Killroy's killing Gray puts it beyond dispute that he shot him deliberately and after caution not to fire, and the witness must have seen the blow if he received any. When you consider the evidence against Killroy, his previous threatening and that repeatedly after admonition . . . and the express evidence of killing Gray and the manner of it, I think you must unavoidably find him guilty of murder. What your judgement should think of the rest, tho the evidence is undoubtedly fullest against him, yet it [is] full enough against the rest."

Evening was flowing into the courtroom as the justices finally called the proceedings to an end, sending the prisoners back to jail for one more night. The trial was coming to an end. Tomorrow they would learn if they were to be free or imprisoned, if they would live or die.

CHAPTER TWELVE

The beginning of December was a time to celebrate in New England. The harvest was done and the hardest days of winter had not yet arrived. There was abundant meat that needed to be eaten before it spoiled, to be enjoyed with newly fermented beer and wine. In parts of Europe and other colonies, preparations were being made to welcome the Christmas season; the following day, the 6th, was St. Nicholas name day, but there was little change to be seen in the town. The Puritans had long ago rejected Christmas, claiming it invoked paganism and idolatry and led to immoral behavior. Public celebrations had been outlawed by the Massachusetts General Court more than a century earlier, and anyone observing that day "by forbearing of labor, feasting or in any other way" could be fined 5 shillings. Private celebrations, wassailing, and the exchange of cards had slowly crept back into favor, and overly aggressive wassailers were known to force their way into homes to partake, but the day still was not fully embraced. The Puritan ethic, embodied by Cotton Mather's warning that "the feast of Christ's nativity" led to "reveling, licentious liberty, mad mirth and lewd gaming" still had its hold on the colony. Though it was known and accepted that children often would sneak off to the Episcopal churches to enjoy the revelry.

But in the courts there was still work to be done. The soldiers' trial was nearing an end, with the trial of the citizens charged with firing muskets from the Custom House still to be held. In addition, Adams had to keep pace with his other cases. Coincidentally, on this momentous day, the 5th of December, he filed a declaration in a property dispute in which he represented John Whiting, a landowner, against a claim made by the daughter and heir of a previous owner, Abiel Hill, who was represented by his co-counsel in the soldiers' case, Josiah Quincy, Jr.

Throughout the trial the weather had remained fair, but on this Wednesday morning, as Paine rose to complete his presentation, it had become warm. Paine spoke for more than two additional hours trying to convince jurors that rather than the prisoners' lives being in jeopardy, the redcoats were out of control, taking advantage of the chaos caused by a small group of rabble-rousers to release their pent-up anger. When he finished, it was time for the judges to charge the jury.

This part of a case is the foundation on which the jury would render its verdict. The judge's charge was an explanation of the law the jury should consider when reaching its decision, what laws apply. In essence, an instruction sheet describing how the puzzle might be put together. And in so doing, the judges could narrow the scope, making conviction more difficult, or broaden it to give greater leeway to the jury. These judges could also share their candid views of the strength or weakness of the evidence as it applied to the law.

Judge Edmund Trowbridge spoke first. Trowbridge was greatly respected as an arbitrator, a teacher and a student of the law. He held no strong political views that might influence his direction; in fact, he had lost respect for the loyalist Hutchinson when the governor had placed his brother, Foster Hutchinson, on the bench.

Trowbridge began by reading the indictment, which charged the prisoners "with having feloniously and of their malice aforethought, shot and thereby killed and murdered" the five victims. Those not charged with giving the mortal wounds were said to be "present aiding and abetting" and therefore charged as principals in the murder. "So far as respects the killing . . . the stroke of one is, in consideration of the law, the stroke of all."

He would not review the testimony of each witness, he explained, but that hardly was necessary. Jurors were permitted to take notes and among them, Edward Pierce, had listed the evidence presented against each defendant. About "John Carrall" (one of the many names he misspelled), for example, he wrote: "Mr. Austin saw Carrall and heard six or seven guns. James Baley saw Carrall fire the second gun. John Danbrooke saw Carrall. Thomas Hall saw Carrol." The most evidence was presented against Matthew Killroy: "Lanksford saw Killroy present his gun and fired and Gray fell at his feat then pushd his bayonet at Lanksford and run it through his clothes. Francis Archible saw Killroy. Hemenway heard Killroy say he would not miss an opportunity to fire . . . Nicholas Firiter saw Killroy . . . Joseph Crosswell saw Killroy . . . Thos Crasswell . . . Jonathan Cary . . ."

Rather than summarize the witness testimony, what he intended to do, Trowbridge continued, was "point out the manner in which various testimonies are to be considered, and how the evidence is to be applied, still leaving it with you to determine how far that which has been testified by each witness is to be believed."

He began with a broad history of law in America, explaining, "The laws of England are of two kinds, the unwritten or common law and the written or statute law . . . the common law is the law by which the proceedings and determinations in the King's ordinary courts of justice are guided and directed. This law is the birthright of every Englishman. The first settlers of this country brought it from England with them."

Under that law, "Homicide is of three kinds, justifiable, excusable and felonious . . . the third is the highest crime against the law of nature. There are also degrees of guilt in felonious homicide, which divide the offense into manslaughter and murder."

Justifiable homicide is the basis of a self-defense claim, meaning it is accepted that "Killing him who attempts to rob or murder me, to break open my dwelling-house in the night, or to burn it, or by force commit any other felony on me, my wife, child, servant, friend or even a stranger if it cannot other-wise be prevented, is justifiable"

This same common law obliges peace officers of any kind to suppress riots and other unlawful assemblies and empowers them to raise a sufficient force to do that. "It is the duty of all persons," he continued, "(except women, decrepit persons and infants under 15) to aid and assist . . . when called upon to do it. They may take with them such weapons as are necessary to enable them effectually to do it, and may justify the beating, wounding and even killing such rioters as resist or refuse to surrender; if the riot cannot otherwise be suppressed . . .

"Homicide excusable in self-defense . . . differs from justifiable self-defense because he was to blame for engaging in the affray and therefore must retreat as far as he can safely . . ."

His lecture continued at some length, discussing the various applications of the different types of killings, until he finally reached felonious homicides and the core distinction between manslaughter and murder: "Malice is the grand criterion that distinguishes murder from all other homicide. Malice aforethought is the dictate of a wicked, depraved and malignant spirit. As when one with a sedate, deliberate mind and formed design kills another." If a quarrel results instantly in a duel and one man is killed, he gave as an example, that is manslaughter; but if they agree to duel at a later time and one is killed, that is murder. Or, if a man maliciously attempts to kill another man, but instead kills a third person, it also is murder.

In this manner Justice Trowbridge guided the jury through the various situations that result in death, explaining to them which is murder and which is a different type of homicide and how they might determine the difference. Citing Blackstone, he advised them, "Where one kills another willfully without a considerable provocation, it is murder, because no one unless an abandoned heart, would be guilty of such an act upon a slight or no apparent cause."

In his role as judge, he explained, his job was "to determine the law arising on the facts, because [the court] is supposed to know it . . ." and then "recommend to the jury to find the facts specially, or direct them hypothetically as, if you believe such and such witnesses who have sworn so and so, the killing was malicious and then you ought to find the prisoners guilty of murder, but if you do not believe these witnesses then you ought to find them guilty of manslaughter only."

As for all the competing claims circulated in the months preceding the trial, those attempts to sway the opinions of the jurymen must be ignored completely. While the politics of the time hung over the case, he warned them not to bring that knowledge or prejudice with them into their deliberations. "You are to settle the facts in this case upon the evidence given to you in court . . . and not collect it from what has been said by people out of court, or published in the newspapers or delivered from the pulpits."

Judge Trowbridge then made suggestions about how they might proceed: first, they had to establish if murder was committed that night. To do that the jury had witness testimony that five persons were shot and thereby mortally wounded that night, and that evidence "must, I think, also convince you that they were killed by the party of soldiers that were at the Custom House that night, or by some of them."

The jury then had to determine if each of the prisoners was at that scene. It only requires the sworn testimony of a single witness for them to make that conclusion, he reminded them, if they believe that testimony. More important, and vital to the fate of each soldier, "You must be fully satisfied upon the evidence given you, with regard to each prisoner, that he in particular did, in fact or in consideration of law, kill one or more of these persons that were slain, or he must be acquitted."

More questions to be answered: Was the sentry legally placed at the Custom House? Was he attacked? Were the prisoners ordered there to support and protect him? These were the great political questions bearing on the trial; Sam Adams had asserted that the very presence of the troops in the town was illegal; and if that were true, their actions must be criminal. The judge suggested otherwise. "The main design of society is the protection of individuals by the united strength of the whole community," Trowbridge said. To accomplish that the King, and only the King has the absolute right to raise fleets or armies. "The Mutiny Acts dictate that with the consent of Parliament the King may keep a standing army not only in the Kingdom, but also in America . . . Placing sentries is a necessary part of the regulation of an army . . . so you have no reason to doubt but that it was legally done."

Was the sentry attacked by the inhabitants? There was no easy path through the conflicting evidence." . . . if witnesses contradict each other, so that their testimonies cannot be reconciled, you must consider the number of witnesses on each side, their ability, integrity, indifference as to the point in question, and the probability and improbability arising from the nature of the thing in question, and upon the whole settle the fact as you verily believe it to be."

Trowbridge led the jurors through the questions as if he were holding their hands. If the sentry was attacked, was it lawful for the prisoners to respond? "Now as this party did not assemble or go there of their own accord, but were sent out by their Captain to protect the sentry, it must be supposed that was their design in going, until the contrary appears." The justice continued, winding the law around the event in response to each of the points raised by both the prosecution and the defense. The witness Fosdick, for example, testified he was pushed with a bayonet while standing peacefully, an action that might be viewed to show "their design was to disturb the peace and not preserve it. But as Fosdick himself says, that upon his refusing to move out of his place they parted and went by him, you will consider whether it is not more reasonable to suppose that what he calls a push was an accidental touch . . .

rather than any thing purposely done to hurt him . . ."

Justice Trowbridge then launched into a long and detailed analysis of the firing of the muskets and what might be gleaned from the fact that the entire party fired almost together, concluding that any or all of the defendants might only be found guilty if "he in particular in fact did kill one or more of the persons slain.

"Some witnesses have been produced to prove that Montgomery killed Attucks; and Langford swears Killroy killed Gray, but none of the witnesses undertake to say that either of the other prisoners in particular killed either of the other three persons or that all of them did it. On the contrary, it seems one of the six did not fire, and that another of them fired at a boy as he was running down the street, but missed him (if he had killed him, as the evidence stands, it would have been murder) but the witnesses are not agreed as to the person who fired at the boy or as to him who did not fire at all. It is highly probable, from the places where the five persons killed fell and their wounds, that they were killed by the discharge of five several guns only. If you are upon the evidence satisfied of that, and also that Montgomery killed Attucks and Killroy

415

Gray, it will thence follow that the other three were killed, not by the six prisoners but by three of them only: and therefore they cannot all be found guilty of it. And as the evidence does not shew which three killed the three, nor that either of the six in particular killed either of the three, you cannot find either of the six guilty of killing them or either of them."

If the jury believed Montgomery had killed Attucks, it then had to determine whether or not it was justifiable, excusable or felonious homicide, and if it was malicious. If the jury was satisfied Montgomery had reason to believe his life was "in immediate danger . . . he ought to be acquitted;" if he was assaulted with clubs and other weapons, he should be found guilty of manslaughter only; but if he fired without first being assaulted he should be found guilty of murder. To make that point known, he added that if the party was pelted with snowballs, ice and sticks — in anger — this must be considered an assault.

Those same circumstances also held true for Killroy. The verdict for him must be the same as Montgomery — unless, Trowbridge cautioned, the threats he made at the Ropewalk are considered material. But even then, he added, "if the assault upon him was such as would justify his firing and killing" it would be manslaughter. "In the tumult of passion the voice of reason is not heard," he concluded, "and it is owing the allowance the law makes for human frailty that all unlawful voluntary homicide is not deemed murder."

There was no testimony given against the other six prisoners that tended to show they had gone to the Custom House "to disturb the peace or, after they got there and before firing agreed to do so; or in case they had actually unlawfully abetted the killing."

Judge Peter Oliver spoke next, and his feelings about the affray were known in the town. Oliver was a wealthy man, having built his fortune as the owner of an iron works. His mansion in Middleboro, with its magnificent gardens and imported woodwork and artwork, was considered among the finest in the entire province. He was a strong supporter of Parliament and its right to tax the colonies, a man who referred angrily to the "Sons of Anarchy" rather than "Liberty" and often railed against smugglers like Hancock, whom he once derided as someone whose "understanding was of dwarf size." Adams had argued several cases in his courtrooms, among them a libel case three years earlier in which he believed one judge was fixed on an outcome, but Oliver was "the fair, candid, impartial judge." He was generally considered a man of integrity and at times had entertained John Adams and Benjamin Franklin at Oliver Hall.

Judge Oliver previously had presided at the murder trial of Ebenezer Richardson and described the inhabitants who crammed into the courtroom as "a vast concourse of rabble." During his final remarks he had argued that the merchant had committed no crime, that guilt lay with "the promoters of the effigies and the exhibitions which had drawn the people together and caused unlawful and tumultuous assemblies."

Several years later the true magnitude of his disgust would be revealed when he wrote about the colonists' *Short Narrative* and the subsequent trials; the narrative "was crowded with the most notorious falsities; which answered the purposes of the faction . . ." In this courtroom, though, Oliver was appropriately subdued as he rambled through the testimony. Addressing the jury, he began, "This is the most solemn trial I ever sat in judgement upon . . . [It is] our part to adore the divine conduct in this unhappy catastrophe and to justify the ways of God to man." He immediately made known his respect for the prisoners, reminding the jurors that "Soldiers, when they act properly in their department are . . . in some cases they are more useful than any other members of society, as we happily experienced in the late war, by the reduction of Canada." And those soldiers, he said pointedly, are entitled to the same protection under the law as any of His Majesty's subjects.

Oliver then spoke out passionately against the propaganda that had preceded the trial but especially an article appearing months earlier in the *Gazette:* "I think I never saw greater malignity of heart expressed in any one piece; a malignity blacker than ever was expressed by the savages of the wilderness, for they are in the untutored state of nature and are their own avengers of wrongs done to them; but we are under the laws of society, which laws are the avengers of wrongs done to us. I am sorry I am obliged to say it, but there are persons among us who have endeavored to bring this Supreme Court of law into contempt and even to destroy the law itself." He continued, "There may come a time when these persons themselves may want the protection of the law and this court, which they now endeavor to destroy, and which, if they succeed in their attempts, it may be too late for them to repair to for justice . . ." These were noble words coming from a man who had no formal legal training, but had served on the bench for nearly two decades. He reminded the jurors, as had Trowbridge, "to divest your minds of every thing that may tend to bias them in this cause: It is your duty to fix your eyes solely on the scales of justice and as the law and evidence in either scale may preponderate, so you are to determine your verdict."

He then acknowledged that Justice Trowbridge had given to the jurors the legal definition of homicide, but felt it necessary to make one addition from Foster's *Pleas,* not necessarily because it bore on this case but rather to take full advantage of the widespread attention it had generated, including many from the country: "If a person drives his cart carelessly," he explained, "and it runs over a child in the street; if he have seen the child and yet drives on upon him, it is murder because willfully done . . . but if he saw not the child it is manslaughter; but if the child had run cross the way and the cart run over the child before it was possible for the carter to make a stop, it is by misadventure."

There also had been repeated demands from patriots that blood be answered by blood; they quoted Moses, as the source of mortal law, "He that killeth a man, he shall be put to death." But Oliver noted that "Moses was the best commentator on his own laws, and he hath published certain restrictions of this law . . ." Moses carefully noted the difference between a killing committed to satisfy hatred and a killing done "without enmity," or by accident. In that latter case he suggested there were sanctuary cities to which the accused might flee, concluding, "to construe that law to Noah strictly is only to gratify a blood thirsty revenge, without any of those allowances for human frailties which the law of nature and the English law also make."

Judge Oliver then reiterated his colleague's instruction that jurors begin their process by first satisfying themselves that the "prisoners at the bar were an unlawful assembly when they were at the Custom House, for on that much depends their guilt or innocence." Then the jury had to determine if the gathering of inhabitants was a lawful assembly, although he objected to the description of them as a mob: "Some delicacy hath been used at the bar in calling those people a mob . . . but I shall use the legal phrase and call such a crowd a riotous assembly if the sound is more agreeable than mob."

Oddly, John Adams, Quincy, Jr., and even Judge Trowbridge had ignored the presence of the man in red, who several witnesses had testified played a role in sparking the events. But now, Oliver did not hesitate to place blame on him, saying that after as many as two hundred men, many of them armed with weapons, had been driven from Murray's barracks, "a tall man with a red cloak and white wig talked to the people, who listened to him and then huzzaed for the Main guard. I cannot but make this observation on the tall man with a red cloak and white wig that, whoever he was, if the huzzaing for the Main guard and then attacking the soldiers was the consequence of his speech to the people, that tall man is guilty in the sight of God of the murder of five persons . . . and although he may never be brought to a court of justice here, yet unless he speedily f lies to the city of refuge, the supreme avenger of innocent blood will surely overtake him."

Even before the trial began there was little doubt where Judge Oliver's loyalty lay, and he had heard nothing during those long days that had changed his mind. Thirty-eight witnesses, he pointed out, among them six defense witnesses, had testified that a "riotous assembly" had collected around the soldiers. The behavior of the soldiers in the face of such provocation had been exemplary, he said: the sentry had "behaved with a good temper of mind" and done much to avoid a dispute. The soldiers coming to his aid gave way to Fosdick when he refused to move. While in front of the Custom House they raised their guns to allow Gridley to pass between them. Even as the assembly closed on them they pushed at them with their bayonets rather than striking and "at the same time bidding them keep off."

As for their being provoked, twenty-five witnesses swore that ice, snowballs, sticks and other objects were thrown at the soldiers; and thirty witnesses testified "to words of provocation uttered against the prisoners . . . threatening to kill them." While words alone cannot legally justify killing, "if threatening expressions are attended with an attempt on the life of a man" such a killing is justified. Justice Oliver overtly questioned testimony from certain witnesses, "that although they were close to the soldiers, they saw nothing of any kind thrown at them, nor heard any huzza or threatening; nay, one witness is so distinct as to tell, in a cloud of smoke, which guns killed the different persons. I know not how to account for such testimonies, unless by the witnesses being affrighted, which some of them say they were not: They themselves perhaps may satisfy their own minds . . .

". . . Ye have one difficulty to solve, Gentlemen," Judge Oliver continued, finally focusing on the question of murder, "and that is that there were five persons killed, and here are eight soldiers charged with murdering them. Now one witness says that the Corporal did not fire, and Thomas Wilkinson says that the guns of the third or fourth man from the eighth flashed, so that there are two guns of eight not discharged — and yet it is said seven were fired. This evinces the uncertainty of some of the testimonies . . . Indeed as to two of the prisoners there is no great doubt of their firing, namely Montgomery and Killroy." After recounting the testimony that showed Montgomery fired only after being struck and threatened, his attention turned to Killroy.

There seemed considerably more evidence against Private Matthew Killroy, he observed, but then proceeded to offer alternative explanations. His bloodied bayonet? Rather than stabbing a mortally wounded victim, as had been alleged, "I have only one way to account for it, if it was bloody . . . that by pushing to keep off Nathaniel Fosdick it might become so by wounding him in the breast and arm." The battle of the rope-walks a week earlier? Nicholas Ferreter "says that Killroy uttered no threatenings but only daring the ropemakers to come out." Hemmingway's claim Killroy had said he would not miss an opportunity to fire on the inhabitants? "How the conversation was had, whether it was maliciously spoke or was jocose talk doth not so fully appear, but it would be extream hard to connect such discourse with this transaction; especially as his being at the Custom House was not voluntary but by order of his officer."

He might have gone further and deeper into the evidence, he said, but he was afraid of becoming tedious. Instead he laid out his opinion on the matter and while doing so gave legal blessing to John Adams's advice to the jury: "If upon the whole, by comparing the evidence, ye should find that the prisoners were a lawful assembly at the Custom House, which ye can be in no doubt of if you believe the witnesses, and also that they behaved properly . . . and did not fire till there was a necessity to do so in their own defense, which I think there is a violent presumption of; and if, on the other hand, ye should find that the people who were collected around the soldiers were an unlawful assembly, and had a design to endanger, if not take away their lives, as seems to be evident, from blows succeeding threatenings, ye must in such case acquit the prisoners. Or if upon the whole ye are in any reasonable doubt of their guilt ye must then, agreeable to the rule of law, declare them innocent."

With that, and references to it from both Adams and Paine in their summations, the doctrine of reasonable doubt entered the language of the law.

Next came Judge John Cushing. At seventy-five he was the oldest judge and Adams had concerns about him. He had argued before Judge Cushing in a 1767 case where Adams's client, Stephen Nye, had sued one Rowland Cotton for slander. Adams felt the judge went out of his way to make things difficult, writing in his diary that the defendant, Cotton, "is not only a Tory but a relation of some of the judges, Cushing particularly . . ." According to Adams, "Cushing was very bitter, he was not for my arguing to the jury the question whether the words were actionable or not. He interrupted me — stopped me short, snapped me up. 'Keep to the evidence.

Keep to the point. Don't ramble all over the world to the ecclesiastical councils. Don't misrepresent the evidence.' This was his impartial language."

While Judge Cushing's instructions were not recorded, it is not surprising that Robert Paine wrote in his notes that the perhaps crotchety judge did say that this was "The longest trial I have ever known."

Finally, Judge Benjamin Lynde addressed the jury. He too explained that their verdict must turn on whether "this meeting of the soldiers was lawful." If that was true "the homicide cannot legally be imputed to them all; only those who did the act can be charged with it."

No specific evidence had been brought against six of them, other than being present, "but there are only two against whom anything certain can be fixed." Lynde agreed with Oliver that the evidence was strongest against Killroy. His own words, his threat that he would fire on the inhabitants, "taken alone would suggest a malicious intent and, had he gone down and joined the soldiers of his own accord this would be more apparent, but that was not the case . . ."

But what bothered him most, he admitted, was the charge that the next morning Killroy's bayonet "was bloody five inches up. If this was done by stabbing the dying man after he was shot down . . ." as two witnesses so said, ". . . it was a barbarous action." It was cruel and inhuman, the mark of a bad mind.

"But whether he can be charged with murder is the question." Considering he had been ordered to assist the sentry, the threatenings, the things flung at the soldiers "and that the person slain was one of the most active . . . these things, together with the real danger they were all in from the numbers surrounding, may lessen his crime, from what he is charged with, to manslaughter."

Finally, he fixed on Montgomery. The witness Bailey "swears he was the first person that fired and Attucks, the mulatto fell by his shot." Another witness swore the same thing, while a third witness named the tallest man, Warren. In defense of Montgomery, Adams had elicited the evidence that the soldier "had a blow given to him . . . and being asked by the prisoner's counsel whether it was a violent one, he answered, Yes; he goes on to say that the stroke given Montgomery brought him to the ground." Other witnesses confirmed that, one adding that "the blow on his head was accompanied with the cry, 'Kill the dog. Knock him overboard.' They say this was done by a large stout man, and describe him in such a manner as we must suppose him to be Attucks." Judge Lynde continued, covering the well-trod ground through the remainder of the morning, and early in the afternoon the case finally was handed to the jury.

Some of the judges had hardly seemed objective, but it was still the jury's decision to make. The jurors retired to begin deliberations. Perhaps to prod them to a decision, they were permitted neither food nor drink, a tradition that harkened back to at least the year 1293 when a French judge was recorded telling a jury to reach its verdict or "You will stay shut up without food or drink till tomorrow morning." Sir Edward Coke advised in his 1628 *Institutes of the Lawes of England,* "a jury after their evidence on the issues ought to be kept together in some convenient place, without meat or drink, fire or candle, which some books call an imprisonment." In 1670, a juryman named Edward Bushell was fined for refusing the court's order to return a verdict against William Penn in an unlawful assembly case. When Bushell refused to pay the fine he was jailed. The Court of Common Pleas ruled in his case that a jury could not be punished for its verdict but that individual members of a jury might be charged for improper actions. This practice of sequestering a jury was summed up for history by Alexander Pope, who wrote in his 1714 epic poem *The Rape of the Lock,* "The hungry judges soon the sentence sign; And wretches hang that jury-men may dine."

There wasn't long to wait this day. The jury returned by four o'clock. "Gentlemen of the jury," the clerk asked, "are you all agreed in your verdict?"

"Yes."

"Who shall speak for you?"

"Our foreman."

The clerk faced the prisoners. "William Wemms, hold up your hand." Wemms did so. "Gentlemen of the jury, look upon the prisoner: How say you, is William Wemms guilty of all or either of the felonies or murders whereof he stands indicted, or not guilty?"

Foreman Joseph Mayo replied, "Not guilty." There is no record of any outburst occurring in the courtroom.

The clerk continued, "Harken to your verdict as the court hath recorded it. You upon your oaths do say that William Wemms is not guilty, and so say all." After a moment he continued, "James Hartegan, hold up your hand . . ." Not guilty.

"William McCauley . . ." Not guilty.

"Hugh White . . ." Not guilty.

"Matthew Killroy, hold up your hand. Gentlemen of the jury, look upon the prisoner: How say you, is Matthew Killroy guilty of all or either of the felonies or murders where he stands indicted, or not guilty?"

"Not guilty of murder . . . but guilty of manslaughter."

William Warren also was not guilty. John Carrol, also not guilty. But Hugh Montgomery, accused of firing the first shot, was also found guilty of manslaughter.

With the verdicts given and received, court was adjourned. The longest trial in colonial history was over, and an impression had been made upon the legal system that would last for centuries.

Six of the soldiers were released immediately. According to the *Gazette,* "The soldiers were discharged from court in high day-light. And went their way thro' the streets with little, if any, notice." Later they were removed from the town to rejoin their regiment which had departed for New Jersey. Killroy and Montgomery remained in jail awaiting sentencing, which was scheduled for the 14th. Manslaughter was a capital offense. They were facing the possibility of the death penalty.

A day later Governor Hutchinson wrote to General Gage, "It is with pleasure that I embrace the first opportunity of advising you that yesterday towards evening the jury gave in their verdict, and found Killroy and Montgomery guilty of manslaughter and acquitted the rest. I do not think there was sufficient ground for the verdict as for the two. Killroy is said to be a bad fellow and, the day before had sworn he would kill some of the people the first opportunity but this ought not to have been connected with the action for which he was charged. Montgomery fired the first gun and it appears probable that he did it to save his own life. The judges shewed great firmness. The foreman of the jury had the character of a Son of Liberty but proved an honest man and would not go against his conscience . . ."

Should General Gage desire to influence opinion about the trial through publication, Hutchinson added some anecdotes, but requested that they be transcribed before submission and the original burned as "My hand is singular and much known . . ."

Privately Hutchinson reveled in the decision, believing it to be a great victory at the expense of the patriots. He wrote, "The issue however is favorable to the cause of government and the counsel for the prisoners have done more to hurt the general cause in which they had warmly engaged than they ever intended."

Captain Preston, who left for England the day after the verdicts, also wrote to Gage offering his congratulations to the general and "all the King's servants together with every honest man in America on this joyful occasion. The Corp' and 5 men are acquitted and two found guilty of manslaughter . . . All arts were used to make this affair appear in the most black and horrid colors and full as much pains was taken to elucidate it . . . but its effects will be felt by every soldier in America and convince the world that a man on duty is sacred."

Sam Adams bitterly denounced the verdicts in the *Gazette.* "As it was said in court that the unhappy persons who fell a sacrifice to the cruel revenge of the soldiers, had brot their death upon their own heads," he wrote under his pseudonym Vindex ". . . in behalf of those who cannot now speak for themselves . . ." He praised the victims and attacked the evidence, describing testimony as mistaken and inconclusive and inaccurate; rather than accusing the important witness, Andrew the servant, of lying, he suggested his testimony was the product of "a fellow with a lively imagination indeed."

But the prevailing view was presented by the respected Boston Reverend Samuel Cooper in a letter to his friend then representing the colonies in London, Benjamin Franklin. The trial was remarkably fair, Reverend Cooper wrote, "In the disposition of judges, in the appointment of the jury, in the zeal and ability of lawyers, in the examination of witnesses and in the length of trial . . . These trials must, one would think, wipe off the imputation of our being so violent and bloodthirsty a people as to not permit law and justice to take place on the side of unpopular men . . ."

There were many who believed the result — six acquittals and two convictions — had served both patriots and loyalists. It kept the cause alive for the patriots, who claimed the acquittals proved that the redcoats could kill with impunity and thus provided a propaganda victory that they would continue to exploit. Sam Adams raged against the outcome and staged annual commemorations supposedly to honor the victims of British brutality. Loyalists believed the convictions demonstrated that the rule of law was respected by the King and Parliament and provided security for the inhabitants.

As might be expected, John Adams fully supported the verdict. He wrote in his diary, "Judgement of death against those soldiers would have been as foul a stain upon this country as the executions of the Quakers or witches, anciently . . . As the evidence was, the verdict of the jury was exactly right."

The two soldiers, Killroy and Montgomery, were returned to the courtroom on December 14th. Once there, they were asked by the court if they knew any reason why the death sentence should not be carried out. In response both men asserted an ancient right: they "prayed clergy." As a result of the battle for power between the church and the Crown in medieval England, a punishment known as "benefit of clergy" was recognized. As originally applied, this allowed a clergyman to avoid punishment in a secular court by proving he was a member of the church; as few commoners could read it was granted to anyone capable of reading aloud Psalm 51, verse 1: "Have mercy on me, O God, according to thy loving kindness: according unto the multitude of thy tender mercies blot out my transgressions." The necessity of actually reading aloud this "neck verse," as it became commonly known, was abolished in 1707, after it became evident that many prisoners were capable of reciting it from memory. It was granted to prisoners who simply pleaded it in court. Killroy, for example, was illiterate, but still received this right.

There was a limitation: a man or woman was permitted to make this lifesaving claim only once. To ensure that, anyone making it was branded on his right hand. Following the conviction of the two soldiers, an appeal for clemency from this branding was made to Governor Hutchinson. He later admitted, "Application was made to . . . remit the punishing of burning in the hand especially with respect to one of them, Montgomery, who had been knocked down with a club and provoked to fire, as appeared in the course of the evidence." Hutchinson rejected this request, he continued, because "it would have a tendency to irritate the people and, being on little consequence to the prisoners, it was thought advisable not to interpose."

The court ordered Sheriff Greenleaf to brand a small permanent mark, the letter "M" for manslaughter, on the brawn of their right thumbs. Remembering that scene many years later their attorney, John Adams wrote that he had "never pitied any two men more than the two soldiers . . . They were noble, fine looking men; protested they had done nothing contrary to their duty as soldiers; and, when the sheriff approached to perform his office they burst into tears."

Having done his service to the law, to Boston and to the King, John Adams quietly returned to the demands of his practice. As he feared would happen, his appearance for the soldiers had reduced his business; by half, he later would estimate. But he still had work to do. In only weeks he would appear for a London supplier of stationery goods, Thomas Longman and his representative in America, John Hancock, attempting to collect a debt of more than £1,600 from the printer of the *Boston Chronicle,* John Mein. It was a complicated action in which Mein claimed that the patriot Hancock had bought his debt, then made a sudden demand for payment that would cause ruin and perhaps force the closure of the loyalist newspaper. Shots had been fired in anger. Mein had been attacked by a mob and found refuge on a ship in the harbor.

This was a political case involving substantial sums in which the law might turn in several directions. A fine case for John Adams. It was time for him to move ahead. His participation in the Boston Massacre trials, "one of the most gallant, generous, manly and disinterested actions of my whole life," was done.

It was what happened in John Adams's life after the trials, in part as a result of them, that would become far more historically significant than the trials themselves.

EPILOGUE

There remained many loose ends to tie down. On December 12th, the trial of the four men accused of firing muskets from the windows of the Custom House, as depicted in Paul Revere's propaganda etching, was held in the Queen Street courtroom. With the disappointing end of the two earlier trials, much of the patriotic fervor for justice had dissipated. Samuel Quincy again prosecuted the case but neither John Adams nor Josiah Quincy was involved. The evidence against the four men, customs official Edward Manwaring, notary public John Munro, Hammond Green and Thomas Greenwood consisted primarily of the testimony of fourteen-year-old Charles Bourgatte, Manwaring's French-born indentured servant. The lad told a fanciful tale about going to the Custom House and being ordered to fire at the inhabitants by a tall man who threatened to run him through with his sword if he did not. After being accused, Manwaring described Bourgatte as "a boy under age, without principle, sense or education and indeed unacquainted with our language."

In the months preceding the trial, Bourgatte had wavered, admitting his story was not true. But after meeting privately with patriot firebrand William Molineux and the woman to whom he had supposedly first told his story, a tailor named Mrs. Waldron, he reaffirmed his original claims. There were others who supported him: in depositions published in the *Horrid Massacre,* seven other townspeople testified they had seen muskets fired from the upper windows. But only two other witnesses were questioned at the trial, one of them described as "dull-witted" and another admitting, "I saw no firing from the Custom House."

Trial records seem to indicate the four prisoners were not represented by defense counsel, which was not uncommon. Instead the accused requested specific witnesses be called: two young women testified they had been inside the Custom House watching the scene unfold from those very windows and there had been no men with guns present. Another witness, Elizabeth Hudson, with whom Manwaring was boarding while in the town, testified he, Munro and the boy had remained in her house throughout the entire event. A debtor who had been imprisoned with the boy swore that Bourgatte admitted to him that his claims were false and he had been persuaded to make them by Molineux, who promised to provide for him, and Mrs. Waldron, who offered him gingerbread and cheese. The fourteen-year-old had also allegedly been warned that the mob would kill him if he did not stand against Manwaring.

Bourgatte was recalled to the stand, questioned this time in French by interpreters, but continued to insist his story was true. It made no difference. The defense case was so compelling that without leaving their seats in the courtroom the jury voted to acquit the four men. The trial, Judge Oliver wrote, "was rather farcical than serious . . . for it was proved that the French boy, the principal evidence against them, was neither present [in the room] himself, nor his master."

Following the trial the boy was indicted and later convicted of perjury. He was sentenced to twenty-five lashes from Sheriff Greenleaf. On April 1st, 1771, the *Gazette* reported that "Charles Bourgette (Known by the name of 'the French Boy') stood one hour in the pillory . . . and on Saturday received 25 stripes at the public whipping post, agreeable to his sentence."

That marked the conclusion of legal matters pertaining to the killings of March 5th. While the passions of the town had been subdued, there remained great interest in the proceedings. On December 27th, printer John Flemming advertised that he would be selling "a coarse version" of the transcript of the soldiers' trial for "three shillings and four pence, lawful money," and a "fine" version "sewed in blue paper" for 4 shillings. The 217-page sewn volume went on sale in late January, "nearly opposite the White Horse Tavern in Newbury Street."

Many questions were left unanswered about the chaos of the evening; Private Hugh Montgomery settled one of them after he had rejoined his unit and was about to depart the town for New Jersey, admitting to one of his defenders that after being knocked to the ground he had indeed shouted, "Damn you, fire!" and fired the first shot.

There also was no further public discussion or investigation into the identity or the actions of the tall man in the red cloak and white wig who had been seen in Dock Square and was believed by some to have instigated the protests. Justice Oliver had suggested in his remarks that he might have egged on the inhabitants but left his guilt and punishment to God. It seemed apparent the man was well-known and respected; after listening quietly to him the inhabitants huzzaed the Main guard. Yet no man admitted knowing him. A loyalist newspaper, the *Evening Post,* claimed that man was Sam Adams but failed to produce any evidence. Adams denied it, demanding the publisher support his claim, writing, "Whether he [the man in red] gave them good or ill advice, or any advice at all, we may possibly form some conjecture concerning it, when his person is ascertained. The sooner it is done the better."

Another newspaper, the *Boston News-Letter,* wrote that the identity of "the person in the red cloak declared by some witnesses to have been very busy at the beginning of the tragedy will be ascertained, if Vindex and his adherents desire it." The implication was quite clear that Sam Adams was somehow involved if not there personally. Ever since there has been speculation about that mysterious tall man, and others who have been named as possibilities include John Hancock, who was known in the town for his height, and William Molineux.

Also never resolved was whether the series of incidents that took place the night of March 5th that culminated in the killings on King Street had been happenstance or by design. Was it the result of a plan to create a disturbance as an excuse to force the British to withdraw from the town? Whatever its origins, it has long been considered one of the most important sparks that eventually ignited the American Revolution.

The participants from the trial also took on roles in history as well. Prosecutor Robert Treat Paine eventually joined John Adams in signing the Declaration of Independence, then continued his distinguished career in Massachusetts as a jurist and elected representative.

His associate, Samuel Quincy, was the only member of his illustrious family to become a loyalist, and as a result, weeks after fighting broke out in Lexington, the man who once was John Adams's close friend left his wife and children in America and fled to England and later Antigua, never to return. Following the Revolution he was banned from returning to Massachusetts and his property was forfeited. He never recanted or appeared to regret his choice. "Be assured," he later wrote to his wife, "if I cannot serve my country, which I shall

444

endeavor to the utmost of my power, I will never betray it." He died on a voyage from Tortola to England in 1789.

His younger brother, the patriot defense attorney Josiah Quincy, Jr., was a leader in the quest to find a path to economic freedom from England without resorting to war. He sailed to London in 1774 and met there with leaders of the British government, including Prime Minister North, but came away disheartened. Writing to Philadelphia's Joseph Reed, a member of the Committee of Correspondence, he said, "Let our countrymen . . . be on their guard at every point . . . Hath not blood and treasure in all ages been the price of civil liberty? Can Americans hope a reversal of the laws of our nature, and that the best of blessings will be obtained and secured without the sharpest trials?" While there he was diagnosed with apparent tuberculosis. He sailed home, but died within sight of Gloucester, Massachusetts.

Justice Peter Oliver had been born in Boston but remained loyal to the Crown. Governor Hutchinson rewarded him for his work in the trials by appointing him chief justice of the superiour court in 1772, but he was impeached two years later after a dispute over the source of funds to pay his salary. He left Massachusetts forever when the British evacuated their troops and loyalists in 1776 and was officially banished two years later. His memoir of the Revolution, *The Origin and Progress of the American Rebellion,* which bitterly denounced patriot leaders for their disloyalty, was published in 1781, and he lived a gentleman's life in England until his death in 1795.

Judge Edmund Trowbridge, later to be described as "a reluctant patriot," resigned from the bench two years after the trial and died in Cambridge in 1793.

Captain Thomas Preston retired from the army following the trial and was believed to have settled in Ireland. John Adams always believed he had not been properly paid for his representation of Preston, which was a sum received from the government after the trial. Adams also noted that Preston never thanked him for his work on his behalf and remembered that when he was living in London as America's minister to Britain, they passed each other on a street and his former client failed to even acknowledge him.

Of the witnesses, the man who most distinguished himself in the Revolution was the rotund bookseller Henry Knox. With the support of John Adams, Knox was commissioned a colonel in the Continental Army's artillery regiment, eventually rising to the rank of general and becoming one of George Washington's most trusted advisors. In the early days of the war, Knox's Noble Train of Artillery literally dragged sixty tons of abandoned cannon and other weapons by oxcart three hundred miles through winter forests and over frozen rivers from Ft. Ticonderoga to the Dorchester Heights; after Washington secretly moved them into position overlooking Boston, the British army was forced to evacuate the town and sailed to Nova Scotia. Following the war, Knox became President Washington's second secretary of war. In recognition of his deeds, numerous places were named after him, among them the city of Knoxville, Tennessee, and the army artillery training center and gold reserve, Ft. Knox, Kentucky.

The eight British soldiers, ordinary soldiers stationed far from home in an inhospitable town had played a central role in one brief but vitally important moment in the glare of history. But among the victims, Crispus Attucks eventually emerged as a symbol of the fight for liberty — for slaves and free black Americans. In the turmoil in Boston, race had less meaning; people of all races and origins lived in the town (if not always equally), even some Native Americans. The term molatto was used primarily as a description just as Patrick Carr was an Irishman — but his race did assist the defense's effort to distinguish him from the mob that night from the other inhabitants. When the abolitionist movement began in earnest in the 1840s, Attucks became a handy symbol, suddenly being positioned as "the first martyr of the American Revolution," honored as a patriot who sacrificed his life for a cause. That legend took root, and two hundred fifty years later the mysterious man with a hazy background remains a central and compelling figure in American history.

Peter Oliver wrote of Samuel Adams that a celebrated American painter had once observed " 'That if he wished to draw the picture of the devil, that he would get Sam Adams to sit for him' . . . He could turn the minds of the great vulgar as well as the small into any course that he might choose . . ." Samuel Adams was one of the leading players directing the steps toward revolution, both publicly and covertly. His writings made the case for independence while it was strongly believed that he was manipulating events from behind the curtain. Wherever

In a bustling port like Boston, sailors and travelers passed through with little attention. Crispus Attucks would have been easily forgotten by history had he not been killed on March 5. Instead, decades later, Michael Johnson, as he was then called, became a martyr to an entirely different cause — freedom for black Americans. Two hundred and fifty years later he has become the most widely known participant in the actual incident; ironic considering at that time no one even knew his real name. COLLECTION OF THE MAS-

SACHUSETTS HISTORICAL SOCIETY

resistance reached the streets, Adams was somehow deemed to be behind it. "Put your enemy in the wrong, and keep him there," he wrote to George Washington's younger brother, John Augustine Washington. His position in the chaos leading to the Boston Massacre was never determined but three years later, he was an instigator of the Boston Tea Party. In 1776, as a delegate to the Continental Congress, he signed the Declaration of Independence. After the Revolution he served four terms as governor of Massachusetts.

While John Adams's initial fears that his defense would damage his standing in the town proved accurate, that opinion was generally replaced with respect for his courage in defending the rule of law. Adams had proved his fidelity to a much greater cause: in the words of the Roman statesman and philosopher Cicero, "We are all servants of the laws in order to be free."

Following the trial, Adams took his place among the Founding Fathers of the country, helping create and pass the Declaration of Independence, negotiating the peace treaty with Great Britain, then serving two terms as the nation's first vice president under George Washington before being elected America's second president in 1796.

The practical side of the man was never satisfied with the payment he received for his representation of Captain Preston and the soldiers, a total of 19 guineas, but even as his political opponents used the cases against him, he never doubted that he had done the right thing. In 1787 he wrote in his own defense, "I begin to suspect that some gentlemen who had more zeal than knowledge in the year 1770 will soon discover that I had good policy, as well as sound law on my side, when I ventured to lay open before our people the laws against riots, routs and unlawful assemblies. Mobs will never do . . ."

In his later years he remained embittered that others failed to appreciate the reasons he had accepted the case. "To this day," he wrote to a friend in 1815, "my conduct in it is remembered, and is alleged against me to prove I am an enemy of my country, and always have been . . . My head or my heart, or perhaps a conspiracy of both, compelled me to differ in opinion from all my friends, to set at defiance all their advice, their remonstrances, their raillery, their ridicule, their censures and their sarcasm . . ."

It will never be known for certain precisely what happened on the streets of Boston the night of March 5th, 1770. The popular story of the Boston Massacre became set in legend long ago. There is little doubt, however, that whatever actually took place, John Adams's controversial role in the trials of Captain Preston and the eight soldiers helped set a critical precedent for the law that would prove to be a foundation of American liberty.

Ironically, the hostilities on King Street were to be repeated after the British army returned to Boston in 1774. Reporting an incredibly similar confrontation, one that raises the question of how any slight difference on that cold March night might have changed history, an unnamed British officer wrote in his diary on the 21st of January, 1775, "Last night there was a riot in King Street in consequence of an officer having been insulted by the Watchman, which has frequently happened, as those people suppose from their employment that they may do it with impunity; the contrary, however, they experience'd last night: a number of officers as well as townsmen were assembled, and in consequence of the watch having brandished their hooks and other weapons, several officers drew their swords and wounds were given on both sides, some officers slightly; one of the watch lost a nose, another a thumb, besides many others by the points of swords, but less conspicuous than those above mention'd. A Court of Enquiry is order'd to set next Monday, consisting of five field officers, to enquire into the circumstances of the riot."

Without a formal trial nor a widely distributed engraved depiction memorializing the event, the fate of those five officers remains unknown.

BIBLIOGRAPHY

Adams, John. *A Dissertation on the Canon and Feudal Law.* Rise of Douai Publisher, 2014.

Adams, Randolph G. "New Light on the Boston Massacre." American Antiquarian Society. https://www.americanantiquarian.org/proceedings/44806960.pdf.

The Annotated Newspapers of Harbottle Dorr, Jr. "The Boston-Gazette, and Country Journal, 28 May 1770." http://www.masshist.org/dorr/volume/3/sequence/172. Last modified 2019.

Bell, J. L. *Boston 1775.* boston1775.Blogspot.com. Last modified November 8, 2019.

Bell, J. L. "Henry Knox at the Boston Massacre." http://www.boston1775.Blogspot.com/2012/03/henry-knox-at-boston-massacre.html. Last modified March 10, 2012.

Blackstone, Sir William. *Commentaries on*

the Laws of England in Four Books, Book I: The Rights of Persons. Oxford, England: Clarendon Press, 1765.

Blackstone, Sir William. Commentaries on the Laws of England in Four Books, Book II: Of the Rights of Things. Oxford, England: Clarendon Press, 1765.

"The Boston Massacre, The British View, 1770." EyeWitness to History. www .eyewitnesstohistory.com. Last modified 2009.

Brown, Jared. The Theatre in America During the Revolution. Cambridge, UK: Cambridge University Press, 1995.

Butterfield, E. H. The Adams Papers, Legal Papers of John Adams Volumes 1-3. ed. L. Kinvin Wroth and Hiller B. Zobel. Cambridge, Massachusetts: The Belknap Press, 1964-5. Also available online, http:// www.masshist.org/publications/adams -papers/index.php/browse/volumes. Last modified 2019.

"Captain Preston's Unknown Biography." Boston Massacre Historical Society. http:// www.bostonmassacre.net/players/preston -biography.htm. Last modified 2008.

The Colonial Society of Massachusetts. "An Overview of Massachusetts History to 1820." Medicine in Colonial Massachusetts

1620-1820, 57 (1980): 3–19.

Forbes, Esther. *Paul Revere and the World He Lived In.* Boston, Massachusetts: Houghton Mifflin Co., 1943.

Founders Online, National Archives. "Editorial Note." https://founders.archives.gov/documents/Adams/05-03-02-0001-0001. Accessed September 29, 2019.

Friedman, Lawrence M. *Law in America: A Short History.* New York, New York: Modern Library, 2004.

Gillis, Jennifer Blizin. *Life in Colonial Boston: Picture the Past.* Chicago, Illinois: Heinemann Library, 2003.

Grant, James. *John Adams: Party of One.* New York, New York: Farrar, Straus and Giroux, 2005.

Hinderaker, Eric. *Boston's Massacre.* Cambridge, Massachusetts: The Belknap Press, 2017.

Hodgson, John. *The Trial of William Wemms, James Hartegan, William M'Cauley, Hugh White, Matthew Killroy, William Warren, John Carrol, and Hugh Montgomery, for the murder of Crispus Attucks, Samuel Grey, Samuel Maverick, James Caldwell, and Patrick Carr.* Boston, Massachusetts: J. Fleeming, 1770.

Kidder, Frederick. "Additional Observations to 'A Short Narrative of the Horrid Massacre in Boston by Soldiers of the XIX Regiment.' " In Kidder, Frederick. *History of the Boston Massacre, March 5, 1770.* Albany, New York: Joel Munsell, 1870.

Kidder, Frederick. *History of the Boston Massacre, March 5, 1770.* Albany, New York: Joel Munsell, 1870.

Linder, Doug. "The Boston Massacre Trials: An Account." http://law2.umkc.edu/faculty/projects/ftrials/bostonmassacre/bostonaccount.html. Last modified 2001.

McCullough, David. *John Adams.* New York, New York: Simon and Schuster, 2001.

McNamara, Martha J. *From Tavern to Courthouse: Architecture & Ritual in American Law 1658-1860.* Baltimore, Maryland: Hopkins University Press, 2004.

Mook, H. Telfer. "Training Day in New England." *The New England Quarterly* 11, no. 4 (December 1938): 675–697. https://www.jstor.org/stable/360640.

Morse Jr., John T. *John Adams.* Boston, Massachusetts: Houghton, Mifflin & Co., 1884.

Nicolson, Colin. "A Plan 'To Banish All the Scotchmen': Victimization and Political Mobilization in Pre-Revolutionary Boston." *Massachusetts Historical Review* 9 (2007): 55–102.

Oliver, Peter. *Origin & Progress of the American Rebellion: A Tory View,* ed. Douglass Adair and John A. Schutz. Stanford, California: Stanford University Press, 1967.

Reid, John Phillip. *In a Defiant Stance.* University Park, Pennsylvania: Pennsylvania State University Press, 1977.

Schneider, Wendie Ellen. *Engines of Truth: Producing Veracity in the Victorian Courtroom.* New Haven, Connecticut: Yale University Press, 2015.

Standerfer, Amanda. "An Organized Incident: The Boston Massacre Re-examined." Independent study paper, Eastern Illinois University, 1995.

Surrency, Erwin C. "The Courts in the American Colonies." *The American Journal of Legal History* 11, no. 3 (July 1967): 253–276.

Trainor, Craig. "The Great Presumption." *The American Spectator,* December 4, 2018. https://spectator.org/the-great -presumption.

Willard M.D., Samuel. *John Adams: A Character Sketch.* Milwaukee: H.G. Campbell Publishing Co., 1903.

York, Nel Longley. "Rival Truths, Political Accommodation and the Boston 'Massacre.' " *Massachusetts Historical Review* 11 (2009): 57–95.

Zobel, Hiller B. *The Boston Massacre.* New York, New York: W. W. Norton & Company, 1970.

Zobel, Hiller B. "The Jury on Trial." *American Heritage,* July/August 1995.

ACKNOWLEDGMENTS

I am occasionally asked "How do you write these books with everything else you do?" My response is always the same: these books do not happen without my partner and literary Sherpa, David Fisher. David continues to amaze me with his remarkable ability to master so much complicated material under significant time constraints. This is now our third collaboration and with each book our partnership has become stronger as we have come to understand each other's thinking that much better. I feel lucky to know, learn from and work with David.

Once again, I would like to thank our constructive and supportive editor, Peter Joseph, from Hanover Square Press, who continues to provide valuable feedback with just a dollop of tough love. Once we decided to release this book to coincide with the two hundred and fiftieth anniversary of the Boston Massacre, a bit of a scramble ensued, and Peter kept us on track and on time (barely). Not only does Peter believe in this series of books on historical trials, he becomes deeply involved in the stories, which helps us immensely. His team at Hanover Square, including Grace Towery and John Glynn, were also very helpful in bringing this to fruition.

I also want to once again thank my chief of staff, Stephanie Alexander, and assistant Gideon Taaffe for their terrific copy-editing and research efforts. Stephanie remains a critical piece of everything that I do and is poised to do great things moving forward, hopefully with me. And, of course, I must thank literary agent Frank Weimann of Folio for his support and for bringing David and me together.

As always there is my family: my sister, Judge Ronnie, and her husband, Greg, and their girls, Dylan, Teddy and Finn. My dad, Floyd, remains my professional counselor in all endeavors, but in particular when there is a legal angle, I am blessed to have the ultimate in-house counsel. He inspired me to appreciate history as a child, the law as an adult, and most important he and my mother, Efrat, served as the perennial parental role models. I can only hope that my now seven-year-old son, Everett, the joy of my life, will look back as fondly on me.

And knowing that he just might search for his name in this book before delving into Captain Preston's defense, I will say, "EVERETT, EVERETT, EVERETT, I love you." But it's really thanks to his mother, Florinka, that Everett has become the happy, confident boy that he is today. He, and I, could not have asked for a better, more devoted mom, and I am confident that when Everett (last reference!) writes his first book, he will devote it to her.

Finally, thank you to the brave patriots of the Revolution. Working on this book reminds us of the incalculable sacrifice they made for all of us two hundred and fifty years ago.

— Dan Abrams

I'd like to begin by acknowledging the effort of my coauthor, Dan Abrams. It remains a great pleasure to work with him. And in every possible way, this book is a joint effort. We are very lucky to have as our editor and publisher Peter Joseph, who really cares about the details, which makes all the difference. And we happily welcome his assistant, Grace Towery, to our team. To ensure historical accuracy, we have been joined by Justice Hiller Zobel, perhaps the greatest living expert on the Boston Massacre, and whose wonderful book *The Boston Massacre* remains an extraordinary account of that event. Dan and I are very grateful for his diligence and his good humor. Nicole McAllister of the Bostonian Society was our guiding light, offering suggestions and providing contacts from the very beginning of this process, and, as she writes, she was always happy to help. The society manages the Old State House and maintains records of historical Boston. They can be found at www.bostonhistory.org. We also greatly appreciate the efforts of Sara Martin, editor in chief of *The Adams Papers* at the Massachusetts Historical Society, who set us on the right path and was consistently generous with her time, effort and knowledge. And finally, and always, my love and appreciation to my wife, Laura, the most supportive person I have had in my life. I am a lucky man.

— David Fisher

The authors gratefully acknowledge the assistance and counsel of Hiller B. Zobel, coeditor of *Legal Papers of John Adams* and author of *The Boston Massacre,* two essential sources for anyone writing about Boston and its townspeople in the years

1760 to 1770. His knowledge of Boston's history and the law and legal culture of provincial Massachusetts helped us gain insight into all aspects of that tumultuous period, suggested appropriate verbal improvements — and saved us from numerous errors; we take full responsibility for any that remain.

The Boston Massacre, published in 1970, is still in print today (through Amazon), as the Massacre approaches its 250th anniversary.

ABOUT THE AUTHORS

Dan Abrams is the chief legal affair correspondent for ABC News as well as the host of top-rated *Live PD* on A&E Network and *The Dan Abrams Show: Where Politics Meets the Law* on SiriusXM. A graduate of Columbia University Law School, he is CEO and founder of Abrams Media, which includes the Law & Crime network. He lives in New York.

David Fisher is the author of twenty-five *New York Times* bestsellers. He lives in New York with his wife, Laura.

Together, they are the authors of the *New York Times* bestsellers *Lincoln's Last Trial,* which received the 2018 Barondess/Lincoln Award, and *Theodore Roosevelt for the Defense.*